P9-CNE-572

HQ 536 .B59 2007

Bianchi, Suzanne M.

Changing rhythms of American
  family life

CHANGIN
AMERIC

DATE DUE

Demco, Inc. 38-293

NEW ENGLAND INSTITUTE OF TECHNOLOGY
LIBRARY

CHANGING RHYTHMS OF AMERICAN FAMILY LIFE

SUZANNE M. BIANCHI, JOHN P. ROBINSON,
AND MELISSA A. MILKIE

A Volume in the American Sociological Association's
Rose Series in Sociology

Russell Sage Foundation • New York

NEW ENGLAND INSTITUTE OF TECHNOLOGY
LIBRARY

3-09   #219 642851

Library of Congress Cataloging-in-Publication Data

Bianchi, Suzanne M.
  Changing rhythms of American family life/Suzanne M. Bianchi, John P. Robinson,
Melissa A. Milkie.
    p. cm.—(The American Sociological Association's Rose series in sociology)
    Includes bibliographical references and index.
    ISBN 0-87154-136-X (cloth) ISBN 0-87154-093-2 (paper)
    1. Family—United States. 2. Parenting—United States. 3. Dual-career families—United
States. 4. Family—Time management—United States. I. Robinson, John P. II. Milkie,
Melissa A. III. Title. IV. Rose series in sociology.

HQ536.B59 2006
306.850973—dc22

                                                                        2006040506

Copyright © 2006 by American Sociological Association. First paper cover edition 2007.
All rights reserved. Printed in the United States of America. No part of this publication
may be reproduced, stored in a retrieval system, or transmitted in any form or by any
means, electronic, mechanical, photocopying, recording, or otherwise, without the prior
written permission of the publisher.

Reproduction by the United States Government in whole or in part is permitted for any
purpose.

The paper used in this publication meets the minimum requirements of American
National Standard for Information Sciences—Permanence of Paper for Printed Library
Materials. ANSI Z39.48-1992.

Text design by Suzanne Nichols.

RUSSELL SAGE FOUNDATION
112 East 64th Street, New York, New York 10021
10 9 8 7 6 5 4 3 2 1

The Russell Sage Foundation

The Russell Sage Foundation, one of the oldest of America's general purpose foundations, was established in 1907 by Mrs. Margaret Olivia Sage for "the improvement of social and living conditions in the United States." The Foundation seeks to fulfill this mandate by fostering the development and dissemination of knowledge about the country's political, social, and economic problems. While the Foundation endeavors to assure the accuracy and objectivity of each book it publishes, the conclusions and interpretations in Russell Sage Foundation publications are those of the authors and not of the Foundation, its Trustees, or its staff. Publication by Russell Sage, therefore, does not imply Foundation endorsement.

BOARD OF TRUSTEES
Thomas D. Cook, Chair

Alan S. Blinder
Kenneth D. Brody
Christine K. Cassel
Robert E. Denham
Christopher Edley Jr.

John A. Ferejohn
Larry V. Hedges
Jennifer L. Hochschild
Kathleen Hall Jamieson
Melvin J. Konner

Alan B. Krueger
Cora B. Marrett
Eric Wanner
Mary C. Waters

EDITORS OF THE ROSE SERIES IN SOCIOLOGY

Douglas L. Anderton
Dan Clawson

Naomi Gerstel
Joya Misra

Randall G. Stokes
Robert Zussman

THE ROSE SERIES IN SOCIOLOGY EDITORIAL BOARD

Karen Barkey
Frank D. Bean
Howard S. Becker
Charles L. Bosk
Maxine Craig
Frank Dobbin
Peter B. Evans
Sally K. Gallagher
Sharon Hays
Pierrette Hondagneu-Sotelo
Miliann Kang
Nicole P. Marwell

Douglas McAdam
Mark Mizruchi
Jan P. Nederveen Pieterse
Margaret K. Nelson
Katherine Shelley Newman
Francesca Polletta
Harriet B. Presser
Jyoti Puri
William G. Roy
Deirdre Royster
Rogelio Saenz
Michael Schwartz

Rachel Sherman
Judith Stepan-Norris
Ronald L. Taylor
Kim Voss
Jerry G. Watts
Julia C. Wrigley
Robert Wuthnow
Alford A. Young, Jr.

Previous Volumes in the Series

Forthcoming Titles

Good Jobs, Bad Jobs, No Jobs: Changing Work and Workers in America
Arne L. Kalleberg

*The Production of Demographic Knowledge: States, Societies,
and Census Taking in Comparative and Historical Perspective*
Rebecca Emigh, Dylan Riley, and Patricia Ahmed

Race, Place, and Crime: Structural Inequality, Criminal Inequality
Ruth D. Peterson and Lauren J. Krivo

*Repressive Injustice: Political and Social Processes in the Massive
Incarceration of African Americans*
Pamela E. Oliver and James E. Yocum

Re-Working Silicon Valley: Politics, Power and the Informational Labor Process
Seán Ó Riain and Chris Benner

Who Counts as Kin: How Americans Define the Family
Brian Powell, Lala Carr Steelman, Catherine Bolzendahl,
Danielle Fettes, and Claudi Giest

*"They Say Cutback; We Say Fight Back!" Welfare Rights Activism
in An Era of Retrenchment*
Ellen Reese

The Rose Series in Sociology

The American Sociological Association's Rose Series in Sociology publishes books that integrate knowledge and address controversies from a sociological perspective. Books in the Rose Series are at the forefront of sociological knowledge. They are lively and often involve timely and fundamental issues on significant social concerns. The series is intended for broad dissemination throughout sociology, across social science and other professional communities, and to policy audiences. The series was established in 1967 by a bequest to ASA from Arnold and Caroline Rose to support innovations in scholarly publishing.

DOUGLAS L. ANDERTON
DAN CLAWSON
NAOMI GERSTEL
JOYA MISRA
RANDALL G. STOKES
ROBERT ZUSSMAN

EDITORS

Contents

About the Authors

Suzanne M. Bianchi is professor of sociology at the University of Maryland.

John P. Robinson is professor of sociology and directs the Americans' Use of Time Project and the Internet Scholars Program at the University of Maryland.

Melissa A. Milkie is associate professor of sociology at the University of Maryland.

Sara Raley is a graduate student in the Maryland Population Research Center at the University of Maryland.

Acknowledgments

THIS BOOK is based on two rounds of new data collection, reanalysis of all the existing U.S. time use data collections dating back to 1965, and a comparison of U.S trends to several other nations. Projects like this do not just happen—they result from the hard work of talented research assistants, the generosity of visionary (we think!) funding organizations, the encouragement of journal and series editors, and the collaborative ties that enhance the research endeavor and make it truly enjoyable and worth doing.

We have had the great fortune of benefiting from research assistance that has grown into collaboration with a number of past and present graduate students. We thank Liana Sayer, now assistant professor of sociology at Ohio State University, who assisted with both data collections and who began her work with us by helping us assess trends in housework (Bianchi, Milkie, Sayer, and Robinson, *Social Forces* 2000). Her dissertation on gender differences in nonmarket time use informs chapter 3, her collaboration with us on changes in parental time with children (Sayer, Bianchi, and Robinson, *American Journal of Sociology* 2004) greatly enhances chapter 4, and her re-conceptualization of leisure activities contributes to chapter 5. Marybeth Mattingly, finishing her dissertation as we finish this book, completed an MA thesis analysis (Mattingly and Bianchi, *Social Forces* 2003) that demonstrated that the quantitative diary data on free time could be used in a more qualitative way. This work informs trends reported in chapter 5 and we draw on Beth's joint work with Liana (Mattingly and Sayer, *Journal of Marriage and Family* 2006) on trends in subjective feelings of time pressure in chapter 7. Beth and Liana undertook a great deal of data collection and management tasks for our project but along the way became true collaborators, often leading the way with their fresh ideas and thoughtful analyses.

As Liana and Beth moved on to other projects, we had the good fortune to sign on Kei Nomaguchi, now an assistant professor of sociology at Northern Illinois University, who swooped in for a year and assisted greatly with analyses of subjective feelings about children and family life (Milkie, Mattingly, Nomaguchi, Bianchi, and Robinson, *Journal of Marriage and Family* 2004; Nomaguchi, Milkie, and Bianchi, *Journal of Family Issues*, 2005). We draw on this collaboration in chapter 7. We also found Sara Raley, who in some ways contributes most to this volume because she joins us as author of chapter 8 on children's time use. Zsuzsa Daczo delved into the analysis of the weekly diaries—going where no one had ventured before. Thanks to her, we were able to include chapter 6 in this volume. Zsuzsa also contributed to the programming of tables throughout the volume. And, finally, thanks to our "angel at the end," Vanessa Wight, who with consummate editorial experience, organization, and skill, handled all the many rounds of edits and revisions, always tackling them with extreme good humor.

We owe special thanks to our international collaborators—Jonathan Gershuny of Great Britain, Michael Bittman of Australia, Andries van den Broek of the Netherlands, Gilles Pronovost of Canada, and Laurent Lesnard and Alain Chenu of France. Their analysis of time-diary data from their respective countries allows us to place U.S. trends in comparative perspective in chapter 9, and their interpretation of trends appears in appendix C.

We are especially indebted to those who funded our data collection and analyses and supported our research and the graduate students working with us: the National Science Foundation, Grant No. SBR 9710662, the Alfred B. Sloan Foundation, particularly Kathleen Christensen, Program Officer for the Working Families Program at the Foundation, and the National Institutes of Child Health and Human Development (NICHD) infrastructure support, 1 R24 HD41041-01 for the Maryland Population Research Center.

We are indebted to the ASA Rose Series Editors, especially Naomi Gerstel, for their helpful suggestions in a preliminary meeting in April 2003 and their patience as we crawled to completion of the first draft in March 2004 and the final draft in June 2005. We benefited from the thoughtful reviews of Andrew Cherlin and Jerry Jacobs and our colleague Stanley Presser, who not only helped collect the time-diary data we use but also read and commented on the complete draft manuscript.

This volume marks a truly collaborative effort among the three of us—John, Melissa, and Suzanne—each with differing strengths, each who at differing times pushed the project forward. We hope the melding of demography, social psychology, and time-use methodology works for the reader. It certainly broadened and enhanced each of our perspectives on family change, as we underwent our own significant family changes. Over the years of our collaboration on this volume, marked from the start of the new time-diary data collections that we feature, one of us became a grandparent for the first time, one of us launched two of her three children from the home, and the other became a parent to one, two, and then three children. In some sense this book is for these precious children, in whose childhoods we, as parents and grandparent, are heavily invested!

═ Chapter 1 ═

Parenting: How Has It Changed?

T HE CULTURAL image of the American mother has changed from the cheery, doting homemaker to the frenzied, sleepless working mom. The conventional wisdom accompanying this change is that as today's mothers juggle the dual roles of worker and family caregiver, they must spend less time with their children, and receive little help from fathers.

Although family incomes have increased with higher maternal employment, social observers worry that this rise is offset by a decline in the quality of family life and in parental supervision and investment in their children. Concern about working mothers forced to endure a "second shift" of labor at home, and "latchkey kids" spending unsupervised time alone each day, sends shudders throughout American society. As this concern transforms into dogma, it seems as if the sky is indeed falling for mothers, their children, and the American family.

However widely these viewpoints are believed, they are largely based on mass media images and familiar anecdotes. This volume moves beyond the dogma, the politics, and the attendant emotions to focus on the scientific evidence from American parents themselves about how they spend their time and how they feel about it. Based on four decades of time-diary surveys in which representative samples describe a typical "day in the life of America," we are able to document more definitively the real changes that seem to have taken place in the American rhythms of time, work, and family.

As it turns out, our conclusions from this evidence stand in sharp contrast to the generally accepted story of modern parenting. In the chapters that follow, we will show that parents are spending as much—and perhaps more—time interacting with their children today than parents in 1965, the heyday of the stay-at-home mother. This might seem to some readers an impossibility: how can parents at once spend more time at work while maintaining the time they spend with their children?

Our data suggest a complex and fascinating set of strategies that working parents have developed to maximize the time they spend with their

1

children. By increasingly engaging in multitasking and incorporating their children in their own leisure activities, parents have deepened their time to circumvent the simple zero-sum trade-off between work and other areas of their lives. Mothers' time diaries contain about as much time for leisure and sleep as in earlier decades. The big difference is that today's mothers spend less time than their mothers doing housework, a deficit partially compensated for by husbands, who have increased the time they spend in domestic chores and fathering over the years.

This book also closely examines another hotly debated issue in American families: the balance of work between the genders. The idea that mothers shoulder a greater proportion of the total workload in families because of their dual work and family responsibilities has become a rarely contested fact among sociologists and the public. They point to Arlie Hochschild's 1989 classic, *The Second Shift*, in which she carefully observed the everyday lives of full-time employed, married mothers in northern California who were raising at least one young child under the age of six. In 2005, only 15 percent of married mothers were in Hochschild's targeted group. The other 85 percent either did not work outside the home, worked part-time hours only, or had older, school-age children in the home when they did work full-time hours.

What we show in this book is that, on balance, married mothers and fathers have about equal workloads. This may seem surprising to many, given the widespread perception that mothers' workloads are heftier than those of fathers. However, we make a simple but critical distinction: employed mothers do put in a long workweek but nonemployed mothers trail behind them. This heterogeneity among U.S. mothers has received too little attention and is the reason why some women are doing double duty, but average workloads are fairly even across the sexes. Even the mothers doing "double duty" because they are employed full-time have total workloads that are very similar to those of employed fathers.

To broaden and enrich our numerical analysis of time, we also examine how American parents feel about the time they have for different activities. Here we do find that today's mothers feel more rushed, as if they are doing everything at once, than their mothers did. This is common across all mothers, though more intense for those who are employed—especially when compared with fathers.

Perspective on the Trends

Before launching into what our data show, however, we need to step back and consider a set of broader societal questions that influence the trends we present in this book and our interpretation of those trends.

First, what are the broad demographic and socioeconomic changes that alter the context in which American families decide how to allocate their time? Second, particularly relevant to the time allocation of parents, how has childhood and our conceptions of what children need changed over time, and how might this be relevant for the time-use patterns of parents that we present in this volume?

As childhood has changed in the United States, has the broader cultural context of motherhood also been transformed? In what ways have the demands on fathers changed or remained the same? Finally, what implications do the changing conditions of family life and changing conceptions of childhood, motherhood, and fatherhood have for the gender division of labor in the home? With this as background, we are in a better position to assess change and stability in family life.

Demographic and Socioeconomic Changes Affecting Parenthood

When thinking about how families with children have changed, two demographic trends seem most likely to have reduced parental time with children: the increase in maternal employment and the increase in single parenting. Mothers' employment within two-parent families increased substantially after 1970, and marriages are less stable than fifty years ago (Casper and Bianchi 2002; Cohen and Bianchi 1999). The sociologist James Coleman (1988) cited these two trends as factors within the family that were reducing the social capital that children could draw upon. He argued that these changes would reduce the time and attention that parents provide children. It would thus erode the quality of the parent-child relationship—the relationship from which children learn valuable skills for later life, internalize parental expectations of achievement and hard work, develop a sense of trust and security, and find love and stability.

Indeed, if these had been the only trends in American families over the last forty years, we calculate that maternal time with children should have decreased by about 40 percent (Sayer, Bianchi, and Robinson 2004). Yet, as we discuss in chapter 4, parental time interacting with children has actually increased in the decades after 1965, when stay-at-home mothers with large families were far more prevalent in America than they are today. Although maternal time with children did dip between 1965 and 1975, the time today's mothers spend caring for their children is as high, or higher, than during the 1960s Baby Boom. Moreover, married fathers' time with children is higher than it has ever been, and increased substantially after 1985.

Decreased Birthrates, More Choice

Underlying these perplexing findings are certain counterbalancing trends that may have shifted child rearing to the forefront of American parents' lives. The social context surrounding childbearing and child rearing is different today than in the mid-1960s in ways beyond increased maternal employment and single parenting. For one, it is more acceptable to forgo having children at all today than in the past, even though the vast majority of American adults continue to want them. Yet when it becomes acceptable to choose not to become a parent, and when the means to avoid an unwanted pregnancy are widely available, who decides to become a parent changes.

The ability to control when childbearing occurs in one's life means that parenthood no longer "just happens" for a growing segment of parents. Baby Boom cohorts of women, those born in the 1950s and early 1960s and now at or near the end of their childbearing years, have higher rates of childlessness than their mothers (Goldin 2004). In fact, the increase in childlessness has spurred books like Sylvia Ann Hewlett's (2002) *Creating a Life,* which laments the high rates of childlessness among high achieving women and urges younger women who want children not to wait until it is too late.

Today, especially for the well-educated, parenthood is a role that can be timed later in life, when adults feel more ready to devote time to rearing children. When childbearing is postponed, a growing proportion of mothers and fathers have already achieved many of their life goals by the time they become parents: completing school, traveling, earning good salaries, and experiencing initial career success. The fact that they are more established in their careers when children arrive creates its own set of problems, particularly for women who curtail labor force participation to provide the lion's share of child care in the household. But the delay in childbearing for a larger segment of the population probably pushes parenting into the adult ages (late twenties through the forties, even fifties) when adults are more economically secure, more emotionally mature, and more ready to take on parenting. The delay in having children is also accompanied by a decline in the number of children mothers have. Today's families are smaller on average than they were in 1965, with each child "invested in" more heavily in terms of time and money than when family sizes were larger.

Education

Another change that has gone hand in hand with postponed childbearing is the increase in educational achievement of parents as a group. In fact, part of the reason that children are timed later in life is precisely so that young adults can stay in school longer. More of today's parents, compared with their parents' generation, are college graduates or have at least some college.

As we see in chapter 4, more highly educated parents not only spend more time with their children, they also tend to do more intellectually stimulating things with their children (Leibowitz 1977; Hill and Stafford 1974). More educated parents have more verbal interchange with children, read more to them, and more often take them on educational outings to museums, zoos, and cultural events. In *Unequal Childhoods,* Annette Lareau (2003) paints an intimate ethnographic picture of parental investment in child rearing and suggests that social class differences in parenting remain strong. Highly educated, middle-class parents cultivate a sense of entitlement in their children by being more actively involved in scheduling and participating in children's events, in emphasizing reasoning and verbal negotiation, and in monitoring their children's activities more intensely. To the extent that her observations hold nationwide, one important consequence of the educational upgrading of society is to propel more and more parents into this more intensive parenting.

Income

Hand in hand with older and more educated parents, a third and sometimes overlooked factor affecting parenting trends is that Americans have become more affluent since 1965. Per capita income has risen and parents' ability to provide for their children has increased. Parents thus buy more and better goods, more often send their children to private schools, take them on more vacations, and often support them fully into adulthood. Today's parents are simply able to provide more for each child. When family size declines, parental time and money is spread across fewer children. Demographers and economists refer to this as the quantity-quality tradeoff—the notion that as parents have fewer children, they have more resources to invest in the quality of life of each child, allowing them to more often realize each individual child's human potential (Becker 1991; Gauthier, Smeeding, and Furstenberg 2004).

Not all children have shared equally in these salutary trends, of course. For example, not all child rearing is planned or delayed until parents are financially secure. Among lower income groups, and particularly among some racial-ethnic groups such as African Americans or Puerto Ricans, women often have children early in life and parenting frequently takes place outside marriage or stable relationships. Family formation may be bifurcating by social class: today's children arrive later and within marriage among the more highly educated, but earlier and often outside marriage among the less educated. This may portend growing inequality, or at least greater heterogeneity, in the time and money investments that children receive depending on their family circumstances.

In addition, not all income trends are positive. Although per capita income has risen on average, this is partly attributable to the rise in dual earning among married couples. Wives' earnings have bolstered stagnating or declining earnings for men, particularly for less-educated men, but income inequality across families has increased (Levy 1998; Neckerman 2004). Many parents report working more hours than they want, and others cannot get enough work to support their families (Rones, Ilg, and Gardner 1997; Jacobs and Gerson 2004).

Documenting Change

Our goal is not to present an overly optimistic view of changes in the family, but rather to suggest that over the past few decades, changes were neither uniformly good nor uniformly bad for children and their parents. Without careful examination of the daily lives of parents with children, it is not obvious how changes in the family may have affected parental time. More working mothers may reduce time in the home, but in so doing they increase the money available to their families. More single mothers probably means reduced time and money for their children, thereby creating greater inequality across family types (Ellwood and Jencks 2004). In contrast, the increase in highly educated, affluent parents probably leads to greater investment of time and money in child rearing.

We cannot stop here, however. Understanding the context that surrounds parenting—whether parents are employed, how much education they attain, whether they marry and remain married, how much money they make, how old they are when they have their children—is only part of the equation in evaluating changes in the everyday lives of American children and their parents. Behavior is guided not only by what is, but also by what we think should be. Parents' beliefs about what constitutes good parenting and what makes for a good childhood also matter.

In our view, changes in beliefs about what makes an ideal childhood have propelled parents to make greater and greater investments in child rearing. At the same time, despite the changed conditions of motherhood—more paid work, more single parenting—there are important cultural brakes that keep mothers from wholesale reallocation of time away from mothering. Along with pressures for more involved fathering, a strong normative emphasis on the importance of a father as breadwinner continues. Notions of good parenting affect parenting behaviors and how equally mothers and fathers share parenting roles. We now turn to a brief discussion of the normative context of family life because it is also important to interpreting the trends presented in the chapters that follow.

How Has Childhood Changed?

Parental investment of time, energy, and material resources in their children does not take place in a vacuum, but in historical settings, with particular conditions of childhood, and with important cultural conceptions about what is appropriate and desirable for children. In *Pricing the Priceless Child*, Viviana Zelizer (1994) argues that, during the latter half of the nineteenth century and the early decades of the twentieth in the United States, a moral transformation occurred in our conception of children's worth and in our notion of what childhood should be. As society became urbanized and industrialized, children, once valued for the labor they could provide on the family farm, the factory floor, or on the streets of the city, became, in Zelizer's words, "economically worthless but emotionally priceless" (3). Childhood was increasingly defined as a period in which children should be able to develop their talents free from the harsh conditions of work. Compulsory school attendance laws were enacted, laws against child labor were passed, and children's safety became a paramount concern as geographic boundaries on children's activities moved indoors or onto playgrounds and off dangerous city streets. Parents were no longer expected to reap the economic rewards from their children's labor but rather to invest heavily in cultivating their children's talents.

Ideas about good parenting evolved along with changing notions of what children were deemed to need. Children who needed constant protection and supervision, guidance, emotional investment, intellectual stimulation and continual monitoring, obviously also needed a far more labor-intensive type of parenting. In the early decades of the twentieth century, this ideal of good parenting was more achievable in the middle-class than in the working and poor immigrant communities of urban areas and in rural parts of the country.

This transformation might be viewed as continuing to the present day. In the late twentieth and early twenty-first century, the notion of childhood as a "protected space" in which to nurture, invest in, and care for children is being extended to older and older ages, at least among families that have the economic means to do so (see discussion of the concept of emerging adulthood in psychology in Eccles et al. 2003). In part due to economic changes of the last two decades, children are increasingly viewed as needing schooling beyond high school if they are to be successful in today's competitive labor market. "Good parents" therefore increasingly support their children (to the extent possible) beyond high school and through college.

Frank Furstenberg and his colleagues (2004) document the extension of adolescence, or quasi-dependence, to later ages and suggest that we need a new label for the period of early young adulthood as one in which it is increasingly assumed that children are not fully launched, thus implying that they will be partially supported by their parents. As transitions to full-time employment, marriage, and parenting are delayed, young adulthood becomes redefined as a period in life in which to experiment with relationships, job options, schooling, and travel. In effect, childhood is elongated and the expectation of parental support is extended to children of increasingly older ages.

To be sure, this rather indulgent elongation of childhood among young adults is not characteristic of all social classes. Linda Burton (forthcoming), for example, talks about early "adultification" among poor adolescents who are often forced by limited financial means or early childbearing to take on adult roles early—and who as teens become caregivers for their own children or siblings and who must thus curtail education in favor of employment. Yet the dominant trend, as society becomes more affluent and parents more educated, is in the direction that Furstenberg et al. (2004) document—dependence on parents well past the teenage years.

The emphasis on investment and production of a "quality" child and childhood puts pressure on parents of today's middle class to make children's activities the focal point of family life. According to Lareau (2003), middle-class families are ruled by the calendar, with each child in two or three extracurricular activities and families rushing from one practice or lesson to another. Most of these activities require the involvement of parents—disproportionately mothers—to schedule, transport, and monitor. In addition, parental vigilance is required to make sure children get the attention they need from schools and the maximum benefit from their participation in their dizzying array of activities. Time must be spent negotiating with children, coaching them to successfully handle adult interaction, teaching them to affect their world and mold it to their needs. Middle-class child rearing is more labor intensive than that of the working class or poor, where parents love and care for their children but invest far less in arranging and monitoring children's activities (Lareau 2003; Miller and Swanson 1958).

This middle-class vision of intensive parental involvement in children's activities to ensure later success is spreading. It was not the norm, even for the middle class in 1965, the beginning point of our story. Lareau's parents do not recall this level of frenetic activity or level of parental involvement in their childhoods. Neither do the grandparents of today's children.

There may be pressures for intensifying parents' involvement in children's activities for all parents, not just the middle class. The middle-class version of family life often defines the culturally dominant ideal, even among those who cannot achieve it (Edin and Kefalas 2005). Also, as parental education rises, as the competitive nature of getting into the right college and then the right job becomes a concern for more and more parents and children, the vision for childhood embodied in the middle class holds sway over large segments of parents. Not to provide a child with every opportunity for new experiences and activities is to risk that child's future. Few are immune from this pressure, not even those least well-equipped to engage in such parenting.

How Has Motherhood Changed?

The biggest change for mothers in the last forty years is unquestionably the increase in their participation in the labor market. This reallocation of time came in response to expanded opportunities in the wake of the civil rights movement of the 1960s and the renewed women's movement of the 1970s (Spain and Bianchi 1996; Blau 1998). Women increased their college attendance and completion, catching up to and even surpassing men by the end of the twentieth century, to the point where it is estimated that women could comprise close to 60 percent of college students in the next decade (Snyder and Tan 2005). Women moved into the traditionally male domains of law, business, and medicine. They found workplaces that, if at first not very receptive or even hostile, became over time more inviting to those who were trained and talented. At the same time, women also confronted workplaces designed largely for men, or at least for workers unencumbered by family responsibilities.

Women with the highest skills entered a workplace where employees were either presumed to have limited family demands, or if they had them, to need someone else to manage them. In *Competing Devotions,* Mary Blair-Loy's (2003) study of top women executives in the financial industry, one encounters the so-called schema of work devotion—the pervasive cultural expectation that becomes internalized among successful workers in the highly remunerative occupations she studies. One's career is a calling or a vocation that requires and deserves single-minded devotion. Those who are viewed as the best in their field and those who are worthy of moving up the corporate ladder must work with intensity and be consumed by their job. To be successful, one must internalize this devotion to work—a schema widely shared by other successful workers, and most important, giving meaning and legitimacy to one's time allocation.

In her book *Unbending Gender,* Joan Williams (2000) describes a similar concept of the ideal worker norm, the organization of market work around the "ideal of a worker who works full time and overtime and takes little or no time off for childbearing or child rearing" (1). Some successful women meet the demands of the workplace by forgoing parenthood. Fully two-thirds of the successful managers who remained in top jobs in the financial industry that Blair-Loy interviewed did not have children. Hewlett (2002) claims similarly high levels of childlessness among the top managers and professionals she interviewed. Claudia Goldin (2004, figure 30) shows rates of childlessness approaching 30 percent among college-educated Baby Boom women. Though this ideal-worker norm does not define all jobs today, according to Williams (2000), "it defines the good ones: full-time blue collar jobs in the working class context and high level executive and professional jobs for the middle class and above" (1).

Women with less than a college education and fewer job skills may not aspire to full-time work, in which the expectation is that women will devote inordinate amounts of time to the job. Yet they too face pressures that can propel them toward more market work. They also typically work in jobs that may hold even less flexibility in hours and schedules than those occupied by highly educated women (see Perry-Jenkins 2005). Faced with the decline in men's wages among the high school or less-educated segments of the population, more families rely on two wage earners to achieve the American dream of owning a home, saving for their children's education, or just making ends meet.

This pressure to "give oneself over to the job" that mothers—particularly highly educated mothers—face in the workplace is difficult to reconcile with the intensive parenting that the contemporary notions of a good childhood we described earlier require. There is a contradiction as women face an equally intense pull to the home in order to involve themselves fully in the lives of their children. Blair-Loy (2003) discusses a "schema of devotion to family caregiving" that is also powerful in women's lives, even among women with high potential for success in the workplace. The schema promises women fulfillment and meaning when they devote themselves to the care and nurturing of their husband and children. It carries with it the assumption that there is a strong biological base for women's greater devotion to children and for men's devotion to paid work. Children are needy, fragile, and worthy of full-time investment by their mothers. Even the highly successful women Blair-Loy interviews often subscribe to this vision of the caregiving required to properly nurture children. Her concept is reminiscent of Sharon Hays's (1996) discussion of the norm of intensive mothering in *The Cultural Contradictions of Motherhood*, a norm that pervades not only the middle class but also the working class. An "ideology of domesticity" assumes that "women belong in the home because of their 'natural' focus on relationships, children, and an 'ethic of care' " (Williams 2000, 1). For many women who prepare for careers but also want children, the dual commitments of devotion to family and devotion to work—of an ideal worker ideology versus an ideology of domesticity—obviously compete. In *The*

Price of Motherhood, Ann Crittenden (2001) argues that these competing claims on mothers are at the root of a system that is unfair to women.

Not surprisingly, the major commodity that must be rationed is time. The hours allocated to paid jobs away from the home are taken from those that can be allocated in the home, and vice versa. Hence the popularization of the notion of what is called the second shift: the unpaid work that employed mothers come back home to each day. Yet Janet Gornick and Marcia Meyers (2003, 42) argue that American mothers have more often met the inherent conflicting time demands between paid and unpaid work through another solution, or trade-off. Forced by the lack of public support for child rearing, Americans have opted to forgo income, by having one parent—overwhelmingly the mother—either reduce hours of employment or work intermittently when children are young. As a result, mothers suffer wage and career penalties. Many terms have been coined to document the resulting earnings and income inequality between child-less women and women with children (or between men and women with children) that this solution fosters: Ann Crittenden talks of a "mommy tax," Jane Waldfogel of a "family gap," and Michelle Budig and Paula England of a "motherhood penalty."

If we accept the fact that once women enter the workforce, they must encounter increasing pressure to reduce time in the home, we can begin to understand the trends in housework described in the following chapters. Yet, if we also acknowledge the powerful normative pull of devotion to family and of creating a good childhood for one's children, we can also begin to understand why trends in child care might be quite different from those for other types of household labor. This also suggests that children continue to create important brakes on women's desire and ability to embrace demanding careers, especially when children are young.

Ultimately, these competing devotions to work and family for women also push the spotlight onto men. A question of increased interest and debate is whether fathers, and fatherhood, are changing in response to the reallocation of mothers' time to market work. Many of the proposed solutions to the work and family conflict of women involve calling on men to reallocate more of their time to caregiving (Gornick and Meyers 2003).

How Has Fatherhood Changed?

Men's lives also change as women work outside the home in greater numbers. For one, today's married men are less likely to have a wife at home full time than in the past. Independently, they also face increased pressures to embrace a new type of fatherhood and involve themselves in caring for their children and maintaining the home. Traditionally, men have defined their worth, their performance as a good husband and father, largely in terms of their breadwinning rather than their direct care-giving responsibilities. In *The Package Deal*, Nicholas Townsend (2002) argues that this definition of men's worth continues. The men he studied emphasized four components that fit together to make the template for a successful adult life: a man should work in a good job, marry well, have children, and provide a home for his family. First is employment. A man must have a job that supports a family. Among the Baby Boom cohort of fathers Townsend interviewed, the ideal often was to be a successful enough breadwinner to support a wife who stayed at home to rear children.

Men in Townsend's study see the importance of their direct involvement in the lives of their children, but also count as important the indirect involvement they provide by financing the reduced labor force participation of their wives. Fathers see the need to develop emotional closeness with their children as one of the important facets of fatherhood. Yet this emotional closeness, from their view, is partly or even wholly achieved by economic provision—providing sufficient material resources and marrying well so that their children have a mother who has the time to devote to rearing them. Providing a home is another way that fathers feel they can show their love for children. Providing for children takes on primacy because it is seen as the way fathers carry out the other essential aspects of parenting. Employment allows fathers to protect their children (by providing safe neighborhoods) and to endow children with the resources that will allow them to grow and prosper (such as providing access to good schools and good peers).

The importance of marriage and employment in defining success for men as fathers—indeed in defining masculinity—is also argued by Steven Nock (1998) in his *Marriage in Men's Lives*. Using quantitative, longitudinal data, Nock shows how patterns of activity change with marriage: men spend less time in risky pursuits and less time with friends in order to reallocate time to family and religious participation—activities that many would attribute to a more stable life style.

The picture from Townsend's ethnographic account and Nock's examination of activity patterns suggests that men are not immune from expectations that ratchet up their involvement in the home. Moreover, they also see their paid work as a powerful way to become more involved with their children. Paid work hours "count" as good parenting for them. This pushes men to work more, not fewer, hours outside the home when they first become fathers (Lundberg and Rose 2000, 2002).

In interviews with mothers, a father's long work schedule is often given as one of the reasons the woman has cut back her employment hours. In Blair-Loy's (2003) study, women cited their husbands' long hours of work as a reason for curtailing their own. Many couples do not even consider that the husband might decrease his hours of employment when children are born, even when the wife is the higher earner. Townsend's and Blair-Loy's studies thus shed light on why men might appear slow to change in this regard. To the extent that providing is the essence of good parenting for men, and to the extent this has not changed as the ideal for them, it is very difficult to cut back on one's role as a provider and still be a "good father."

In chapter 4, we provide evidence that men are indeed changing in their role as parents. They are spending more time with their children. Yet their labor market hours seem relatively unaffected by the number and ages of children, whereas mothers' labor force activities appear highly responsive to their children's need for care. The primacy of employment for men helps place in perspective what has changed, and what has not, for men since 1965.

How Has the Gender Division of Labor in the Home Changed as a Result?

Even as women have changed their economic behaviors, powerful normative schemas may retard movement toward similar patterns of paid work and caregiving among women and men—particularly in families with children. Many accounts suggest that men do not do their fair share of household work and there are strong suggestions in the literature that employed women—but not men—are burdened by their second shift and, by implication, their long paid *and* unpaid work hours. However, the gender differences in our time diaries in families with children show that men have increased the housework they do and that total workloads of men and women are actually remarkably similar. At the same time, the gender specialization of women into the unpaid work of family caregiving and of men into family providing via paid work remains very strong in families with children, particularly if young children are involved.

In *It's About Time*, Phyllis Moen (2003) argues that couples typically do not pick one path or even stick to just one earnings profile over the life course. Nonetheless, it remains most common for couples to follow what is termed a neo-traditional model—with a wife's career and labor force participation taking a backseat to a husband's career advancement, especially when children are young. Townsend would suggest that for many men, this is a desirable way for children to be reared, because it fulfills men's parenting responsibilities. Blair-Loy would suggest it also aligns with the powerful devotion to family schema that sees women as the more appropriate caregiver in couples.

Others suggest that we are slowly but inevitably on a path toward more gender equality. Nock (2001), for example, argues that we are rapidly moving toward couples who are "mutually economically dependent." The number of marriages in which the wife provides income equivalent to the husband's is on the rise, and the percentage in which the wife rather than the husband is the major breadwinner is also slightly higher (Raley, Bianchi, and Mattingly 2006). Still, Moen's neo-traditional couple remains the modal type of dual-earner family, especially among those with children. This suggests that though change has taken place, widespread gender specialization (and inequality) remains in both the home and the labor market.

Many have prescriptions for change that endorse the goal of greater gender equality. Janet Gornick and Marcia Meyers (2003) discuss the ideal as being a dual-earner, dual-career society in which mothers and fathers share earning and caregiving equally. Public support ensures adequate time for caregiving when children are young without long-term career penalties for either women or men. Williams (2000) argues that the "ideal worker norm" is discriminatory to women, but also to many men, and that we need to move away from this ideal. Blair-Loy (2003) discusses women who seem to be trying to slowly change both the schemas of devotion to work and to family. Among her high profile workers, those who work part-time while adhering rather strongly to a schema of devotion to family caregiving, and those who have children despite working full-time and adhering to a schema of devotion to work, may actually be agents of change.

To effect change, we must take stock of where we are, how we got here, and where we might be headed. This leads to the central question of this volume: as mothers dramatically increased their paid work outside the home and as single parenting increased, what was going on inside the home? What has changed and what has not changed, and how can we understand it?

Organization of the Volume

There is a compelling case for taking stock of changes in the way American parents use their time and for doing it with data that allow us to examine reallocation across the broad spectrum of daily activities. In *Time for Life*, John Robinson and Geoffrey Godbey (1999) used time-diary data from the United States to chart changes in the activities of the American population. This book follows in the tradition of *Time for Life* but focuses specifically on families with children, the population subgroup at the center of debates about time pressures in American society. These are the families whose time is most affected by the rise in women's employment: it includes those with presumably the most difficulty balancing paid work and family caregiving, those experiencing the most severe time pressures and "leisure deficits," and those for whom the consequences of increased stress in daily life activities could be consequential for the health and well-being of the next generation.

We combine numerous perspectives to inform this analysis of family change, drawing on insights from demography, social psychology, and time-use methodology to provide a unique understanding of the changing dynamics of parenting and American family life. Our collaboration in this volume combines complementary strengths in these areas: Suzanne Bianchi is a family demographer with long-standing research interest in the changing lives of women and children's well-being. Melissa Milkie adds a social psychological and gender perspective on the cultural meanings behind family changes and the related parental feelings about time. John Robinson contributes career expertise in the methodology of time-diary data to track and analyze American activity patterns.

Changing demographics, economic structures, and norms about gender roles, parenting, and children's needs act in concert to alter the family context for the rearing of children in contemporary American society. If time pressures are intense in families with children, as many assert, questions arise about the quality of care children receive today. How differently are children being raised today? Are they being deprived of either maternal time or paternal time? What sacrifices do parents make to devote time to child care and market work?

Answering these questions compels us to move beyond the standard data sources that are typically used to study changes in the family and instead to assess trends with time-diary data that we have collected from American families. Time-diary data capture the full array of life's activities. Because these data are less well-known than the Current Population Survey (CPS) or census data commonly used to assess changing labor force participation and family composition, an introduction to the time-diary methodology is presented in chapter 2. Some readers will need the introduction in chapter 2 to evaluate the evidence provided in subsequent chapters. Readers familiar with the basics of time-diary data collection may wish to move directly to our empirical analysis in chapter 3.

Chapter 3 combines CPS time-estimate data with our time-diary data to assess trends in labor force participation and the total weekly workload (paid and unpaid) of parents. One of the first questions to answer is whether more work (paid and unpaid) is crowding the lives of parents today more so than in the past, and whether it is affecting mothers, fathers, or both. Our focus on paid work provides perspective on only a slice of a busy parent's lifestyle. We begin here because this is where most of the previous research has been concentrated.

The examination of paid work and total (paid and unpaid) workloads of parents in chapter 3 sets the stage for the in-depth look at parental child care and time with children in chapter 4, which is the heart of our analysis. Although mothers now spend more time working outside of the home, we find that parents have adjusted to preserve the amount of time they spend with their children. We use the time-diary data to measure the total number of hours that married mothers, married fathers, and single mothers spend with their children in both primary and secondary activities. By all our measures, we find that parents are spending at least as much time, if not more, caring for their children in 2000 than in 1975. A large portion of this expansion is attributable to parents combining child care and leisure activities, indicating that either child care has become more oriented towards "fun" activities, or that parents are more frequently including children in their own leisure activities. In addition, we find that though married mothers still put in more time than married fathers, men have been closing the child care gap in recent decades.

In chapter 5, we ask what else, apart from time with children, changed as American women of childbearing age dramatically reallocated their time to market work. What must be sacrificed in family life as couples juggle more combined hours of paid work, and as more single mothers rear children on their own? We examine other aspects of family life, including changes in the allocation of parents' time to personal care, sleep, housework, and free time. Whereas many observers surmised that more paid work meant that mothers would have to give up time for sleep or leisure, our data suggest that neither of these have changed much for mothers in the last four decades. Rather, today's mothers appear to be spending less time engaged in core household work and civic activities, and are increasingly multitasking in order to get everything done.

In chapter 6, the focus is more explicitly on the issue of gender equality and the joint nature of mothers' and fathers' time allocation in families with children. Using unique new data from the first weekly time-diary data collection in the United States, we explore patterns in the gender division of paid work, housework, child care, and leisure in middle-class families. Here again, we find that total household work time is roughly equal for mothers and fathers, with fathers performing more paid work and mothers doing more household work. Examining how correlated the time allocations of mothers and fathers are, we find that children who have high levels of contact with one parent tend to have significant contact with the other parent as well. We also find that increased market work for fathers is associated with increased child care time for mothers, but that the increased market work for women is not associated with greater child care by fathers.

In chapter 7, we examine the subjective dimension of time—how people feel about their time allotments and whether they feel pressured to find time for certain activities. It is hard to deny that American parents feel time pressured—expressions of "too little time" are ubiquitous. The first inclination is to assume this is the result of too much work, the thesis of Juliet Schor's (1991) immensely popular book, *The Overworked American*. Not only is this too simple an explanation, it also does not fit with much of the evidence we present in this volume. We suspect that normative expectations about good parenting may be changing and contributing to the sense of time pressure. Our data show that married mothers crave more time alone and with their husbands, whereas married fathers wish they had more time with their children. Unsurprisingly, we find that single mothers feel the most harried. Overall, it appears that parents are giving themselves over to rearing children to the extent possible, given other demands on their time and limited resources in some families. Yet they often feel as if their efforts are not enough.

In chapter 8, with collaborator Sara Raley, the focus is on how children themselves spend their time. The examination of children's time use is more limited than for parents' time use because trend data are far less readily available. Time diaries have been recently collected in the Panel Study of Income Dynamics–Child Development Supplement (PSID-CDS). We assess children's time use and see how it varies depending on maternal employment and whether the child has a single parent. Using our weekly diaries, we can also examine the correlation in activity patterns and interconnections in the lives of parents and children. These data show that children are quite busy, spending the equivalent of a full-time job (35 plus hours per week) in educational activities, on top of chores, jobs, and extracurricular activities. Their behavior also shows gendered patterns similar to those among their parents.

Chapter 9 places the U.S. trends in international perspective by providing comparable trends for parents in Great Britain, France, Canada, the Netherlands, and, to a more limited extent, Australia. How similar or dissimilar are changes in parents' time use in the United States compared with those in selected other Western economies that have undergone similar "revolutions" in mothers' market work? Although there are variations between the countries, it appears that parents in all countries except France are averaging more time with their children, despite working longer hours. Presence of preschool-age children is the strongest predictor of child care time in each country for both mothers and fathers, even after the other predictors are taken into account. Employment is negatively associated with child care time for both mothers and fathers in nearly all countries as well.

Chapter 10 concludes with a summary of findings and returns to the issues raised in this introduction. We comment on the role that apparently changing norms about childhood, motherhood, and fatherhood play in altering behavior and influencing the sense of time pressure. The likely future demographic shifts in the family and what these portend for families' time use are considered. We return to the issue of gender and its relationship to changing expectations and behaviors in American families. What has changed in U.S. family life, what has remained the same, and how does that picture foreshadow the future?

Chapter 2

Measuring Family Time

THIS BOOK takes advantage of a unique social science measurement
technique for examining family change: the time diary. Most of
what is known about changing family life is based either on small
observational studies of unknown generalizability, or on surveys that
measure market work but provide relatively little information on other
spheres of life, such as family caregiving and leisure activities.

These studies have left unresolved questions about time allocation
outside the market. The answers require data that assess all productive activities, not just market activities. Time diaries cover all daily
activities—market work and also leisure, personal, and family care
activities. Moreover, as we will show, they suggest a rather different set
of conclusions about family life than research using other measurement
techniques (Robinson and Godbey 1999).

Measuring Family Time Use

Most of what we know about time use comes from questions embedded
in surveys that ask respondents to estimate how much time they spend
on an activity during a particular time period (for example, a typical
week). A rich body of historical data from national samples relies solely
on estimates to measure time spent working (from the Current Population
Survey), doing volunteer work (from Independent Sector organizations),
traveling (from the U.S. Department of Transportation), and watching
television (from the Roper Organization and the General Social Survey).

The most widely used measure of market work hours comes from the
Current Population Survey (CPS), in which respondents estimate how
many hours they worked in the previous week and report the usual hours
per week they worked in the preceding year. The CPS has been the gold
standard for assessing change in the work patterns of men and women,
mothers and fathers. One advantage of CPS-type estimate questions is
that they take a respondent three to ten seconds to answer, whereas the
complete time diary takes up to fifteen minutes. That makes it quite cost
effective to ask estimate questions of much larger samples, such as the

19

CPS, which surveys all workers in about 50,000 households every month. In contrast, time-diary studies are based on samples of 1,000 to 5,000 respondents and have been mainly done once a decade.[1] Another advantage is that the CPS has been administered since the late 1940s, whereas the first national diary study was not conducted until 1965 and had notably lower response rates.

Moreover, the time coverage of the estimate question—a week—is far broader than that of the diary, which has usually been only for a single day. Thus, over the thirty-five years of time-diary research in the United States, studies cover a grand total of about 2,000 weeks (or 14,000 days) among those age eighteen to sixty-four, compared to CPS estimates covering millions of respondent weeks. The CPS also makes it possible—as we do in the first part of the next chapter—to examine detailed breakouts of work hours by gender, by marital status, by presence and ages of children, and the like.

Estimate questions have drawbacks, however. Recalling details about time spent in an activity involves complicated calculations. Asking someone, "How many hours do you work?" assumes that each respondent interprets work in the same way, searches memory for all episodes of work, and is able to properly add all the episode lengths across the day or across days in the last week.

Obtaining accurate responses on time use is particularly difficult in the survey context, in which respondents are expected to provide on-the-spot answers in a few seconds. What seems at first to be a simple estimate task turns out to involve several steps that are quite difficult to perform, even for a respondent with regular and clear work hours and a repetitive daily routine. One consequence is that, when asked to provide daily and weekly estimates of several activities, survey respondents give estimates that add up to considerably more than the 168 hours of time each week (Chase and Godbey 1983; Hawes, Talarzyk, and Blackwell 1975; and Verbrugge and Gruber-Baldine 1993).[2]

The appeal of the time-diary approach is that respondents are not asked to make complex, vague, and changing calculations, but to simply recall their activities sequentially for a specific period, usually the previous day. That way, it is possible to reduce the respondents' recall period and reporting task, first to cover all daily activity, and second to ensure that the resulting account respects the zero-sum property of time—in that the activities total exactly 24 hours in a day.

In the process of collecting such data, it is possible to augment them with information on where the activity took place, when it took place, with whom it was done, and what other activities were taking place at the same time. Sometimes diary studies have asked diary keepers how much they enjoy each activity, for whom the activity was undertaken, and the quality of the environment among other aspects of daily life.

Moreover, considerable evidence supports the reliability and validity of such diary data (Robinson and Godbey 1999; Juster and Stafford 1985). That is, the various diary accounts are consistent with each other and with other ways of collecting time data by observation.[3] Indeed, the diary can be seen as a type of social microscope, offering unique insights into the minutiae of daily life. It has the dynamic flavor of watching everyday life unfold across the hours of the day.

That is not to say that the diary method is without flaws. Respondents can still distort, embellish, or even lie about what they do. When asked to recall, many simply cannot remember and may substitute a habitual activity for what actually took place. The method is also demanding of interviewer and respondent time and effort.

As much as an analyst might wish for fuller or more verifiable accounts of activity and more satisfactory ways of accounting for behavior, the diary still presents us with a far richer and persuasive source of family activity patterns than any present alternative. Moreover, the results from diary data challenge so many existing beliefs that they deserve detailed research attention.

Diary Methodology

Here we discuss the measurement logic behind the time-diary approach used in the first American diary study, which was undertaken as part of the most extensive and well-known of diary studies—the 1965 Multinational Time Budget Study (Szalai 1972). In that study, respondents age nineteen to sixty-five in urban employed households from each of twelve countries kept a diary account of a single day. The same procedures and activity codes were used in each country. Respondents were chosen in such a way that each day of the week was equivalently represented; in subsequent U.S. studies all seasons of the year were covered as well.

In each of the U.S. time-diary studies, a standard series of questions has been used to collect the time diary by sequentially "walking" respondents through a 24-hour period. Question wording from one of our recent studies is shown in table 2.1. Starting at some point in the day, usually midnight of the previous day, a respondent is asked: "What were you doing?" (Q1). Responses to this query are commonly known as primary activities because they are thought to be the most salient activity for respondents. Respondents are also asked: "Did you do anything else?" (Q4) at the same time they did each primary activity. These anything else reports are referred to as secondary activities because they capture time spent in simultaneous activities that are not the major focus of attention. For example, respondents might report getting a child dressed for school (primary activity) while listening to

Table 2.1   Time-Diary Question Wording

Next, I would like to ask you about the things you did yesterday. I want to know only the specific things you did yesterday, not the things you usually do. Let's start at midnight [fill day of week before diary day], that is, the night before last.

Q1)	What were you doing [fill in day of week before diary day] at midnight?
	***If person reported traveling, ask question Q2B
Q2A)	Where were you?
Q2B)	How were you traveling?
Q3)	What time did you finish?
Q4)	At any time while you were (REPEAT ACTIVITY) did you do anything else? (like talking, reading, watching tv, listening to the radio, eating, or caring for children)
Q5)	While you were (REPEAT ACTIVITY) who was with you?
Q6)	What did you do next?

Source: CATI Transcript, 1998–99 Family Interaction, Social Capital, and Trends in Time Use Study (FISCT). Bianchi, Robinson, and Presser (2001).

the radio (secondary activity). Respondents also report the location of each (primary) activity (Q2A) and identify the other people present during the activity (Q5).

Table 2.2 shows the diary entries for one respondent in our 2000 diary study, a forty-three-year-old employed married woman who completed her diary in late June. Totaling her day, she put in more than 6 hours of housework. Getting her children up took another three-quarters of an hour. She spent only 5.5 hours sleeping, 1.5 hours eating and an hour grooming. She watched 2.5 hours of television, which was her only free time during the day. She was on the road for a little over an hour and spent 6.5 hours at her workplace. The remaining 16 plus hours of the day she spent at home, mostly with her children when she was not alone.

The task of keeping such a diary may create some recall difficulties, but is fundamentally different from the task of making long-term time estimates. The diary keeper's task is to recall one day's activities in sequence. This may be similar to the way the day was structured chronologically for the respondent and to the way most people may store their activities in memory. The respondent need only focus attention on a single day (yesterday). Rather than working from some list of activities whose meanings vary from respondent to respondent, respondents simply describe their day's activities in their own words.

The diary technique also presents respondents with a task that gives them minimal opportunity to distort activities in order to present

Table 2.2 Sample of Completed Time Diary

Married Woman, Aged Forty-Three, with Two Children Under Age Eighteen (Diary Completed on a Thursday in June)

What Did You Do?	Time Began	Time Ended	Where You Were	With Whom?	Doing Anything Else?
Working	Midnight	12:20	Work	Coworker(s)	No
Traveling home from work	12:20	1:00	Car	—	Listening to the radio
Watching television	1:00	1:30	Home	—	Cleaning house
Washing dishes	1:30	2:15	Home	—	No
Sleeping	2:15	7:45	Home	—	No
Drinking coffee	7:45	8:15	Home	Spouse	Talking
Woke sixteen-year-old son	8:15	8:30	Home	Children	No
Washing clothes	8:30	11:00	Home	Children	Additional clothes care
Watching television	11:00	11:30	Home	—	Additional clothes care
Woke fourteen-year-old daughter	11:30	12:00	Home	Children	Watching television
Eat lunch	12:00	12:30	Home	Children	Watching television
Cleaned up and dusted	12:30	2:00	Home	—	Clothes care
Watching television	2:00	2:30	Home	Children	No
Paid bills	2:30	3:30	Home	—	Watching television
Watching television	3:30	4:30	Home	—	Clothes care
Bathing, showering	4:30	5:00	Home	—	No
Dressing	5:00	5:30	Home	Children	Watching television
Eating dinner	5:30	6:30	Home	Spouse, Children	Talking
Traveling to work	6:30	7:00	Car	—	Listening to the radio
Working	7:00	Midnight	Work	Coworker(s)	Visiting and socializing

Source: 2000 National Survey of Parents (NSP).

themselves in a particular light. They are given few clues about a study's interest in one activity or another, because the diary is intended as a complete and simple record of all activity. Some respondents may wish to portray themselves as hard workers or light television viewers, but to do so they must fabricate the activities that lead and follow the one they want to exaggerate. Further, it is only a one-day account, and on any given day respondents probably realize that they may work less or watch television more than usual. Moreover, respondents are not pressured to report an activity if they cannot recall it or do not wish to report it.

Automatic procedures are built into the diary recording procedures that are now conducted by computer-assisted telephone interviewing (CATI) to ensure accurate reporting. Whenever respondents report consecutive activities that involve different locations, they are reminded that some travel episode must connect them. Activity periods that last more than 2 hours automatically involve a probe: "Were you doing anything else during that time or were you doing (activity) for the entire time?" Moreover, all periods across the day must be accounted for in order that the diary account does total to all 1,440 minutes of the day (across the 24 hours).

Activity Coding

The largely open-ended diary reports are coded using the basic activity coding scheme developed for the 1965 Multinational Time Budget Research Project (as described in Szalai 1972). As shown in outline in table 2.3, the Szalai code first divides activities into nonfree-time activities (codes 00–54, 59) and free-time activities (codes 55–58, 60–99). Nonfree-time activities are further subdivided into paid work and related commuting, which is usually referred to as contracted time in the time-diary literature; three categories of family care (housework, child care, and obtaining goods and services, or unpaid work that is often referred to as committed time in the literature); the three basic aspects of personal care (sleeping, eating, and grooming); and educational activities. The remaining free-time activities are coded under the five general headings of information seeking, organizational activity, entertainment and socializing, recreation, and communications. The main value of the open-ended diary approach is that activities can be recorded or recombined, depending on the analyst's unique assumptions or purposes.

Activity categories are typically coded in minutes per day and then converted into hours per week after ensuring that all days of the week are equally represented. In other words, the sampling units are person-days rather than persons, because subjects were interviewed only about a single day's activities. The data are weighted by demographic variables

Table 2.3   Basic Two-Digit Activity Code

00–54, 59 Non-free time

00–09 Paid work
  00 (Not used)
  01 Main job
  02 Unemployment
  03 Work travel
  04 (Not used)
  05 Second job
  06 (Not used)
  07 (Not used)
  08 Breaks
  09 Travel to and
     from work

10–19 Household work
  10 Food preparation
  11 Meal cleanup
  12 Cleaning house
  13 Outdoor cleaning
  14 Clothes care
  15 Car repair
  16 Other repair
  17 Plant, garden care
  18 Pet care
  19 Other household

20–29 Child care
  20 Baby care
  21 Child care
  22 Helping, teaching
  23 Talking, reading
  24 Indoor playing
  25 Outdoor playing
  26 Medical care-child
  27 Other child care
  28 (Not used)
  29 Travel, child care
30–39 Obtaining goods or
  services
  30 Everyday shopping
  31 Durable, house shop
  32 Personal services
  33 Medical services
  34 Government,
     financial services
  35 Car repair services
  36 Other repair
     services
  37 Other services
  38 Errands
  39 Travel, goods,
     services

40–49 Personal care
  40 Washing,
     hygiene, etc.
  41 Medical care
  42 Help and care
  43 Eating
  44 Personal care
  45 Sleep
  46 (Not used)
  47 Dressing
  48 NA activities
  49 Travel, personal
     care

50–54, 59 Educational
  50 Attend classes
  51 Other classes
  52 Other education
  53 (Not used)
  54 Homework
  59 Travel, education

55–58, 60–99 Free time

55–58 Information
  technology,
  information seeking
  55 Using library
  56 Using the Internet
  57 Playing games
     on a PC
  58 Other PC use

60–69 Organizational
  60 Professional, union
  61 Special interest
  62 Political, civic
  63 Volunteer helping
  64 Religious groups
  65 Religious practice
  66 Fraternal
  67 Child, youth, family
  68 Other organizations
  69 Travel,
     organizational

70–79 Entertainment or
  social
  70 Sports events
  71 Entertainment
  72 Movies
  73 Theater
  74 Museums
  75 Visiting
  76 Parties
  77 Bars, lounges
  78 Other social
  79 Travel, social

80–89 Recreation
  80 Active sports
  81 Outdoor
  82 Exercise
  83 Hobbies
  84 Domestic crafts
  85 Art
  86 Music, drama, dance
  87 Games
  88 Computer use games
  89 Travel, recreation

90–99 Communications
  90 Radio
  91 Television
  92 Records, tapes
  93 Read books
  94 Magazines, etc.
  95 Reading newspaper
  96 Conversations
  97 Writing
  98 Think, relax
  99 Travel,
     communication

Source: 1998–99 Family Interaction, Social Capital and Trends in Time Use Study, derived from Szalai (1972).

to match the March CPS characteristics (for example, gender, age, education, and employment status). All estimates we discuss throughout the book are weighted to match CPS characteristics and to provide equal representation of all seven days of the week.

The Szalai code has several attractive features. First, it has been tested, found reliable, and used in several countries. Second, extensive prior national normative data are available for comparison purposes. Third, it can be easily adapted to include new code categories of activities of interest to researchers who are looking into different scientific questions from various disciplines. The location coding can be aggregated to estimate time spent in travel, outdoors, or at home, which are all important parameters for analyzing trends in use of time.

When aggregated, then, activity-diary data have been used to provide generalizable national estimates of the full range of alternative daily activities in a society, from contracted time for an employer, to the committed time for unpaid housework and family caregiving, to personal care for body and mind, and to all the types of activities that take place in free time. The multiple uses and perspectives afforded by time-diary data have led to a recent proliferation of research and literature in this field. Comparable national time-diary data have been collected in more than forty countries over the last two decades, including virtually all European countries.

Time-Diary Samples

In the United States, the first national diary study was conducted in 1965, and has since been replicated in 1975, 1985, and 1995, as shown in table 2.4.[4] These are the main data collections analyzed in the chapters that follow. In addition, we examined two new data collections for this volume: one a cross-sectional time-diary study of adults conducted in 1998 and 1999 and the other a national time-diary study of parents conducted in 2000 and 2001. These are described in the two right columns of table 2.4. The parents in these studies are combined for the year 2000 time point shown in our tables and figures.

There are methodological differences across the surveys (a detailed comparison is shown in table 2.4). The 1965 and 1975 studies were done in person and had higher response rates than subsequent studies but were not spread over the entire year. Beginning in 1985, studies were done in part or entirely by telephone and had lower response rates, but they were spread over the entire year.[5] The 1975 study also included diaries with spouses of married respondents and three follow-up interviews conducted in 1976. For comparability with other time points, we exclude spouse interviews but use some of the follow-up data with respondents in our assessments of multitasking and subjective well-being in chapters 5 and 7.

It is also possible that change between earlier and more recent diary collections may be due to different methods of survey administration. Respondents in the 1965 survey completed tomorrow diaries (that is, diaries for the day subsequent to a personal interview), whereas respondents in the more recent surveys completed yesterday diaries provided during a computer-assisted telephone interview. The 1985 survey included three methods of survey administration: a personal interview with a tomorrow diary, a telephone interview with a yesterday diary, and an initial telephone contact followed by a mailback diary. In analyses not shown, we determined that the differing survey methods in 1985 had minimal effects on trends, and hence we combine all three to increase sample sizes (see also appendix A in Robinson and Godbey 1999; more detail on the earlier time-diary collections taken in 1965, 1975, 1985, and 1995 can be found in appendix B).

We also draw on a number of other data sources, such as the family composition and labor force trends that are captured each March in the major labor force survey in the United States, the CPS. Questions on subjective feelings about time with children, spouse, and self were included in the 2000 General Social Survey. Questions on the gender division of parenting were included in a 1999 all-purpose Omnibus Survey conducted at the Survey Research Center of the University of Maryland. Some questions had been asked in two surveys on the workforce: the 1977 Quality of Employment Survey and the 1997 National Study of the Changing Workforce. Finally, we examine children's time use with the Child Development Supplement to the Panel Study of Income Dynamics. Details of these studies are also included in appendix B. Because two of the collections are in some sense being unveiled or analyzed for the first time in this volume, we now turn to a more detailed description of those studies.

The National Survey of Parents (NSP)

With funding from the Alfred P. Sloan Foundation's Working Families Program, we interviewed a national sample of 1,200 parents living with children under age eighteen in 2000 and 2001. Parents were asked an array of attitudinal questions about their activities with children and their feelings about the time they spent alone, with children, and with a spouse. Embedded in the study was a one-day, yesterday diary of time expenditures. The data were collected in computer assisted telephone interviews, with a 64 percent response rate. This is the main data set examined in this volume.

Table 2.4 Methodological Features of U.S. National Time-Diary Studies

	1965[c]	1975[d]	1985[e]	1995[f]	1998[g]	2000[h]
Survey organization	University of Michigan	University of Michigan	University of Maryland	University of Maryland	University of Maryland	University of Maryland
Funder	NSF	NSF	NSF; ATT	EPRI	NSF; NIA	Sloan
Sample size	Total = 1244 Parents = 742	Total = 2406 Respondents = 1519 Spouses = 887 Parents = 1087	Total = 5358 Parents = 1612	Total = 1200 Parents = 493	Total = 1151 Parents = 496	Total = 1200 Parents = 1200 Weekly Diaries[b] = 128
Age range	Nineteen to sixty-five	Eighteen and older	Twelve and older	Twelve and older	Eighteen and older	Eighteen and older
Months	November 1965 to December 1965 March 1966 to April 1966	October 1975 to December 1975 Reinterviewed: February, May, and September 1976	January 1985 to December 1985	January 1995 to December 1995	March 1998 to December 1999	June 2000 to May 2001
Mode and response rate	Personal (72%)	Wave I-Personal (72%) Wave II-III-Telephone	Mailback (51%) Telephone (67%) Personal (60%)	Telephone (65%)	Telephone (56%)	Telephone (64%)
Diary type	Tomorrow (1244) Yesterday (130)	Yesterday (2406)	Tomorrow (3890) Yesterday (1468)	Yesterday (1200)	Yesterday (1151)	Yesterday (1200)

Sample restrictions	Residents of labor force families in nonfarm, urban locations[a]	Excludes households on military reservations	Households in the contiguous United States (forty-eight states and D.C.)	Households in the contiguous United States	Households in the contiguous United States	Parents living with children under age eighteen in households in the contiguous United States
Parent ID?	"Do you have any children eighteen years of age or younger living in this household?"	Constructed from household roster: the number of children aged seventeen or younger in household	Variable indicating children under eighteen years of age in household	Variable indicating children under eighteen years of age in household	Flag created by Liana Sayer based on marital status and number of adults in home	Interviewer asks if there are children under eighteen in the household and asks to speak with parent

Source: Authors' compilations from data documentation deposited with the Inter University Consortium for Political and Social Research (ICPSR). Ann Arbor: Institute for Social Research, University of Michigan.

a. In 1965, at least one member of the household had to be employed. Rural households excluded.
b. Married parents, where both spouses worked at least 10 hours per week for pay and at least one of the parents had some college education were given weekly diaries.
c. 1965–66 Americans' Use of Time Study
d. 1975–76 Time Use in Economic and Social Accounts
e. 1985 Americans' Use of Time
f. 1995 Electric Power Research Institute (EPRI) Study
g. 1998–99 Family Interaction, Social Capital and Trends in Time Use Study
h. 2000 National Survey of Parents

Family Interaction, Social Capital, and Trends in Time-Use Study (FISCT)

The 2000 to 2001 Sloan study of parents followed a full national diary data collection that included nonparents as well as parents. In 1998 and 1999, we conducted a national study of adults, age eighteen and over, in which 1,151 adults were interviewed (Bianchi, Robinson, and Presser 2001). Respondents were interviewed by telephone and completed a one-day, yesterday diary. The overall response rate was 56 percent. The study, conducted with funding from the National Science Foundation (NSF) and supplementary funding from the National Institute on Aging for interviews with the population age sixty-five and older, was designed to be comparable to earlier national time-diary data collections. For many of our analyses, the sample of parents from the NSF study are combined with the Sloan sample of 1,200 parents to augment the sample sizes on which the diary estimates for the most recent time point are based.[6]

These data collections were the first in the United States since 1985 that asked adult respondents about not only their primary activities, but also their simultaneous or secondary activities and with whom they spent their time on the diary day. Interviews for both studies were conducted by telephone using the same survey procedures and the same survey organization (the Survey Research Center of the University of Maryland). Nondiary questions in the NSF study were more limited, less focused on child rearing, and more methodological than in the Sloan study, but similar demographic information was collected in both.

Sloan Weekly Diaries

A major limitation of the one-day diary reports is that they might be collected on a nonstandard or an atypical day and may not adequately represent an individual's time allocation. One of the innovations attempted in the 2000 National Survey of Parents was to collect weekly diaries from all family members for a middle-class, dual-earner subsample of our respondents in the one-day diary study. Broadening the time collection window to a week provides more sampling points for each respondent and increases the likelihood that unusual time allocation on one day is balanced out on subsequent days. For example, if we capture an unusually short workday on Monday because of a child emergency, Tuesday may be more typical and, indeed, that Monday work loss may be made up on following days. Second, the weekly time frame captures time spent on weekend days—which one-day studies show are dramatically different from weekdays—for each individual and in its proper proportion. These data offer a broader perspective on family time use than the usual one-day diaries collected in previous studies. New insights from these weekly diaries are discussed in chapter 6.

At the end of the telephone interview, middle-class parents in our Sloan national survey were recruited to participate in a further weekly diary study. Those parents who were married and employed, whose spouses were also employed, and who had at least some college education (or whose spouse was college educated) were asked to participate in a weekly diary study to be completed by mail. Participants were offered between $70 and $100 to participate, depending on the number of children in the family.

NSP families who agreed to participate were then mailed a weekly time-diary packet, which contained a separate diary for each parent and all children in the household. Each diary was for all seven days of the week, asking for each activity for the 24 hours of each day, the time each activity began and ended, the location, and other persons present (secondary activity data were not collected). The persons present—or with whom—entry identified each child by whether he or she was the oldest child in the household, the youngest, or a middle child. Interviewers at the Survey Research Center called each family by telephone about a week after the packet was mailed to determine whether they had received it and understood its instructions. They were then called a few days later to further confirm participation and instructions, particularly the need to have completed diaries for all members of the family. After completing the weekly diaries, each family mailed them back to the University of Maryland. Only 450 of the original sample of 1,200 families met the criteria: namely, being a parent in a middle-class family in which both parents worked at least 10 or more hours per week.[7] Of these, 128 accepted, completed, and returned a mail-out diary covering an entire week.

Because of the small sample size, low response rate (128/450 or 28 percent), and the high cost of reaching and recruiting cooperating families, a more cost-efficient method of locating families was needed. That involved using the samples of two organizations that already had recruited large national panels of respondents willing to participate in various surveys. Because of their large sample base and previous determination of the demographic composition of their samples, both firms were able to contact families meeting the study's strict sampling criteria (roughly one eligible family for each eight to twelve telephone numbers called). The two panel sample studies—one from Market Facts and the other from National Family Opinion (NFO)—were conducted separately using diary forms, data collection procedures, and payment schedules determined to be most appropriate for each organization. In both studies, about one-third of the panel families contacted returned satisfactorily completed family diaries. These samples also completed other survey questions asked of parents in the University of Maryland NSP.

Comparison of the weekly time diaries showed rather consistent results across the three data collection efforts. Parents in the commercial panel samples reported somewhat more time in religious and other organizational activities in their diaries than those in the University of Maryland survey (both the weekly diary and the initial NSP telephone survey), and the mothers in these samples reported somewhat less time at work. Overall, however, the three samples reported weekly behavior similar enough to warrant combining them into the single sample examined in chapter 6.

Even more important, when we compared the estimated weekly activity patterns (one-day diary reports times seven) of the 450 respondents eligible to receive weekly diaries in the University of Maryland study to the activity patterns actually reported in the weekly diaries that were returned by the three subsamples (the 128 respondents from the University of Maryland sample and the NFO and Market Facts samples), they were very similar.

Although our samples of weekly diaries are not drawn from probability samples, they represent the only weekly data collection in the United States and provide information on the time use of multiple family members. Although the use of nonprobability and low-response rate samples can be a source of concern, we take encouragement from Robert Putnam's (2000) findings about similar trends and conclusions on a wide variety of topics from commercial panel versus probability samples, and by the findings of Richard Curtin, Stanley Presser, and Eleanor Singer (2000) and Scott Keeter and colleagues (2000) about convergent conclusions from high and low response rate surveys. Obviously, though we would prefer to have had high response-rates and probability samples (rather unlikely given the heavy respondent burden associated with weekly diaries from multiple family members), our several methodological checks indicate that the results from the weekly diaries do not seem out of line with those from more representative samples used for single-day diaries. We also are reminded of Howard Schuman and Stanley Presser's (1981) finding that although one may find notable differences in frequency distributions across various samples, the conclusions from correlations across disparate samples seem less affected by such biases. That type of correlational analysis is a main focus of our analysis of weekly diaries in chapter 6.

A further concern in our weekly diary samples is that they include only middle-class parents with both spouses working at least 10 hours per week. These sampling criteria were introduced to focus on the families of interest to the sponsor, the Sloan Foundation's Working Families Program. Thus, these parents are likely to be busier than the overall parent population. That is, this Sloan sample reflects time pressure at one of the busiest points in the life course because these are college-educated working parents, often in demanding jobs, who must combine many hours of market work with their child care and housework responsibilities. Also, because our weekly diary sample of parents is somewhat better educated than the general population of parents—even middle-class ones—and education is positively correlated with employment opportunities (and work hours), parents in our weekly sample are likely to have longer paid work weeks than the average American or American parent. Finally, the higher educational level of our middle-class parents may predispose them to be relatively more egalitarian in their division of labor compared to all parents—another reason we compare our sample of middle-class parents with all married parents in chapter 6.

Time Diaries Versus Direct Survey Questions

Research has shown that time-diary estimates of paid work hours are typically lower than estimates derived from the CPS (Robinson and Bostrom 1994). Perhaps because of the diary's implicit constraint on 24 hours per day, respondents report fewer hours at work per day or week than in survey estimate questions. John Robinson and Jonathan Gershuny (1994), have found consistent overreporting of paid work hours by employed people, not only in the United States but also in ten other Western countries. Using the standard labor-force question, "How many hours do you usually work?," workers within the more normal range of 35- to 45-hour work weeks give relatively consistent reports in time diaries and in survey estimate questions, but those who work longer hours have greater gaps between their estimates and diary figures (Robinson and Bostrom 1994). Workers estimating 60- to 80-hour work weeks have the greatest gaps. These findings suggest one tendency of time estimation to follow the adage, "The higher the estimate, the greater the overestimate."

To date, much of the methodological work comparing survey estimates with time diaries has focused on market work. Our 1998 to 1999 NSF-funded study collected data on selected nonmarket activities like housework using both the diary format and standard survey-estimate questions. In the survey portion of the study, we had respondents estimate their time doing various housework activities and compared these estimates directly with the reports in their diaries. The housework estimate questions—taken directly from the 1984 to 1986 National Survey of Families and Households (NSFH)—were of particular interest because they dealt with family-care activities and because they had been extensively analyzed in the literature.

Table 2.5 shows the results of this comparison separately for men and women. The first two columns show results from estimate questions covering two reference periods—housework done over a week

Table 2.5   Estimates from Survey Questions Versus Time Diaries of Housework (Hours per Week; 1998 to 1999 Data)

	Men				Women			
	Estimated Hours		Time-Diary Hours		Estimated Hours		Time-Diary Hours	
Activity	(1) Weekly[a]	(2) Yesterday[b]	(3) Primary	(4) Primary + Secondary	(1) Weekly[a]	(2) Yesterday[b]	(3) Primary	(4) Primary + Secondary
Preparing meals	4.1	5.1	2.3	2.7	7.5	6.8	4.4	5.0
Washing dishes	2.6	1.7	0.6	0.7	5.5	3.8	0.8	1.1
Cleaning house	3.3	2.9	2.2	2.5	7.1	7.5	3.1	3.7
Doing other chores	4.1	4.1	2.8	2.9	3.0	2.8	1.8	2.1
Washing and iron clothes	1.5	1.4	0.6	1.2	3.7	4.4	2.2	2.9
Paying bills	1.5	2.2	0.5	0.6	1.8	1.7	0.6	0.7
Doing auto repair	1.2	2.6	0.3	0.3	0.5	0.4	0.2	0.2
Household shopping	1.6	1.8	0.5	0.8	2.9	2.7	1.0	0.3
Chauffeuring	1.1	1.8	0.4	0.4	2.5	2.1	0.6	0.6
Total	21.0	23.6	10.2	12.1	34.5	32.2	14.7	16.6

Source: Presser and Robinson (2000). Authors' compilations from 1998–99 Family Interaction, Social Capital and Trends in Time Use Study (FISCT) (Bianchi, Robinson and Presser 2001).

a. Responses to question, "What is the approximate number of hours per week that you spend _____?"

b. Responses to question, "How much time did you spend yesterday _____?"

and housework done yesterday. The sample was randomly split in two, and half were asked about activities yesterday and the other half about a typical week. The third and fourth columns show housework time as reported in the diary: estimates of housework time as the primary activity (column 3) and estimates that added in time when housework was reported as either a primary or a secondary activity (column 4). All one-day reports, from the diary and from yesterday estimate questions, have been multiplied by seven to facilitate comparisons with weekly estimate questions asked of half the sample.

Comparing the first and third columns, it can be seen that in virtually all housework activity comparisons, the estimated hours are notably higher than times reported in diaries. In the first activity of meal preparation, for example, the estimates from the survey question asking respondents to report how many hours of housework they do in a week are almost twice as high as the primary activity times reported in diaries (4.1 estimate hours versus 2.3 diary hours for men and 7.5 hours versus 4.4 hours for women), and that pattern is replicated for most other activities. Indeed, when all these activities are summed, the estimates (21 hours for men and 35 hours for women) are again more than double their diary hours (10 hours and 15 hours for men and women).

One might think that overestimates result from the weekly time referent being too difficult for respondents to cope with in the immediacy of the interview situation. For that reason, our 1998 experiment also asked daily estimate questions under the assumption that yesterday estimates might yield results that were similar to the diary. Column 2 suggests that virtually the same overestimates are given with the yesterday format. In other words, it is not just the lengthy estimated time period that produces these results: respondents have the same difficulty estimating time spent on housework activities yesterday.

Differences between the diary and the estimate questions might also occur if many of these housework tasks are multitasked, and respondents count all time doing housework. Therefore it is important to compare diary estimates that add together primary and secondary time in housework as in column 4. However, doing housework as a secondary activity totals fewer than 2 hours per week for men and 3 hours for women, far short of the 11- to 18-hour gap between estimates and diary figures.

Figure 2.1 arrays a measure of the gap between estimated hours and diary hours according to the size of the estimated time in each of four housework tasks: cleaning house, preparing meals, washing clothes, and washing dishes. The graphs indicate that for respondents giving lower estimates, the diary and the survey estimate questions produce rather similar results. But as estimates rise, the discrepancy between the estimates and diaries also rises. Assuming the diary responses are more

**Figure 2.1   Differences Between Estimated Hours and Diary Hours as a
Function of Estimated Hours**

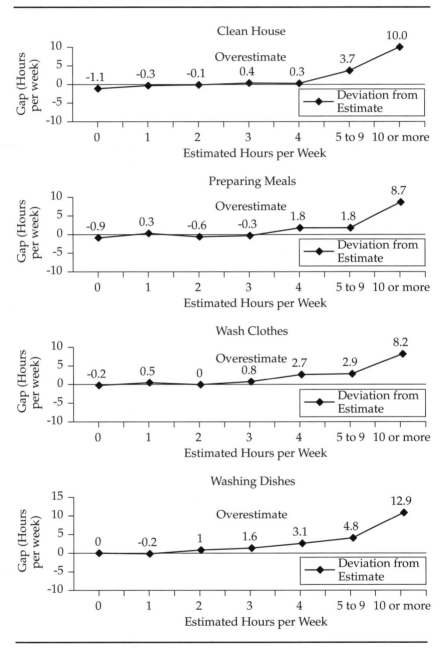

Source: Authors' calculations from the 1998–99 Family Interaction, Social Capital and
Trends in Time Use Study (FISCT) (Bianchi, Robinson, and Presser 2001).

accurate because the task is cognitively easier, the results suggest an overall pattern of rising overestimation for higher estimates. They also suggest why we find it important to use time-diary assessments in this book: to provide a more accurate and complete assessment of changing activities in families with children over the 1965 to 2000 period.

Summary and Conclusions

We rely heavily on time-diary evidence for two reasons. First, estimates from time diaries seem superior to survey-estimate questions for assessing individuals' time expenditures. Second, the time diary allows us to assess all types of activities, not just market work. Because diaries cover the full 24-hour period, they provide information on time spent in productive activity in and for the household—the "second shift" of interest to family researchers.

Diaries also allow us to examine all of the personal care and discretionary pursuits that could be affected by the busy schedules in working families. Because many nonmarket activities are done in bits and pieces across the day, before and after work, on weekends rather than weekdays, weekly hours in these activities may be even more difficult to estimate than weekly hours of employment by means of survey-estimate questions.

Nonetheless, survey estimates can provide a broad perspective on family change and do reflect how survey respondents perceive they spend their time. The next chapter begins with an assessment of trends in market work using the CPS. An important reason to begin with these data is to make sure that trends parallel those in the time diaries. Our diary studies were also embedded in surveys that asked respondents questions about their estimated time use and about their feelings about various activities. These include parenting practices, feelings of time pressure, and the like. We draw on these estimate and attitude data in subsequent chapters to enrich the picture that the diary evidence can provide of changing rhythms of American family life.

Chapter 3

Changing Workloads: Are Parents Busier?

THERE HAS been considerable debate in the United States about what has been happening to work hours over the past two decades. On the one hand are those who argue that total work hours have expanded, driven by consumer aspirations, acquisitions, and debt, as well as by shifts in the economy. Juliet Schor's (1991) *The Overworked American: The Unexpected Decline of Leisure,* argued that Americans were working more, driven by competitive pressures in the workplace and ever increasing demands for consumption in the home. The pressure on individuals to work longer hours to maintain living standards, Schor argued, was crowding out leisure activities and diminishing the quality of American life.

Schor's work spurred many to reexamine trends in labor force participation rates and work hours. It also sparked interest in trends that could not be easily assessed with standard measures of productivity, namely, the trends in unpaid work such as housework and child care. Her critics also asked for more direct evidence of declining leisure and free-time pursuits, declining investment in families, and declining civic participation. The evidence was at best mixed.

Data from time diaries were at odds with the picture Schor provided. Robinson and Godbey's (1999) *Time for Life* showed that work hours as measured in time diaries were actually decreasing for some groups, and that time spent doing housework was spiraling downward for those who did most of this type of work—namely women. If anything, discretionary time was on the increase, though much of it seemed to be spent in front of the television set.

Current Population Survey (CPS) estimate data on annual hours of employment per worker did show an increase in employment hours, mostly because workers reported working more weeks per year. But estimated average weekly employment hours changed minimally between the 1970s and the mid-1990s—although the dispersion of hours across workers was growing (Rones, Ilg, and Gardner 1997; Jacobs and Gerson

2004). There was indeed an increasing group of workers estimating long work weeks, but this was counterbalanced by growth among other groups who were working relatively short work weeks. For example, Mary Coleman and John Pencavel (1993a, 1993b) showed that weekly and annual labor market hours declined between 1940 and 1988 for both women and men with less than a college education, but increased for college-educated women and men.

Arlie Hochschild's (1997) *The Time Bind: When Work Becomes Home and Home Becomes Work* supported Schor's contention that Americans were working more, but maintained that they did so largely by choice. Workers sought to escape the increasingly complex, often unpleasant negotiations of family life by spending ever greater amounts of time and energy in the calmer, more controlled domain of work. Although criticized by Jill Kiecolt (2003) and others, Hochschild's research hit a nerve: could it be true that family life had become so demanding that members would do anything, including more paid work, to avoid it?

A search for confirming evidence began. Jerry Jacobs and Kathleen Gerson (2004) examined the National Survey of the Changing Workforce to see whether workers were forgoing vacation days in order to work more. They were not. Karen Gareis, Rosalind Barnett, and Robert Brennan (2003) looked at job-role quality among a sample of 105 female physicians who had voluntarily reduced their hours of paid employment, as had their employed husbands. They found no evidence of psychological distress among the wives. Indeed, among both the wives and their husbands, positive assessments of the wife's reduced work schedule was associated with a higher job-role quality. David Maume and Marcia Bellas (2001) examined the Survey of Ohio's Working Families to assess whether those who preferred work over home tended to work long hours to avoid home. They found that respondents who favored work over family were no more likely than others to work long schedules or to work on weekends. These analyses found explanations for the overworked American that countered Hochschild's argument. Whereas in the single organization that Hochschild studied intensively, workers may have been abandoning home for the office, there did not seem to be a widespread desire to work more among Americans. In fact, Jacobs and Gerson (2004) found reasonable evidence that parents actually wanted to devote more attention to their families rather than to the workplace.

How could experts on American work and family life come to such different conclusions about time in the workplace and time in the home? The answer is this: there isn't one story about how work and family life are changing in the United States. What may be happening is too much work at some stages of life and too little work at others (Jacobs and Gerson 2004).

The group for whom it is clearest that market work has increased is women, especially mothers. To fit the pieces together requires trend evidence on the paid and unpaid work of those at the busiest stages of the life course, when workers are mired in both parenting young children and working for pay. Two groups seem especially susceptible to overwork—single parents and dual-earner married parents.

A quarter century ago, Clair Vickery (1977) argued that single mothers were not only at heightened risk of financial poverty, but that they also suffered a severe time deficit. The same might be argued for mothers (and fathers) in dual-earner families with children, given the heavy demands of paid work and family caregiving. Here we combine CPS data with our time-diary evidence to chart the growth in the types of families that may face significant challenges in finding enough time both to financially support their families and to care for them. We try to answer the question of how time-bound or busy today's parents are, and whether they became busier between 1965 and 2000.

Providing and Caring: The Dilemma of Working Families

Families with children must solve the problem of how to provide adequate financial support to children while making sure children have the parental time and supervision they need to grow and prosper. In midtwentieth century America, providing for a family largely took place within a two-parent context where gender roles tended to be highly specialized. Fathers provided economic support, and mothers supplemented this by taking care of the home and children.[1]

In 1965, when our assessment of changing family patterns begins, 90 percent of families with children were two-parent families (see appendix table 3A.1). By the beginning of the twenty-first century, the majority of families with children still included two parents, but the majority was 70 percent rather than 90 percent, and a greater proportion of two-parent families included a stepparent rather than both biological parents.[2] Figure 3.1 displays the changing distribution of families by number and employment status of parents.

Much attention has been given to the Ozzie-and-Harriet family of the 1950s and 1960s. Hence it may come as a surprise that the father breadwinner, mother full-time homemaker family accounted for only a little over half (57 percent) of families with children, even in 1965. The ensuing decades saw this percentage fall to 21 percent by 2000, by which time no family type accounted for a clear majority, though dual-earner parents constituted 41 percent of families with children—up from 24 percent in 1965. Over the 1965 to 2000 period, the share of all families with a single

Figure 3.1   Distribution of Families with Children Under Age Eighteen by Number and Labor Force Status of Parents, 1965 to 2000

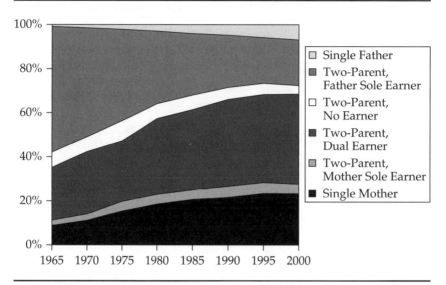

Source: Authors' calculations from the 1965, 1970, 1975, 1980, 1985, 1990, 1995, and 2000 March Current Population Surveys (CPS).
Note: Universe restricted to parents who are householders.

mother increased from 9 to 23 percent and the share with a single father increased from 1 to 7 percent (see appendix table 3A.1).

In the latter half of the twentieth century, the gender-specialized division of labor with mother in the home full-time became less universal, less desirable, and perhaps less attainable as dual wage earning increased in two-parent families, and more families had only one parent to both earn income and care for children. Yet it would be a mistake to conclude that the gender specialization of mothers in the home and fathers in the workplace had disappeared. As we suggested in chapter 1, powerful norms about the need for mothers to devote themselves to the care of their children and for fathers to spend their time providing financially for their families persist.

Figure 3.2 illustrates the employment patterns of parents in two-parent families with children under age six. The percentage of those relying solely on the father for earnings has declined significantly, from 65 to 37 percent (see appendix table 3A.2 for the estimates graphed in figure 3.2.). Yet this type of highly gender-specialized family breadwinning and caregiving pattern remains fairly common when children are young, now characterizing nearly two in five couples with preschoolers.

Figure 3.2   Joint Labor Market Status in Two-Parent Families with Children Under Six

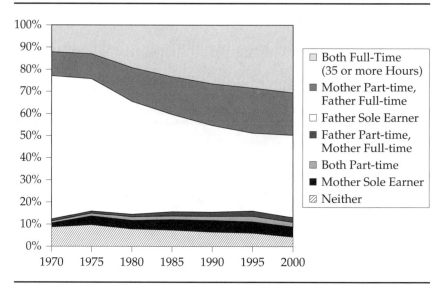

Source: Authors' calculations from the 1970, 1975, 1980, 1985, 1990, 1995, and 2000 March Current Population Surveys (CPS).
Note: Universe restricted to all couples who are householders and the woman is age twenty-five to fifty-four.

Among families with young children, the percent with both parents working full-time hours to provide financially for the family increased from 12 to 31 percent, but this group remains somewhat less common than the father as sole breadwinner group. Another 19 percent of couples with young children (up from 11 percent in 1965) have what Phyllis Moen (2003) has labeled a neotraditional arrangement, one in which the father is employed full-time but the mother works part-time hours—presumably allowing her time to handle the child rearing demands of young children. Relatively few families with young children have neither parent employed (4 percent), only the wife employed (5 percent), or the husband working part-time (less than 35 hours per week) and the mother working full-time (2 percent).

These figures illustrate why it is difficult to determine whether families have changed dramatically, or whether there is continuity with the past in family breadwinning and caregiving. There is not one dominant model, one clear solution for balancing work and family that most families, or most new fathers and mothers, settle upon. Instead, there is a great deal of churning as parents experiment with different strategies. Mothers who may have thought that they would remain committed to full-time employment often reassess this after their children are born. Sizable subgroups of women continue to drop out of the labor force for at least a few years or cut back their hours of work when their children are young. This does not happen for sizable subgroups of men when they become fathers.

On the other hand, mothers as a group have greater commitment and attachment to the labor force during their child-rearing years than they did in the past. Still, there is enough diversity to fuel tensions among mothers who choose full-time parenting, those who choose full-time employment, and those who try to straddle both worlds. No one is completely sure who has it right—or whether it is even possible to settle on an ideal solution to the inherent conflict between work and family life. As Jacobs and Gerson (2004, 53) note, "new generations are seeking a balance between home and work that remains elusive."

Mothers' Work Outside the Home: The Big Change in Working Families

The basic work and family dilemma has not changed, in that families still must figure out how to care for and financially support their children in as optimal a fashion as they can. However, the social context surrounding family decision making most assuredly changed over the 1965 to 2000 period because women became more powerful economic actors in families. There was a dramatic increase in paid employment of women between 1970 and 1990, particularly among married women with children. Jacobs and Gerson (2004) argue that the major change in family life that leaves more families feeling time-pressured is just this increase. In a growing share of families with children, all adults work at least some hours outside the home. Mothers' employment has increased in all developed countries, although Gornick and Meyers (2003) show that employment levels vary enormously across developed economies, from a low of around 40 percent of mothers employed in Luxembourg to a high of 85 percent in Sweden. Rates for American mothers are near the average across developed countries: although lower than in Scandinavia, they are higher than in most countries in continental Europe.

Table 3.1 shows changes between 1965 and 2000 in mothers' (age twenty-five to fifty-four) employment based on CPS data. Changes are tracked in the percent employed at least one week in the previous year, the likelihood that mothers were employed all weeks of the year and the number of hours worked per week and weeks worked per year. The top panel of table 3.1 shows estimates averaged over all mothers, including those who were not employed that year; the bottom panel restricts the analysis to mothers who were employed at the time of the survey.

Table 3.1 Employment of Mothers with Children Under Age Eighteen

	1965	1970	1975	1980	1985	1990	1995	2000
All mothers with children under age eighteen								
Percentage employed previous year	44.7	52.2	56.1	65.7	68.7	73.8	75.1	78.1
Percentage employed year round (fifty or more weeks)	19.1	25.5	29.6	35.6	41.8	47.2	51.9	56.5
Average hours worked per week	11	13	14	18	20	22	23	25
Average weeks worked per year	16	20	22	27	29	32	33	36
Estimated annual hours[a]	444	552	606	800	895	1,022	1,081	1,172
Sample size (N)	(9,382)	(17,984)	(16,007)	(22,200)	(19,502)	(19,097)	(18,286)	(15,633)
Employed mothers with children under age eighteen[b]								
Percentage employed year round (fifty or more weeks)	50.2	57.2	60.5	61.2	67.0	69.7	74.6	76.9
Average hours worked per week	34	33	33	34	35	35	35	36
Average weeks worked per year	38	41	42	42	44	45	46	47
Estimated annual hours	1,367	1,406	1,435	1,497	1,565	1,633	1,662	1,711
Sample size (N)	(3,106)	(7,055)	(6,784)	(11,791)	(11,185)	(11,939)	(11,830)	(10,679)

Source: Authors' tabulations from the 1965, 1970, 1975, 1980, 1985, 1990, 1995, and 2000 March Current Population Surveys (CPS).
Note: Analysis restricted to mothers who are householders or spouses ages twenty-five to fifty-four.
a. Hours employed last week multiplied by weeks employed last year.
b. Women employed 1 or more hours in the previous week.

Typically, those who assess trends concentrate on the top line in the table, the increase in labor force participation of all mothers, and then the bottom panel, changes in hours and weeks worked among the employed. We show both panels because focusing only on trends for employed mothers can give the impression that the level of maternal employment in the United States is actually higher than it is. The point to make is this: although there is no question that maternal employment has increased dramatically, the averages across all mothers for the current level of employment and hours worked falls considerably short of a full-time, year-round labor force commitment for the majority of mothers in the United States.

In 2000, 78 percent of mothers were employed, a tremendous jump from the 45 percent in 1965. Employed mothers also increased their year-round labor force attachment: whereas half worked year round in 1965, more than three-quarters did so in 2000. The average number of weeks worked jumped from thirty-eight to forty-seven. What did not change much was the average number of hours per week: 34 hours in 1965, up slightly to 36 hours in 2000. Hence, an employed mother in 1965 was juggling about as many hours of paid work per week as she would in 2000—but that was a lot more common in 2000 than in 1965.

If one stops here, the picture is of very high employment levels for mothers. Three-quarters are employed, three-quarters of these work year round and average full-time hours (as defined by the Bureau of Labor Statistics at 35 or more hours per week). Where this picture is misleading is that it leaves out the 22 percent of mothers who worked no weeks during the year. If one puts them back into the calculations of mothers' labor market time, as in the top panel of table 3.1, the estimate is that only a little over half (57 percent) of all mothers are employed across the entire year. Averaged across all mothers, hours employed per week are 25 rather than 36, and weeks worked are 36 rather than 47.

One can take estimates of weeks worked per year and hours worked per week to derive an estimate of annual hours worked per year for mothers. A person employed for 52 weeks in a year and paid for 40 hours per week would average 2,080 hours of paid employment. Table 3.1 shows that employed mothers in 2000 averaged almost 1,700 annual hours—a 21-percent increase over the 1,400 hours of 1965. Annual hours averaged over all mothers, including those not employed, more than doubled from 450 to almost 1,200 hours.

One of the ways that mothers, even working mothers, preserve time for the kinds of activities charted in the subsequent chapters—time with children, time in housework and shopping, and free time—is by curtailing their hours of employment. These annual averages of 1,200 (across all mothers) or 1,700 (across employed mothers) fall short of the

2000-plus average that would prevail if all mothers worked full-time, year-round. Mothers' employment is also far more responsive to the number and ages of their children than fathers' employment is. In two-parent families, fathers' employment hours vary little by age of the youngest child, as shown in table 3.2. Despite the media attention to stay-at-home dads, the CPS numbers suggest that about 90 percent of fathers are employed, and average 45 to 47 hours of market work per week—no matter how many children they have or how young those children are.

Mothers' estimated employment hours and probabilities, on the other hand, are very responsive to the age of their youngest child. Only 46 percent of those with at least one child under the age of one were employed in the week before the survey, but this rises to 73 percent when all children are older than six. Employed mothers also average fewer work hours than employed fathers, averaging 36 hours per week when all children are older than six, dropping to 31 hours per week when at least one child is less than a year old. Because so many fewer mothers than fathers are employed when children are young, and because even when employed mothers work fewer hours than fathers, these CPS estimates suggest that mothers contribute almost 40 percent of a family's combined labor market hours when all children are older than six—compared to only about 25 percent when the couple has a child younger than one.

The best available evidence suggests that, if anything, fathers tend to increase hours of market employment after the birth of a child (Lundberg and Rose 2002). Mothers, on the other hand, exercise a wider array of options: some return quickly to their employer (often to full-time work), but a sizable group curtails employment hours or takes some time out of the labor force after the birth of a child, a sorting that continues after the birth of the second child (Klerman and Leibowitz 1999).

In the past, women's labor force participation declined at the time they married, but this is no longer the case (Cohen and Bianchi 1999; Goldin 1990). Now the decrease in women's hours of employment comes with the birth of the first child—even though women are also now much more likely to return to work within six months of a birth than they were twenty years ago (Smith, Downs, and O'Connell 2001). Mothers continue to curtail hours of employment after they have children, and, perhaps not surprisingly, a wage penalty continues to be associated with motherhood (Waldfogel 1997; Budig and England 2001). Earnings contributions to the family become less equal between mothers and fathers once children arrive, in part because mothers cut back on their employment but fathers do not. Gornick and Meyers (2003) show that mothers' wages lag behind fathers' in virtually all developed economies: U.S. mothers average about 28 percent of a family's labor market earnings, which places

Table 3.2   Labor Market Hours in Two-Parent Families, 2000

	Sample Size (N)	Mother's Weekly Hours			Father's Weekly Hours			Parents' Combined Hours	
		Percentage with Any Hours	Average Hours Per Worker	Average Hours All Mothers	Percentage with Any Hours	Average Hours Per Worker	Average Hours All Fathers	Number	Percentage Contributed by Mothers
Children									
Ages of children									
All over age six	(6,781)	72.8	36.0	26.2	89.4	45.8	40.9	67.1	39.0
At least one under age six	(5,109)	58.4	33.6	19.6	90.8	45.6	41.4	61.1	32.2
At least one under age four	(3,671)	56.0	32.8	18.3	91.1	45.7	41.7	60.1	30.5
At least one under age one	(918)	46.3	31.3	14.5	91.0	46.6	42.4	56.8	25.5
Number of children									
One	(4,249)	72.1	36.5	26.3	89.4	45.2	40.4	66.7	39.5
Two	(4,954)	67.8	34.7	23.5	90.6	45.9	41.6	65.1	36.1
Three	(2,116)	60.1	33.9	20.4	89.9	46.3	41.6	62.0	32.9
Four or more	(896)	47.4	32.4	15.3	85.9	45.3	38.9	54.2	28.3

Source: Authors' tabulations from the 2000 March Current Population Survey (CPS).
Note: Analysis restricted to all couples who are householders and the woman is age twenty-five to fifty-four.

U.S. families in the middle of the distribution of countries they examined (ten European countries plus Canada and the United States).

How Many Hours Do Families Give the Labor Market and Has This Changed?

Gornick and Meyers (2003) claim that where American families are exceptional, relative to their European counterparts, is in terms of the total number of hours families commit to the labor force. When one adds mothers' and fathers' estimated annual hours, American parents have less vacation and work the longest annual hours of parents in any country—even Japan. Gornick and Meyers also find that a higher percentage of American dual-earner couples work long work weeks than their counterparts in other countries.

The percentage of dual-earner couples in the United States who put in a long combined work week (of 80 plus or 100 plus estimated hours per week) may be on the increase, especially among highly educated workers (Jacobs and Gerson 2001, 2004). Dual-earner parents, both having professional or managerial jobs, may be especially time-pressed. Both Jacobs and Gerson (2004) and Gornick and Meyers (2003) argue that not enough is done in the United States to assist parents in shouldering the double burden of family caregiving and paid market work.

Figure 3.3 uses CPS data to show the joint employment hours of couples with children—that is, the average weekly hours of the husband and the wife combined. (Appendix table 3A.3 provides the estimates that are graphed in figure 3.3.) Across all two-parent families with children (panel A of figure 3.3), the mean combined labor market hours of husbands and wives grew from 52 to 64 hours per week between 1965 and 2000. These estimates actually dipped slightly between 1965 and 1975 to 51 hours, but then rose steadily as more wives entered the labor force.

However, if the time trend is restricted only to dual-earner couples, one sees little change. As shown in panel B of figure 3.3, dual-earner families with children averaged about 80 hours of market work at each time point. Wives supplied about 35 of those hours, on average, and husbands put in about 45 hours per week (see appendix table 3A.3). The work weeks of dual earner couples changed little, but the number of these kinds of families grew.

Figure 3.4 graphs the percentage of all couples (and of dual-earner couples with children) in which the combined work hours of mother and father equaled or exceeded 80 hours. Also shown is the subset of couples who report 100 or more hours (combined) of market work per week in the CPS. The percentage of couples working at least 80 hours

Figure 3.3   Joint Weekly Market Hours in Two-Parent Families with Children Under Age Eighteen

Panel A: Two-Parent Families

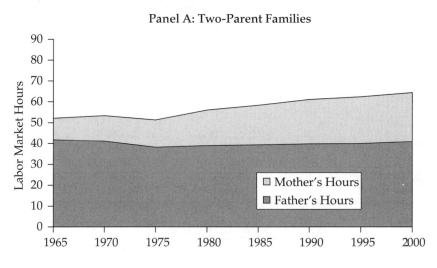

Panel B: Dual-Earning Two-Parent Families

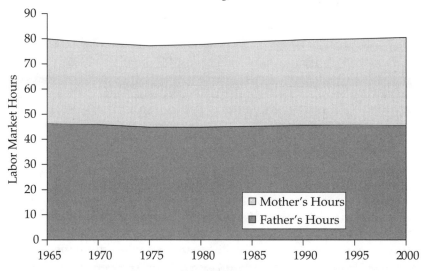

Source: Authors' calculations from the 1965, 1970, 1975, 1980, 1985, 1990, 1995, and 2000 March Current Population Surveys (CPS).
Note: Universe restricted to all couples who are householders and the woman is age twenty-five to fifty-four.

Figure 3.4   Long Work Hours of Couples with Children

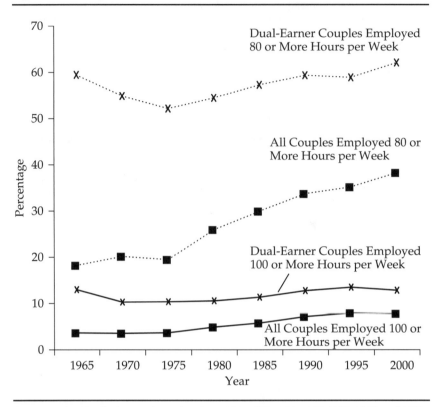

Source: Authors' calculations from the 1965, 1970, 1975, 1980, 1985, 1990, 1995, and 2000 March Current Population Surveys (CPS).

per week dipped slightly as fathers' hours fell between 1970 and 1975. After 1975, the percentage of all couples with a combined 80-hour work week almost doubled, from 20 to 38 percent. The proportion of those with a 100-hour work week also doubled over roughly the same period, from 4 percent in 1965 to 8 percent in 2000. When the comparison is restricted to dual-earner couples, the patterns are less dramatic, though the levels are much higher. Among these, there was a drop from 60 percent to 52 percent working more than 80 hours between 1965 and 1975. By 1990, this figure had returned to the 1965 level of 60 percent. About 13 percent of dual-earner couples with children worked 100 or more (combined) hours in 2000, up from 10 percent in 1975, but that was similar to the estimated levels of 1965. The percentage of sole breadwinner fathers who estimated putting in a 50-hour or more workweek also increased, from about 27 percent in 1975 to 36 percent in 2000 (estimates shown in appendix table 3A.3).

This pattern of a dip in market work estimates between 1965 and 1975, with increases after 1975, is also present in our time-diary data, giving us greater assurance that the curvilinear pattern is real. It suggests that a small subset of dual-earner parents in 1965 were already quite busy. What changed after 1975 was that those busy patterns became more widespread, as more and more couples with children joined the ranks of dual earners. The increase in workloads of 80 or 100 hours also suggests that a growing proportion of children have both parents working full-time, due primarily to an increase in mothers working full-time, with the majority of fathers already doing so.

The last half of the 1990s saw a dramatic upsurge in employment rates of single mothers, especially less-educated single mothers. By 2000, almost half of single mothers were putting in a 40-plus-hour work week, a higher percentage that at any earlier time. The percentage of single mothers working more than 50 hours more than doubled over the period, from 4.2 percent in 1965 to 8.6 percent in 2000 (see appendix table 3A.3).

Trend analyses by Jacobs and Gerson (2004) also suggest that work hours have become more unequal across workers, with low-skill workers often unable to get enough hours of paid work to adequately support their families—in contrast to high-skill workers with the opposite problem— plenty of income but long hours and too little time. Table 3.3 provides a snapshot of employment rates, rates of full-time year-round work, and average weekly hours of employment by educational attainment for three groups of parents—married fathers, married mothers, and single mothers. Employment rates are highest for married fathers, followed by single mothers and then married mothers. Within each group, employment rates are positively correlated with educational attainment: more highly educated workers have higher employment rates, a higher likelihood of working full-time, year-round—and in the case of married fathers and single mothers (but not married mothers), somewhat longer work weeks than less-educated parents.

A number of other features stand out in table 3.3. College-educated single mothers have very high employment rates—almost as high as married fathers. Married mothers with postgraduate education also have very high employment rates, but are considerably less likely to work full-time, year-round than similarly educated single mothers or married fathers. Only 41 percent of married mothers with a postgraduate education work full-time year-round, compared with 69 percent of single mothers and 79 percent of married fathers. Highly educated, married mothers average 34 hours of employment per week compared with 42 hours for comparably educated single mothers and 47 hours for married fathers. Hence,

Table 3.3 Employment Rates of Parents by Educational Attainment, 2000

	Married Fathers			Married Mothers			Single Mothers		
	Percentage Employed	Percent FTYR[b]	Weekly Hours	Percentage Employed	Percent FTYR[b]	Weekly Hours	Percentage Employed	Percent FTYR[b]	Weekly Hours
Parents total	93.9	77.0	44.6	70.0	36.6	33.5	77.3	48.3	36.9
With at least one child under age eighteen									
Less than high school	82.2	59.4	41.6	45.5	22.0	34.7	54.1	26.7	33.4
High school only	92.1	74.6	43.9	68.1	36.6	34.1	77.1	47.3	36.4
Some college[a]	93.3	76.5	44.9	71.9	36.5	33.1	84.8	54.6	36.9
College graduate	97.3	82.3	45.6	72.6	36.1	32.6	90.3	62.5	40.1
More than a bachelor's	96.5	79.2	47.2	81.6	41.0	33.5	94.9	69.0	41.5
With at least one child under age six									
Less than high school	88.0	65.3	41.9	39.4	16.6	33.5	51.1	21.7	32.1
High school only	94.0	75.2	43.3	60.1	30.3	32.6	70.9	39.3	34.7
Some college	94.8	77.1	44.3	63.7	29.4	31.3	79.5	45.8	36.4
College graduate	98.3	83.1	45.2	65.2	29.5	30.5	89.8	62.1	40.5
More than a bachelor's	97.9	79.5	47.7	75.8	33.0	31.4	94.3	70.4	40.3

Source: Authors' tabulations from the 2000 March Current Population Survey (CPS).
Note: Analysis restricted to all parents who are householders or spouses age twenty-five to fifty-four. Full-time employment status is assessed using "hours worked last week" (full-time = 35 or more hours). Employment status is self-reported ("ESR" variable). Respondents missing on education or employment status have been dropped.
a. Includes associate's degrees
b. FTYR = Full-time, year-round employment (year-round = fifty or more weeks worked in previous year).

although highly educated married mothers are much more strongly attached to market work than less-educated married mothers, their allocation of time to market work lags behind that of their husbands and their single unmarried counterparts.

Total (Paid and Unpaid) Work Hours

Work-family stress is not only about paid work hours, it is also about the double burden of unpaid family caregiving on top of paid work hours—the second shift popularized by Hochschild (1989). There is a persistent claim that mothers' work hours are far longer than fathers', an argument bolstered by statistics on women's greater hours of housework (Bianchi et al. 2000). Women do about twice as much child care and housework as men (Robinson and Godbey 1999), but men work more hours for pay. Because both unpaid (nonmarket) work and paid (market) work are necessary for families, it is useful to examine the total amount of work effort that is being expended by mothers and fathers in caring and providing for their families.

To examine trends in total work time, we now turn to our time-diary evidence, which gives us a one-day snapshot, one that we can aggregate across individuals to represent all days of the week and all weeks of the year. The diaries can thus provide annual estimates for comparing the total work hours of single and married parents, both mothers and fathers. The few studies comparing the total workload of mothers and fathers have suggested that total work or productive hours may not be that different for men and women in the United States (Robinson and Godbey 1999; Marini and Shelton 1993; Zick and McCullough 1991). Recent international comparisons by Michael Bittman and Judith Wajcman (2000) show that gender differences in total work hours vary somewhat across countries, but that, in general, gender differences are rather small. For example, total hours of work (paid-market and unpaid-nonmarket) are lower for men in Italy, Canada, the United Kingdom, Finland, Norway, and Sweden, ranging from five fewer hours in Italy to one fewer in the United Kingdom. By contrast, women actually have a lighter total workload than men in Australia, Denmark, and the Netherlands, from only a 25-minute difference to almost a 3-hour-per-week difference in the Netherlands.

Most claims about women's overburdened lives[3] note the large increase in employment of women (hours of work in the first shift) and then focus solely on the disproportionate share of housework that women do. In contrast, we combine paid and unpaid work to examine a measure of total (market plus nonmarket) work. Our measure of total work hours includes what time-diary researchers have typically labeled as contracted time and committed time. Contracted time includes not only time at work but also travel time to work. Committed time is time that is necessary to the functioning of domestic life, and includes time spent in household chores, child care activities, shopping, and providing services for the family (shown in coding categories in chapter 2, table 2.3). These unpaid activities are as essential for individual and family functioning and consumption as is the income generated from remunerated hours in the paid labor market.

Table 3.4 shows weekly hours spent in market work, nonmarket work, and combined workloads for the three groups of parents for whom we have sufficient numbers of cases to track with the time diaries: married mothers, married fathers, and single mothers. Sample sizes are much smaller for the time-diary data than for the CPS, and hence sampling variability may affect trends—particularly for single mothers. Also, the CPS estimates do not include commuting. Despite these differences, trends for market work are quite similar for the three groups in both data sets (CPS numbers are included in appendix table 3A.3). In general, the estimates suggest that the total workload of married mothers and fathers and single mothers was greater in 2000 than earlier. The pattern of total work hours is one of a dip between 1965 and 1975 and a rise thereafter. From the low point of 1975 to 2000, total work hours increased from 55 to 65 hours per week for married mothers, from 59 to 64 hours for married fathers and from 51 to 66 hours for single mothers. In 2000, a married father averaged 64 hours a week in market plus nonmarket work (or a 9-hour work day averaged across the week), a married mother closer to 65 hours (also a little over a 9-hour work day, 7 days a week), and a single mother 66 hours (more like a 9.5 hour work day across the week).

Gender specialization in the market and in the home declined over the period. In 1965, time-diary estimates of married mothers' market work are low relative to CPS. Hence, married fathers' weekly market work hours were almost eight times married mothers' hours in the time diary, but four times as high in the CPS. Throughout the 1970s and 1980s, married mothers' hours of employment rose relative to married fathers' hours and hence by 2000, the ratio of married fathers' to married mothers' market hours declined to 1.8.

With respect to nonmarket work hours, married mothers' hours declined between 1965 and 1975, and fathers' hours held steady before rising between 1975 and 1985. Hence, across the 1965 to 1985 period, the ratio of married fathers' to mothers' nonmarket work hours increased: fathers did only 20 percent as much nonmarket work as mothers in 1965, but 50 percent as much in 1985 and at subsequent time points.

At all time points, the ratio of total work hours of married fathers and mothers hovers around equality, a point to which we return in chapter 6.

Table 3.4   Total Work Hours (Paid and Unpaid) of Parents with Children Under Age Eighteen

	1965	1975	1985	1995	2000
	Market Work[a] (Contracted Time)				
Married mothers	6.0	15.2	19.7	24.9	23.8*
Married fathers	47.8	47.2	42.5	39.8	42.5*
Ratio (married fathers to married mothers)	7.9	3.1	2.2	1.6	1.8
Single mothers	28.4	18.9	24.5	27.7	28.9
Ratio (married mothers to single mothers)	0.2	0.8	0.8	0.9	0.8
	Nonmarket Work (Committed Time)				
Married mothers	52.7	39.9	39.7	40.5	41.1*
Married fathers	12.3	12.0	18.9	20.9	21.5*
Ratio (married fathers to married mothers)	0.2	0.3	0.5	0.5	0.5
Single mothers	30.8	31.9	25.8	25.8	36.7
Ratio (married mothers to single mothers)	1.7	1.3	1.5	1.6	1.1
	Total Work				
Married mothers	58.8	55.0	59.4	65.4	64.9*
Married fathers	60.1	59.2	61.4	60.8	64.0
Ratio (married fathers to married mothers)	1.0	1.1	1.0	0.9	1.0
Single mothers	59.2	50.8	50.3	53.4	65.6
Ratio (married mothers to single mothers)	1.0	1.1	1.2	1.2	1.0

Source: Authors' calculations from the 1965–66 Americans' Use of Time Study; the 1975–76 Time Use in Economic and Social Accounts; 1985 Americans' Use of Time; the 1995 Electric Power Research Institute (EPRI) Study; and the combined file of the 1998–99 Family Interaction, Social Capital and Trends in Time Use Study and the 2000 National Survey of Parents.
a. Includes time spent commuting to and from work.
*2000 estimate differs significantly from 1965, $p < 0.05$.

However, gender specialization continued in 2000, with married fathers spending almost twice as many hours in the labor market each week as married mothers, but with mothers doing twice as many hours of nonmarket work as fathers. Throughout the period, married mothers spent fewer hours in the labor market than single mothers, but spent more hours on nonmarket work.

Liana Sayer (2001, figure 6.2) shows that, in addition to parents, another group stands out as having unusually long (total) work days: married childless women whose market work hours are now similar to married childless men, but who still do an hour more nonmarket work per day than married childless men. This is consistent with longitudinal evidence suggesting that marriage increases women's (but not men's) time in housework activities (Gupta 1999; Robinson and Godbey 1999, 333), and with findings that the nonmarket gender work gap is larger for married than for single individuals (South and Spitze 1994).

A Note on Employed and Nonemployed Mothers

Much of the literature focuses on the overwork that comes with the second shift for working mothers—their need to continue to do large amounts of unpaid work in the home, even as they add substantial paid work to their daily schedules. Figure 3.5 contrasts the overall workload for employed and nonemployed mothers in 1975 and in 2000. These estimates are not standardized for compositional differences between the two groups of mothers—that is, the fact that nonemployed mothers at both points have more and younger children and are also somewhat younger and less educated than employed mothers.

As shown on the bottom of figure 3.5, 45 percent of mothers of children under eighteen were employed and 55 percent were not in 1975. By 2000, this had shifted to a 70-30 split as more mothers joined the paid labor force. Our diary figures indicate that an employed mother at either time averaged the same number of hours of paid employment—36 hours per week. But in the intervening period, unpaid family work increased. At each point, nonemployed mothers spent far more hours in unpaid family work than did employed mothers, as overall workloads increased for both groups. In 2000, total workloads were almost 20 hours per week higher for employed mothers than for nonemployed mothers. Employed mothers averaged a 71-hour weekly workload, compared with 52 hours for nonemployed mothers (and 64 hours for fathers married to employed or nonemployed wives).

Summary and Conclusions: Parents' Total Workload Has Increased

Are parents busier today than they were in the past? Our examination of family change in this chapter, using both the CPS and our time-diary data, leads us to conclude that they are. More now are single parents. In two-parent families there has been a rather dramatic increase in mothers' labor force participation. Labor force rates are especially high for highly educated married and single mothers. Mothers also report working more weeks per year, and they are more often employed full-time throughout the year than in the past.

Total workloads, the combined hours given over to market and nonmarket work, have risen and remain high for all three groups: married

Figure 3.5   Mothers' Total Weekly Work Hours

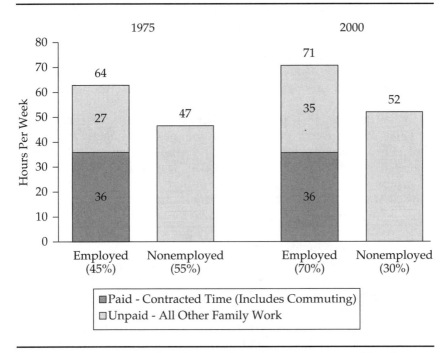

Source: Authors' calculations from the 1975–76 Time Use in Economic and Social Accounts and the combined file of the 1998–99 Family Interaction, Social Capital and Trends in Time Use Study and the 2000 National Survey of Parents.
Note: Difference between workloads of employed and nonemployed significant at p < 0.05 in both 1975 and 2000. Differences between 1975 and 2000 total workloads statistically significant at p < 0.05 for both employed and nonemployed groups.

fathers, married mothers, and single mothers. Parents average a 9-hour to a 9.5-hour workday, 7 days a week, when one adds unpaid work in the home to paid work outside it. Employed mothers' workdays are even longer, averaging 10 hours a day. Moreover, the growing ranks of employed mothers have far greater total workloads than stay-at-home mothers. Hence we conclude that there has been a significant ratcheting up of time pressures in American families—especially in single-parent and dual-earner families.

However, not every trend examined here suggests a family life that is more pressured than in the past. For example, employed mothers do not work appreciably more hours for pay per week. Other trends suggest that families take steps to reduce time pressures that come with paid work and parenting. Working full-time year-round is still not the modal situation for mothers of young children, at least not married mothers of young children. This is true even among the most highly educated mothers: here only 41 percent of married mothers with a postgraduate education work full-time, and this reduces to 33 percent for those with at least one child younger than six. Married mothers' participation in the workforce remains highly responsive to the number and ages of their children—employment falls appreciably, the more children and the younger the children.

In contrast, the participation of fathers is invariant across family size and ages of children. Fathers' employment has not changed much over time either. It may vary somewhat with the business cycle, but employment rates are well over 90 percent—indeed usually over 95 percent—for all groups, except those without a high school degree. These trends are consistent with the cultural brakes scenario on family change that has emerged in the ethnographic literature and that we discussed in chapter 1: fathers continue to concentrate on breadwinning and mothers continue to concentrate on caregiving (Hays 1996; Townsend 2002).

In sum, CPS data on estimated paid work hours show that the combined paid work hours for mothers and fathers rose from 52 to 64 hours between 1965 and 2000, with the proportion of couples working more than 80 hours rising from 18 percent to 38 percent. Single mothers with long paid work weeks are also increasing. The time-diary figures, which add unpaid work hours to paid work hours, also show an increase in mothers' and fathers' total workload, one that parallels the CPS trends—but the change is not as great. The workloads are high however: diary estimates suggest that parents average a 9-hour work day, 7 days a week.

The evidence in this chapter thus leaves a seemingly inevitable conclusion: due to higher parental paid workloads, there must be less time available to interact with children, less leisure, and less time for other activities in these families. Whether this conclusion is correct is the topic of the next two chapters.

═ Chapter 4 ═

Parental Time with Children: More or Less?

I N 1999, the president's Council of Economic Advisers (CEA 1999) estimated that parents today were spending 22 fewer hours in the home
per week compared with 30 years earlier. The CEA arrived at the number by adding the average estimated labor market hours of mothers and
fathers in the Current Population Surveys (CPS), reviewed in chapter 3,
and comparing the two time points of 1968 and 1998. That 22-hour figure
was featured in a May 1999 commencement speech by President Clinton
to illustrate how increasingly difficult working parents were finding it to
spend time with their children (Babington 1999).

At first, it seems reasonable to expect that parental investment in
child-rearing would have declined over the past forty years. After all, the
typical, middle-class American child of 1960 did live in a family like that
of the Cleaver boys from television's *Leave it to Beaver*. As shown in the
last chapter, half of 1965 families with children had a breadwinner father
and a stay-at-home mother and 60 percent of all children lived in such
families (Hernandez 1993). If only about 20 percent of today's families
with children fit this mold (about 30 percent of children living in two-
parent families with a homemaker mother), some social observers rea-
soned that there must have been a corresponding reduction in the amount
of time that children spend together with their parents (Daly 1996)—
because there is ample evidence, other things equal, that mothers who
spend more time in paid employment have less time to spend with children (Aldous, Mulligan, and Bjarnason 1998; Coverman 1985; Coverman
and Sheley 1986; Marsiglio 1995; Zick and Bryant 1996). Moreover, there
is the evidence from children's diaries that children in single-parent families spend less time with their custodial parent (Robinson 1989; Sandberg
and Hofferth 2001), as well as less time with their noncustodial parent
than children in two-parent families (McLanahan and Sandefur 1994).

However, the evidence that parents average less time today caring for
their children than decades ago is inconclusive. First, parents can also
give up other activities—housework, sleep, socializing with friends

and other adult leisure and volunteer activities—in order to maximize time for parenting (a topic pursued in the next chapter). As shown in chapter 3, mothers often adjust their market work to coincide with their children's needs. That is, they often work part-time, or take some time out of the labor force when children are young. They may also try to arrange hours of employment to overlap with their children's school hours in order to maximize their availability in the home.

Second, a mother's increased employment may induce greater father involvement in child rearing (Bianchi 2000). For example, Richard Peterson and Kathleen Gerson (1992) showed that when mothers worked longer hours outside of the home, fathers were more likely to be involved in caring for the family's children. Mothers in Ann Crouter and Susan McHale's (2005) Pennsylvania sample of dual-earner families often reduced their work hours in the summer (when children were out of school), and fathers' involvement was correspondingly higher during the school year (when their wives were more fully employed) than during the summer (when their wives were home more hours).

Chapter 1 highlighted other changes that might predispose parents toward greater involvement in child rearing. Because it is more socially acceptable to remain childless today than in the past (Thornton and Young-DeMarco 2001), and given that effective means of contraception are widely available, those uninterested in raising children can opt out of parenting altogether. As those who opt to delay their childbearing, it is plausible that they may be timing children at a point later in their life when they want to spend time with those children. Declining fertility could lead to an increased emphasis on child quality and on the importance of spending time with each child, ratcheting up per-child investments (Bryant and Zick 1996; Gauthier, Smeeding, and Furstenberg 2004).

Delayed childbearing is also associated with increased educational achievement of parents and more highly educated parents spend more time in child rearing (Bianchi, et al. 2004). Parents who are older when their children are born may also focus more of their attention on child rearing, with some studies finding a positive association between age and spending time with children (Coltrane 1988; Cooney, et al. 1993; Coverman and Sheley 1986; Zick and Bryant 1996), although others have found no association (Pleck 1997; Sandberg and Hofferth 2001).

Early time-diary studies also showed that as education increased (especially for mothers) so did time with children, particularly time in interactive activities (Hill and Stafford 1974, 1980; Leibowitz 1974, 1977). Finally, parenting practices are affected by cultural norms and values that convey notions of appropriate parental behavior. Historical change in parental time with children likely results from shifts in values as well as from demographic factors (Gershuny and Robinson 1988; Sandberg and Hofferth 2001; Sayer, Bianchi, and Robinson 2004). Ethnographic studies of parenting practices suggest that parental behavior has changed with the emergence of norms of "intensive mothering" and "involved fathering" in recent decades (Blair-Loy 2003; Coltrane 1996; Deutsch 1999; Hays 1996; Lareau 2003).

Here we use our time-diary data to measure more directly the time parents report spending in activities with their children. Between 1965 and 2000, did mothers and fathers increase their child care activities and overall time with children, decrease it, or was there no change? The picture that we paint is unexpected—and quite compelling. When we directly measure parents' time allocation, trends suggest that parent-child interaction may be higher than ever.

A Note on Measurement

Our time-diary data provide a unique window into changes in the United States for the period from the 1960s to the beginning of the twenty-first century. As described in chapter 2, in each of the U.S. time-diary studies, a standard series of questions was used to construct a day in the life of respondents by sequentially walking them through a complete day.

We can construct three measures based on the hours in child care activities reported by parents on the diary day (Robinson 1989):

Primary Child Care Activities   Activities captured in response to the question, "What were you doing?" and "What were you doing next?" are known as primary activities because they are considered the most salient activity for respondents. Thus, our first measure is the amount of time parents report in primary child care activities—activities where parents report directly engaging in caregiving or other activities thought to promote children's well-being and where the main focus is the child.

Secondary Child Care Activities   Child care activities mentioned when respondents were asked, "Were you doing anything else?" as they reported each primary or main activity during the day are considered secondary activity time. A more expansive measure of child care time involves adding together primary child care time with this additional secondary time. So, for example, if a father reports watching television but also reports looking after his two-year-old for an hour at the same time, that caring for the two-year-old would be coded as one secondary activity hour and then added to his primary activity time devoted to child care. Obviously, parents can be more or less engaged with children when doing something else: a father absorbed in a television football broadcast may be less focused on the child than when the two of them are watching *Sesame Street*. Lacking such level of detail about each activity, we must assume that children and parents can benefit from the interaction that takes place when care is secondary, even though there may be great variability in the intensity of the interaction between parent and child.

"With Children" Time   Respondent reports of who was "with him or her" while the activity was taking place were also collected in our latest time diaries. This is the largest and most expansive measure of child interactive time. Here we add to the measure of primary plus secondary child care time all other additional time when respondents report that one or more of their children were present, even if no direct child care activity was reported.

Our analysis begins by first examining trends in primary child care time, the most conservative measure, one that adheres to the 24-hour constraint because no time is double counted.[1] Then we expand the analysis to measures that incorporate secondary activity time and next to all the time spent with children.

Finally, we supplement these diary-based measures with additional survey questions related to quality care—frequency-estimate questions about specific parental activities with children, parental monitoring of children, and parental reports of emotional closeness to their children. These non-diary questions were asked only in our 2000 data collection, with the goal of providing a more comprehensive picture of parenting behavior and parental involvement. Because estimates can only be provided for the most recent survey, no trend implications can be drawn from them.

Parents' Time with Children

In recent decades, policy makers, academics, teachers, and parents themselves have been increasingly concerned about children not receiving enough parental time. These concerns about unsupervised latchkey kids (young children left without quality care) stem directly from the demographic shifts in family structure noted in chapter 3—the increasing proportion of mothers of young children who are employed and the growing number of absent fathers.

Figure 4.1 shows overall primary child care hours reported by all mothers and fathers living with children under age eighteen at five points in time: 1965, 1975, 1985, 1995, and 2000. The entries show weekly hours of child care that are estimated by averaging the one-day diary reports of all parents (including those spending no time in child care activities on the diary day), and then multiplying by seven to derive a

Figure 4.1   Primary Child Care, Average Weekly Hours

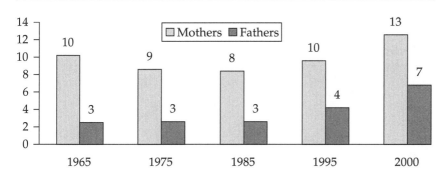

Source: Authors' calculations from the 1965–66 Americans' Use of Time Study; the 1975–76 Time Use in Economic and Social Accounts; 1985 Americans' Use of Time; the 1995 Electric Power Research Institute (EPRI) Study; and the combined file of the 1998–99 Family Interaction, Social Capital and Trends in Time Use Study and the 2000 National Survey of Parents.
Note: 2000 estimate for mothers is statistically significantly greater than in all previous years, $p < 0.05$; 2000 estimate for fathers is statistically significantly greater than in all previous years, $p < 0.05$.

weekly estimate. Figure 4.1 first suggests a dip in maternal child care time between 1965 and 1985 from about 10 hours to 8 hours per week, one that is consistent with the drop in the number of children per family—from the large Baby Boom households of the 1960s to the smaller families of the Baby Bust period of the 1970s and early 1980s. This decline also occurs at the same time that maternal employment and single parenting was rising most sharply.

After 1985, however, maternal child care time rebounded, ultimately surpassing 1965 levels by the year 2000. In contrast, fathers' child care time showed little change over the 1965 to 1985 period but steep increases by the end of the 1990s. This pattern parallels those in other countries, as is discussed in chapter 9 (see also Gauthier, Smeeding, and Furstenberg 2004).

Table 4.1 looks more closely at the child care activities among the three subgroups of parents for whom we have large enough samples to assess trends: married fathers, married mothers, and single mothers. In 1965 and 1975, married fathers averaged a little over 2.5 hours per week in child care activities. Married fathers' child care time increased to 3 hours in 1985—and then jumped to almost 7 (1 hour a day) in 2000. That is, married fathers' child care activities almost tripled over the period, with most of the change occurring after 1985.

Table 4.1   Weekly Hours of Child Care

	1965	1975	1985	1995	2000	Percent Increase 1965 to 2000
Married fathers						
All child care activities	2.6	2.7	3.0	5.0	6.5*	153
Routine activities	1.3	2.0	2.0	3.1	4.1*	209
Interactive activities	1.2	0.6	1.1	1.9	2.4*	94
Sample size (N)	(326)	(239)	(583)	(133)	(550)	
Married mothers						
All child care activities	10.6	8.8	9.3	11.0	12.9*	21
Routine activities	9.1	6.8	7.3	7.7	9.5	5
Interactive activities	1.5	2.1	2.0	3.3	3.3*	124
Sample size (N)	(358)	(278)	(673)	(198)	(700)	
Single mothers						
All child care activities	7.5	8.0	5.8	6.4	11.8*	57
Routine activities	6.2	6.6	4.6	5.5	9.0	43
Interactive activities	1.3	1.5	1.2	0.9	2.8	121
Sample size (N)	(59)	(91)	(230)	(109)	(299)	

Source: Authors' calculations from the 1965–66 Americans' Use of Time Study; the 1975–76 Time Use in Economic and Social Accounts; 1985 Americans' Use of Time; the 1995 Electric Power Research Institute (EPRI) Study; and the combined file of the 1998–99 Family Interaction, Social Capital and Trends in Time Use Study and the 2000 National Survey of Parents.
*Difference between 2000 and 1965 statistically significant, $p < 0.05$.

For married mothers, child care time dropped by almost 20 percent between 1965 and 1975, from 10.6 to 8.8 hours per week. After 1985, there was a 4.1 hour per week increase in child care time, with married mothers reporting about 13 hours per week (almost 2 hours a day) in child care in 2000, 3.6 hours per week higher than in 1985. Hence we conclude that married mothers' average time in child care activities began to increase in the mid-1980s and that it is currently about 20 percent higher than in 1965—and almost 50 percent higher than in 1975.

The child care time reported by single mothers in 2000 was also higher than in any earlier time diaries, although single-mother reports are less stable because of small sample sizes, especially in the early time-diary collection when relatively few children lived only with their mother.

Somehow, then, despite the concerns of policy makers and others that children are not receiving sufficient parental time, parents seem to have compensated for family and work arrangements that at first glance should have taken time away from child rearing. Other historical and cross-national data corroborate these U.S. time-diary findings. For example, using a sample of white married women, Bryant and Zick (1996) showed that U.S. mothers' time with children per child was higher in the 1980s than in the 1920s—though lower on a per family basis. Data collected in the Middletown community surveys of 1924, 1977, and 1999 show a substantial increase over the twentieth century in the time mothers and fathers spend with children (Caplow, Hicks, and Wattenberg 2001, 88–89). Using a multinational archive of time-diary studies from a number of countries, Anne Gauthier and her colleagues (2004) also show an overall increase in parental time in primary child care activities. Finally, child diary studies from the United States and parent diaries from other Western cultures suggest similar (though smaller) increases in the time children spend interacting with parents, especially fathers, over the last two decades (Bittman 1995; Fisher, McCulloch, and Gershuny 1999; Neimi 1988; Sandberg and Hofferth 2001), a topic to which we return in chapter 9.

Routine Caregiving Versus Enriching Activities

We can also use the time-diary data to separate activities parents do with their children into two types: the first are routine, custodial daily care activities (such as feeding or dressing them), and the second are interactive activities that represent greater parental "investment" in or "enrichment" for their children and are probably considered more enjoyable as well (Robinson and Godbey 1999, 374). The coding of routine child care activities includes baby or child care, medical care of children, other child care, and travel associated with child care activities, and interactive activities include time helping or teaching children, talking or reading to them, and indoor or outdoor playtime.[2] Table 4.1 distinguishes these two types, with the last column showing the percentage change between 1965 and 2000 time investments.

Why separate routine from interactive activities? First, if mothers' child care time remains high, perhaps it is because most of mothers' primary child care time is spent in the routine caregiving that probably cannot easily be curtailed no matter how busy they are. Although more interactional activities may give way to time pressures, routine care may not. Teaching and playing with children might be more sensitive to changing investment in child rearing, though still responsive to factors such as average family size or fertility, where economies of scale come into play, such as when feeding or supervising more than one child at a time is possible. The more interactive parental time may also signal parental time investments of greater quality and thus may have a stronger relationship with child well-being (Zick, Bryant, and Osterbacka 2001).

A second reason for disaggregating the two types of care is that it is often claimed that fathers tend to neglect basic child care tasks and instead devote their child care time to the more enjoyable activities of teaching and playing with children (Robinson and Godbey 1999, 374). Does the increase in married fathers' time in child care merely represent more fathers skimming off the most enjoyable aspects of child rearing? Or are fathers doing more of their fair share of the routine care that children require as well?

For married fathers, both types of child care time have increased, but the increase has been greater in routine care activities—more than a three-fold increase, versus a doubling of their time in interactive activities. For married mothers, by contrast, time in routine child care was quite similar in 2000 to 1965, but higher than at some time points between 1965 and 2000. However, time in interactive activities, such as teaching and playing, doubled. For single mothers, our estimates are more volatile because of small sample sizes, but in 2000, single mothers report about 40 percent more routine care than in 1965—and over twice as much time in interactive activities with their children.

At all time points, far more time is spent in routine care of children than in interactive time with them. However, by 2000, married mothers reported almost 3.5 hours per week (about half an hour per day) in interactive activities with their children. Married fathers (and single mothers) were not far behind, spending almost 2.5 hours per week in interactive activities. These figures clearly refute any notion that quality activities have been sacrificed as time constraints on employed parents and single mothers have increased.

With respect to the question of whether married fathers are doing their fair share and whether they skim off the most enjoyable child care and neglect the rest, the answer depends on whether the focus is on trends or on current levels. Figure 4.2 graphs these ratios of married mothers' to married fathers' time in child care activities, first overall and then for routine care and interactive activities. Trends suggest more gender egalitarianism in child care activities. Current levels, on the other hand, show that mothers continue to do almost twice as much routine child care as fathers, though fathers do participate much more equally in interactive activities.

In sum, married fathers are participating much more in both routine and interactive aspects of child care. Yet, mothers in 2000 still do most of the routine care and fathers continue to devote proportionately more of their time with children to interactive activities. Another way to summarize the table 4.1 results is that whereas married mothers' routine care was similar in 1965 and 2000, single mothers increased theirs by 40 percent and married fathers theirs by 200 percent. Both mothers and fathers approximately doubled their interactive care time over the thirty-five years.

Figure 4.2   Ratio of Married Mothers' to Married Fathers' Child Care Time

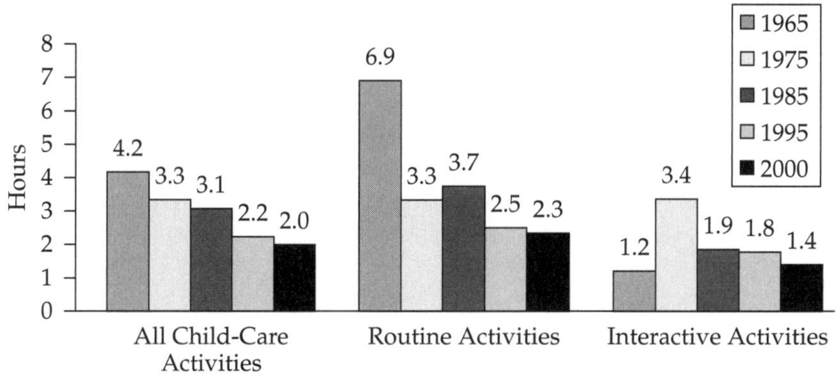

Source: Authors' calculations from the 1965–66 Americans' Use of Time Study; the 1975–76 Time Use in Economic and Social Accounts; 1985 Americans' Use of Time; the 1995 Electrical Power Research Institute (EPRI) Study; and the combined file of the 1998–99 Family Interaction, Social Capital and Trends in Time Use Study and the 2000 National Survey of Parents.

What About "Missing" Fathers?

Overall, then, the time-diary results suggest that children's time with married parents has not decreased. However, the analysis still does not capture time with the growing number of nonresidential parents (usually fathers), and it is clear from research using children's time diaries that children report fewer activities and much less time being cared for by stepfathers and by absent biological fathers (Hofferth 2003). In the United States, only about two-thirds of children under five years old now live with married parents (biological, step, or adoptive), and this declines to about 55 percent for children age fifteen to seventeen (Casper and Bianchi 2002, table 8.2).

The increase in children who do not live with both parents thus results in increased heterogeneity in children's experience of parental time. Children in two-parent families are receiving an increasing amount of parental time as married fathers expand what they do for children. In contrast, children with single parents effectively receive day-to-day caregiving from only one parent. The absence of fathers from single-mother households probably further contributes to the inequality in parental time that children receive. In table 4.1, children living with two married parents might average almost 6 hours per week of parental contact in interactive activities when both mothers' and fathers' time in these activities are combined.[3] A child living only with a single mother receives about half that time in 2000, and much less in earlier years.

Secondary Child Care Time

As noted, secondary child care time is additional time in child care that parents report while involved in primary activities that are not described as child care. We do not double-count time when two different child care activities are reported simultaneously (for example, talking with a child and driving them to a doctor's appointment), but we do pick up secondary child care time reported in conjunction with a primary other activity (making dinner while answering questions from one's twelve-year-old, for example). The secondary time thus expands substantially the time spent on child care activities (Robinson 1977; Robinson and Godbey 1999).

Two questions motivate this examination of secondary child care time. First, was there an increase in secondary child care time, similar to the increase in primary child care time since 1975?[4] Second, how often is child care undertaken in conjunction with other activities and how has this changed over time? Are parents increasingly multitasking when providing child care? Are parents perhaps less focused on children when caring for them than in the past because they are more often doing housework or involved in other activities?

Table 4.2 contrasts the weekly hours of secondary child care activity reported at two time points, 1975 and 2000. The amount of secondary child care time reported in these diaries is substantial. In 1975, married fathers averaged 2.7 hours per week in primary activities but almost as many hours (2.1) in secondary activities, leading to a total time of 4.8 hours per week. In 2000, fathers were averaging 8.6 hours per week of child care time (primary plus secondary). Thus, although fathers' primary activity time caring for their children increased by 144 percent between 1975 and 2000, combining it with secondary time indicates a smaller but still substantial increase of 80 percent.

For married mothers, adding secondary to primary time increases estimates of time caring for children by about half (58 percent in 1975 and 47 percent in 2000). Married mothers' combined child care increased from 14 to 19 hours per week, a 36-percent increase in child care.

For single mothers, primary time was again almost 50 percent higher in 2000 than in 1975, but because estimates of secondary time were actually 9 percent lower in 2000, single mothers' combined child care time rose from 13.4 to 16.7 hours per week, an overall increase of 24 percent.

As shown earlier, 1975 child care estimates are the lowest of any, and 2000 figures are the highest. A 1975 to 2000 comparison may there-

Table 4.2   Hours in Primary and Secondary Child Care Activities

	Hours per Week		Change	
	1975	2000	Hours	Percent
Married fathers				
Primary child care activities	2.7	6.5*	3.8	144
Nonoverlapping secondary				
child care activities	2.1	2.1	0.0	0
Primary + secondary activities	4.8	8.6*	3.8	80
Ratio secondary to primary	0.8	0.3		
Married mothers				
Primary child care activities	8.8	12.9*	4.0	46
Nonoverlapping secondary				
child care activities	5.1	6.0	0.9	18
Primary + secondary activities	13.9	18.9*	5.0	36
Ratio secondary to primary	0.6	0.5		
Single mothers				
Primary child care activities	8.0	11.8*	3.8	47
Nonoverlapping secondary				
child care activities	5.4	4.9	−0.5	−9
Primary + secondary activities	13.4	16.7	3.3	24
Ratio secondary to primary	0.7	0.4		

Source: Authors' calculations from the 1975–76 Time Use in Economic and Social Accounts and the combined file of the 1998–99 Family Interaction, Social Capital and Trends in Time Use Study and the 2000 National Survey of Parents.
*Difference between 2000 and 1975 statistically significant, $p < 0.05$.

fore exaggerate the change for parents. The larger increases in primary than in secondary time may also indicate a change in how parents report child care: it may more often be reported in 2000 as the primary activity a parent is doing than was the case in 1975.[5] That is, as the perceived societal importance placed on investing time in children increased, parents might be more sensitive about reporting more primary child care in their diaries.

With these caveats in mind, it still seems very likely that average parental child care time has increased. Although primary activity time may underestimate the amount of time parents spend caring for their children, nothing about the trends in this more expanded measure of child care presented in table 4.2 alters our central conclusion: both fathers and mothers have increased their time in child care activities.

Multitasking Child Care Time

With a diary that captures both primary and secondary activities, we can also measure how often parents report providing child care along with something other than child care, which is one indicator of how focused child care time is. Table 4.3 arrays the percentage of time that child care activities are combined with selected other activities.[6] In 2000, when par-

Table 4.3   Hours per Week Spent in Child Care and Overlap of Child Care with Other Activities

	1975	2000
Married fathers		
Total hours	4.8	8.6*
Percentage of child care time spent:		
Child care only	37.4	24.4
Child care with free time[a]	40.3	60.7*
Child care with television	23.7	18.8
Child care with housework	10.3	6.7
Child care with personal care	6.4	7.4
Married mothers		
Total hours	13.9	18.9*
Percentage of child care time spent:		
Child care only	48.9	26.9*
Child care with free time	23.3	43.3*
Child care with television	9.9	13.6*
Child care with housework	19.0	20.3
Child care with personal care	18.8	7.1*
Single mothers		
Total hours	13.4	16.7
Percentage of child care time spent:		
Child care only	40.7	24.9
Child care with free time	34.6	47.4*
Child care with television	16.3	14.1
Child care with housework	12.3	13.5
Child care with personal care	9.0	11.4

Source: Authors' calculations from the 1975–76 Time Use in Economic and Social Accounts and the combined file of the 1998–99 Family Interaction, Social Capital and Trends in Time Use Study and the 2000 National Survey of Parents.
a. Free time includes television.
*Difference between 2000 and 1975 statistically significant, $p < 0.0.5$.

ents reported providing child care, they reported focusing solely on child care less often than they did in 1975: a decline from 37 to 24 percent for married fathers, from 49 to 27 percent for married mothers, and from 41 to 25 percent for single mothers.

As reports of multitasking have increased, what activities are parents now combining with child care? Year 2000 parents were spending more hours engaged both in child care and in a free-time activity. In 1975, about 40 percent of all child care hours of married fathers occurred when the father was also engaged in a free-time activity, including watching television. In 2000, this increased to 61 percent.

The increase in child care combined with free time was especially accentuated among married mothers. Only 23 percent of their child care time in 1975 was in conjunction with a free-time activity, but the proportion grew to 43 percent in 2000. Either there was a shift toward more fun activities while parenting, or parents became increasingly likely to include children in their own (adult) activities, such as socializing or fitness.

On the one hand, the argument could be made that, because child care time is now more often multitasked, children may be getting less undivided attention from their parents. However, this argument would be easier to make if the multitasking were occurring during parents' paid work or household work. Instead, it seems to be largely when parents are engaged in a free-time activity that they report also caring for their children. If free time actually represents more relaxed time, children may be a greater focus of parental attention today. Also, the bulk of the combined child care time with a free-time activity is not television, but more active forms of free time. For instance, 59 percent of married fathers' child care time in 1975 that was combined with a free-time activity was watching television, whereas by 2000 this number had declined to 31 percent.

Total Time in the Presence of Children

The most inclusive measure of parenting captured in the 1975 and 2000 time diaries involves when respondents were asked who they were with during each primary activity. Our final assessment thus centers on all times during the day when parents reported being with their children. Busy working parents might continue to devote time to child care but let total time fall by the wayside—especially those looking to increase quality time with children to offset quantity reductions.

Figure 4.3 graphs the 1975 to 2000 total diary figures for time spent with children. For both married mothers and fathers, total hours per week with children are again higher in 2000 than in 1975.[7] For single mothers, on the other hand, they are lower.

Figure 4.3   Total Weekly Hours with Children

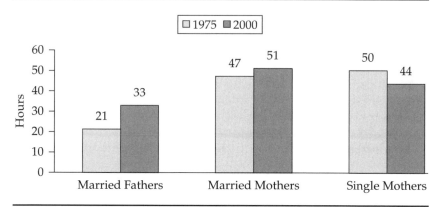

Source: Authors' calculations from the 1975–76 Time Use in Economic and Social Accounts and the combined file of the 1998–99 Family Interaction, Social Capital and Trends in Time Use Study and the 2000 National Survey of Parents.
Note: Difference between 2000 and 1975 estimates statistically significant at p < 0.05 for married fathers.

Thus married mothers and fathers seem to have adjusted how they spend their time to more than compensate for changes that should have decreased parental availability to children. If the only thing that had changed was the increase in married mothers' employment, time with children would most certainly have declined—a point to which we return later in this chapter. But parents have instead altered their behavior: spending both more time in primary child care in 2000 and as much (or more) total time during the day than in earlier decades.

Contrary to the conventional wisdom, then, changes in American families have not reduced married mothers' and fathers' child care time. Although fewer mothers are married, and single mothers face more difficulty than married mothers in devoting large amounts of time to their children, we conclude that, overall, mothers' time caring for their children has not declined drastically, as many have feared, but has actually increased.

There are at least two qualifiers to this optimistic picture. The first has to do with what the time diary cannot capture: accessible time, when parents and children are in enough proximity for control or supervision, but parents do not even record being with their children in their diaries. Although primary and secondary activities and total time with children reflect much of what parents are doing for their children, they do not tell the whole story. As Michelle Budig and Nancy Folbre (2004) rightly argue, measures that focus on the time parents spend actively engaged in activities with children, or with children in the same room, understate the important role of parental availability and temporal flexibility. It is certainly possible that children in the 1960s may have had mothers who were more directly accessible to them on a regular basis. For example, children playing in the backyard or watching television in the living room after school while their mother was doing laundry in the basement (mother-child contact that is probably rarely picked up by our diaries) may have been more common then than now.

The second concern involves single mothers. Whereas children with single mothers clearly get only one parent's attention at a time, those who live with two can get time from both. In this way, as married fathers' child care time has increased, time allocation has become more unequal for children in one-parent versus two-parent households. As much as single mothers may try to devote more time to direct child care to make up for the missing father, they seem to be unable to devote the amount of total time to children that they could manage in the past—or that married parents can afford. Although single-parent families are smaller than in the past—so that per child there may not have been a decrease in single mothers' time with children—the suggested growing inequality between children in one- versus two-parent families becomes an area of policy concern.

Another Dimension of Inequality: Education of Parents

Early time-diary studies suggested that college-educated mothers devote more time to child rearing than less-educated mothers, especially in enrichment activities (Leibowitz 1974), like more time reading to and less time watching television with their children (Timmer, Eccles and O'Brien 1985). College-educated mothers were also found to spend more time in direct child care, and mothers' time with children declined less steeply with the age of the children among college-educated than among less-educated mothers (Hill and Stafford 1985).

Children's diary activities also differ significantly by the educational level of their mother. In a diary study of California children, those with college-educated mothers studied more, read more, and watched less television than those with less-educated mothers (Bianchi and Robinson 1997). Sandra Hofferth and John Sandberg (2001b) report similar differences by parental educational attainment among a 1997 national sample of children. In her ethnographic work, Lareau (2002, 2003) has observed similar class differences in child rearing practices, differences that she argues create and sustain intergenerational inequality, such as children's later ability to attend college.

Research on educational differences in fathers' involvement is more mixed, with some studies finding no educational differences in father involvement, in physical care of children, or in time with school-age children. However, other studies find that college-educated fathers spend more time playing with, reading to, and going on outings with preschool-age children, as well as more time with school-age children (see Bianchi et al. 2004 for a review of these findings).

In figure 4.4, which graphs weekly hours of primary child care among college-educated and less-educated mothers and fathers, all the diary surveys show parents with a college degree spending more time in primary child care. College-educated mothers spent about 2 more hours per week in child care than less-educated mothers, and fathers with a college education about 3 more hours per week. These differences persist even after controlling for age, marital status, number of children, age of youngest child, and employment of the parent (see Bianchi et al. 2004). They also have not changed significantly over time. Time devoted to child care has moved upward at about the same rate for less-educated mothers and fathers as for college-educated mothers and fathers.[8] Hence, although the differentials by parental education are sizable, they have not grown significantly larger (nor narrowed) in recent decades.

Employed Versus Nonemployed Mothers

Although figures 4.1 to 4.3 document that mothers' child care time was at least as high in 2000 as earlier, it is still puzzling that child care time could rise as more mothers entered the workforce. Table 4.4 sheds light on the size of the differences between employed and nonemployed mothers and their changes between 1975 and 2000. The two survey data sets assess not only primary child care time but also secondary care and total diary time with children. Table 4.4 shows how many fewer hours per week an employed versus a nonemployed mother spends with her children. It is important to note that, on average, mothers who are not in the labor force are younger and less educated, and have spouses who work more hours per week and have larger, younger families than mothers who are employed.

Because all of these factors can affect how much time mothers spend with children, we show unadjusted averages and differences and also use ordinary least squares (OLS) multivariate regression techniques to adjust

Figure 4.4 Mothers' and Fathers' Primary Child Care Time by Educational Attainment

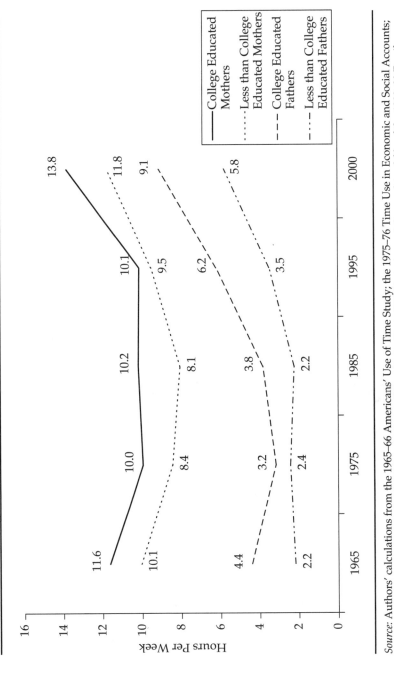

Source: Authors' calculations from the 1965–66 Americans' Use of Time Study; the 1975–76 Time Use in Economic and Social Accounts; 1985 Americans' Use of Time; the 1995 Electric Power Research Institute (EPRI) study; and the combined file of the 1998–99 Family Interaction, Social Capital and Trends in Time Use Study and the 2000 National Survey of Parents.
Note: The gap between college educated parents and less than college educated parents did not grow wider over the 1965–2000 period (see Bianchi, Cohen, Raley, and Nomaguchi 2004).

Table 4.4   Change in Employed and Nonemployed Mothers' Average Child Care Time

	1975	2000	Combined
Primary child care			
Employed mother's hours	6.0[a]	10.6[ab]	9.7[a]
Nonemployed mother's hours	10.7[a]	17.2[ab]	14.5
Difference (unadjusted)	−4.7	−6.6	−4.8
Difference (OLS adjusted)	−4.1*	−4.9*	−4.6*
Year (2000) (OLS estimate)	—	—	4.8*
Secondary child care			
Employed mother's hours	3.1[a]	3.9[a]	3.7[a]
Nonemployed mother's hours	6.8[a]	10.1[a]	8.7
Difference (unadjusted)	−3.7	−6.2	−5.0
Difference (OLS adjusted)	−4.0*	−4.8*	−4.4*
Year (2000)	—	—	1.5*
Primary + secondary child care			
Employed mother's hours	9.1[a]	14.5[ab]	13.5[a]
Nonemployed mother's hours	17.6[a]	27.2[ab]	23.2
Difference (unadjusted)	−8.5	−12.7	−9.8
Difference (OLS adjusted)	−8.1*	−9.6*	−9.0*
Year (2000)	—	—	6.4*
All time with children			
Employed mother's hours	38.0[a]	42.3[a]	41.5[a]
Nonemployed mother's hours	56.0[a]	64.7[a]	61.1
Difference (unadjusted)	−18.0	−22.4	−19.6
Difference (OLS adjusted)	−14.9*	−16.5*	−15.8*
Year (2000)	—	—	5.9*
Sample size (N)	(369)	(999)	(1,368)

Source: Authors' calculations from the 1975–76 Time Use in Economic and Social Accounts and the combined file of the 1998–99 Family Interaction, Social Capital and Trends in Time Use Study and the 2000 National Survey of Parents.
Note: OLS regression is used to produce an estimate of the employment difference net of associations of child care time with number of children, presence of children age 6 or younger, educational attainment, age, marital status. The interaction of year and employment was never statistically significant. Year change estimated by OLS regressions with concatenated 1975 and 2000 data.
a. Employed and nonemployed statistically significantly different at $p < 0.05$.
b. 1975 and 2000 statistically significantly different at $p < 0.05$.
*$p < 0.05$.

the comparisons for the differences between employed and nonemployed mothers in terms of their age and education, as well as family characteristics like the age of their children or their spouses' employment. Finally, we combine data for the two years and estimate whether child care time increased or decreased significantly between 1975 and 2000 (the year effect under the combined column in table 4.4).[9]

Focusing on the entries in the third column of the table (where we combine data for the two years to estimate the association between time with children and a mother's being employed), the relationships are always negative and statistically significant. In contrast to 1975, the estimated time with children is always higher in 2000 (the year coefficient is always positive and significant) for both groups of mothers.

In these analyses, employed mothers average 4.6 fewer hours per week in primary child care than mothers who are not employed. Interestingly, the year estimate is as large but in the opposite direction as the employment effect, suggesting that an employed mother in 2000 spent as much time in direct child care as her nonemployed counterpart in the 1970s.

This is also clear in the unadjusted estimates. Employed mothers in 2000 averaged 11 hours per week in primary child care, virtually the same that nonemployed mothers reported in their diaries in 1975. Part of the reason that child care averages remain high, despite the increase in the proportion of mothers employed, is that time spent in primary child care activities moved upward for mothers, and this upward shift was significant enough to offset the movement of more mothers into the employed category (where they tend to provide less child care).

This pattern is repeated in the diary measures that add in secondary time and time with children, except that with these more inclusive measures, the year effect does not fully compensate for the lesser time working mothers spend with their children compared to nonemployed mothers. The year effect might be thought to counteract about two-thirds of the 9-hour deficit in secondary plus primary time. Put another way, although employed mothers in 2000 still average 9 hours a week less caregiving time than nonemployed mothers, both groups together now average almost 6.5 more hours per week than their counterparts did in 1975.

When total time with children is the focus of the analysis, the employment difference in time in child care is even greater. Here, employed mothers are estimated to spend almost 16 fewer hours per week with their children than nonemployed mothers, other things equal, with a little over one-third of this time counteracted, in some sense, by the year difference. Thinking about these numbers in terms of there being five workdays per week, these regression estimates suggest that the cost of employment for mothers in terms of forgone time with children is about an hour per work day of primary child care, close to 2 hours per workday in primary plus secondary child care, and about 3 hours per workday in total time with children. These sizable differences suggest how much time with children employed mothers would sacrifice if they made no adjustments to their employment status when they had young children.

These estimated employment differences tend to be larger than previous estimates, in part because most studies focused solely on primary child care time, which can be measured comparably over the entire 1965 to 2000 period (as in Sayer, Bianchi, and Robinson 2004). Nock and Kingston's (1988) study of all unpaid family work, including housework, found that nonemployed mothers spent a relatively small proportion of their time in the home engaged in primary child care activities, which tended to minimize differences between employed and nonemployed mothers. Cathleen Zick and Keith Bryant (1996) estimated that a mother employed throughout her child's life would spend 82 percent as many hours directly caring for children as a stay-at-home mother. Time-diary studies conducted in other Western countries also indicate employed mothers devote less time to their children than their nonemployed counterparts—but that the difference is small relative to the gap in time devoted to paid work (Gauthier, Smeeding, and Furstenberg 2004).

Sandberg and Hofferth (2005) estimate that children age twelve and under spend almost 15 percent less time directly engaged in activities with an employed mother as with a nonemployed mother (20 versus 23 hours per week). (Our unadjusted estimates from a mother's point of view would be 14 versus 27 hours in primary plus secondary child care.) Children's total time with an employed mother was estimated to be 39 hours versus 47 hours per week for those with a nonemployed mother. Our estimates of total time differences by employment status are much larger: in 2000, unadjusted estimates are 42 hours for employed mothers compared to 65 hours per week for nonemployed mothers. The mothers' estimates of time with children may be larger than the children's time with a mother, because mothers' diaries include time with multiple children.

Differences between employed and nonemployed mothers in our study may be greater because they include mothers with children up to age eighteen, compared with Sandberg and Hofferth's child diaries for children under age thirteen. As children age, employed mothers take on more paid work and thus less family care. Also, those who remain at home full-time when children are older become an extremely select group, probably those most likely to devote large amounts of time to child rearing.

In summary, and as expected, employed mothers spend less time with their children than nonemployed mothers. However, our reference group of employed mothers in 2000 spent almost as much time in primary child care as nonemployed mothers did in earlier decades. This suggests an increased propensity of mothers to maximize whatever time they have to be with their children. It is as if a cultural shift occurred that propelled all mothers toward spending more time with children.

Estimated Daily Activities with Children

In an attempt to enrich our picture of parents' investment in children, we also included a number of time-estimate questions in our 2000 National Survey of Parents to supplement each parent's time diary. These questions focused both on specific daily activities with children and on parental emotional investment in children and child rearing. These respondent estimates of activities and ties with children enlarge the picture of parenting in the contemporary United States, though they do not track change over time. They do indicate that 2000 parents report a very high level of investment in their parenting role.

The format of these 2000 estimate questions was typically, "How many days a week do you [fill in activity] with your child or children?" This included the estimated days that these parents read to a child, helped a child with homework, drove a child to activities other than school, watched a child participate in extracurricular activities, had a child help with housework chores, and ate their main meal together with their entire family.

With few exceptions, reports of doing the activity with children and the estimated frequency tend to be highest for married mothers and lowest for single mothers. Table 4.5 shows that relatively high percentages of mothers and married fathers report doing these activities with their children during a given week (shown in the first panel).

Although mothers report reading to children significantly more than fathers do, fathers' estimates tend to be only a little lower than for mothers in other areas. Single mothers are less likely to report that they help children with homework, drive them to activities, or watch or supervise children's activities. Their estimated number of days on each of these activities is also lower than for married mothers. Many mothers in both groups report that they frequently eat as a family and involve children in household chores. Overall, again, the general impression is of a fairly high level of parental involvement in these activities with their children.

Quality of Time

We asked parents to estimate how much one-on-one time they had with their youngest child—where estimates were expected to reflect a quality dimension of parental time. Fathers' answers reflect significantly fewer such hours with children, with mothers estimating 16 versus the fathers' 12 hours (data not shown).

We asked parents three further questions about the quality of parental monitoring and interaction with children: how often they knew the loca-

Table 4.5   Percentage of Parents Doing Child Care and Average Days per Week Parents Do Selected Child Care Activities

	Married Fathers	Married Mothers	Single Mothers
Percentage who do the activity			
Read to child[d]	66.7	82.8	78.6[ab]
Help child with homework[e]	70.7	73.2	61.8[bc]
Drive child to activities	66.5	70.7	61.8[c]
Supervise and watch child's activities	64.1	70.8	54.0[abc]
Have child help with chores	89.5	93.0	89.4
Eat dinner as a family	97.0	95.7	92.7[b]
Average days per week all parents			
Read to child[d]	2.5	4.2	3.7[ab]
Help child with homework[e]	2.7	3.3	2.9[a]
Drive child to activities	2.0	2.5	1.8[ac]
Supervise and watch child's activities	1.9	2.2	1.7[c]
Have child help with chores	4.5	4.8	4.8
Eat dinner as a family	4.8	4.6	4.2[bc]
Average days per week across participants			
Read to child[d]	3.8	5.1	4.7[ab]
Help child with homework[e]	3.8	4.4	4.6[ab]
Drive child to activities	3.0	3.6	3.0[ac]
Supervise and watch child's activities	3.0	3.1	3.2
Have child help with chores	5.1	5.1	5.3
Eat dinner as a family	4.9	4.8	4.5[b]

Source: Authors' calculations from the 2000 National Survey of Parents.
a. Married fathers differ from married mothers, $p < 0.05$.
b. Married fathers differ from single mothers, $p < 0.05$.
c. Married mothers differ from single mothers, $p < 0.05$.
d. Asked only of parents with children aged three through twelve.
e. Asked only of parents with children aged five through seventeen.

tion of their youngest school-age child both after school and on weekends, the frequency with which they praised their children, laughed with them, and expressed love to them in the form of hugs or kisses, and their enjoyment of selected child-rearing activities (using a scale of one to ten, with ten being "enjoy a great deal").

As shown in figure 4.5, almost 80 percent (or more) of all groups of parents claimed to know their children's whereabouts "almost all of the time," both after school and on weekends.

In terms of the more emotional dimensions of parenting, figure 4.6 graphs the percentage of married fathers, married mothers, and single mothers who estimated they do certain child-centered behaviors every day. Again, between 80 and 90 percent of parents reported laughing

Figure 4.5   Parents Aware of Children's Whereabouts Almost All of the Time, 2000

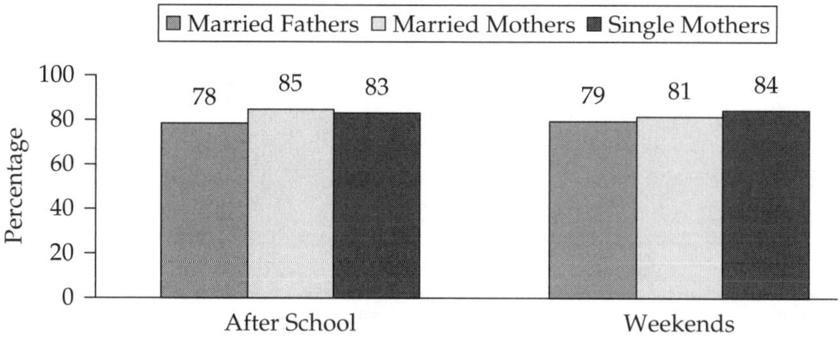

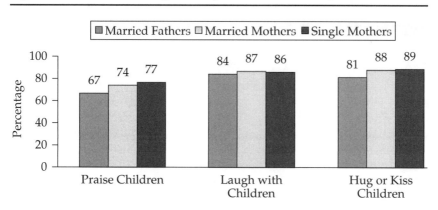

■ Married Fathers □ Married Mothers ■ Single Mothers

Source: Authors' calculations from the 2000 National Survey of Parents.
Note: Married mothers' estimates for after school awareness greater than married fathers' estimates, p < 0.05.

Figure 4.6   Parents Who Report Daily Positive Interaction, 2000

■ Married Fathers □ Married Mothers ■ Single Mothers

Source: Authors' calculations from the 2000 National Survey of Parents.
Note: Married mothers' estimates for praising and hugging children greater than married fathers', p < 0.05. Single mothers' estimates for praising and hugging children greater than married fathers', p < 0.05.

Figure 4.7   Parents Rating Parenting Activity as a 10 in 2000

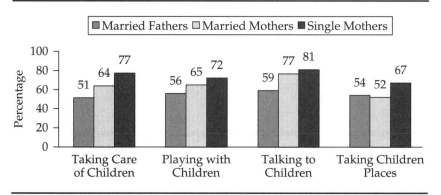

Source: Authors' calculations from the 2000 National Survey of Parents.
Note: Rating of 10 on a 10 point scale means parent "enjoys a great deal." Single mothers' estimates for caring for and taking children places greater than married mothers', p < 0.05. Married mothers' estimates for caring for, playing with, and talking to children greater than married fathers', p < 0.05. Single mothers' estimates for all activities greater than married fathers', p < 0.05.

with and showing affection to their children on a daily basis. Praise for children on a daily basis was a little less frequent, but 67 percent of married fathers, 74 percent of married mothers, and 77 percent of single mothers said they did so.

Finally, in terms of rated enjoyment of selected child-rearing activities, Figure 4.7 shows the percentage rating as a ten (on a ten-point scale) their enjoyment of four activities: taking care of their children, playing with their children, talking to their children, and taking their children places. Single mothers reported the highest levels of enjoyment, followed first by married mothers and then by married fathers. However, at least half of all married fathers rated enjoyment of each activity a ten, and very few parents rated any of the activities below an eight. Taking children places was least highly rated of the four activities, but even it was viewed as highly enjoyable by the majority of parents.

The enjoyment of these child-rearing activities had also been asked in the third wave of the 1975 study, and we show the change over time for married fathers and married mothers in appendix table 4A.1 (small sample sizes prohibit the examination of single mothers). Married mothers rated three out of the four activities—taking care of their children, playing with their children, and talking to their children—significantly higher in 2000 than in 1975, and married fathers generally rated their enjoyment similarly. In fact, fathers were slightly less likely to rate taking care of their children, talking with their children, and taking their children places as a ten in 2000 than in 1975. Given that fathers are undertaking more child care today than in earlier years, they may be less likely to view such interaction as a fun or novel activity. Overall, however, both married mothers and fathers report very high levels of enjoying activities with their children in both years.

Although these subjective responses may simply represent socially desirable responses about parenting, the high values given suggest that parents' emotional investment in child rearing (or their beliefs about how invested they should be) is quite high in contemporary U.S. society.

Parenting does not come without its stressful aspects, and there was more variation on three other survey questions: views on whether spanking was "never, sometimes, or usually okay"; estimates of having to discipline children by how often they had to raise their voice, with responses ranging on a six-point scale from one (daily) to six (never); and how satisfied they were with how well their children were doing in life, with responses ranging from a low of one (not satisfied) to a high of ten (completely satisfied).

Almost 80 percent of parents reported that they believed it was usually or sometimes okay to spank their children, with single mothers more likely to say it was never okay to do so (27 percent) than married mothers or fathers (18 percent).[10] The frequency of having to raise one's voice diminished when children in the household were older. In terms of satisfaction with how children were doing, levels were again relatively high with the average being a rating of nine on the ten-point scale. Feeling completely satisfied with how their children were doing in life (a ten on the ten-point scale) was less common for single mothers than for married mothers and fathers, however.

Employed Versus Nonemployed Mothers

On the parenting activities of reading to a child, helping with homework, driving to and supervising children's activities, having children do housework, and eating dinner as a family, only two activities showed a difference by the employment status of the mother, and even these differences were small. Employed mothers reported reading to their children and eating their main meal together as a family about one less day per week than nonemployed mothers (data not shown).

Table 4.6 summarizes the differences by mothers' employment status on other questions, again with few statistically significant differences in parental monitoring and the subjective assessments of the quality of the parenting experience. For example, there were no significant differences between employed and nonemployed mothers in their enjoyment of caring for children, playing with children, talking with children, and taking children places. There were also no significant employment dif-

Table 4.6   Mothers' Ratings of Parental Activities, 2000

	Employed	Nonemployed
Percentage "enjoying a great deal" 10 on scale of 10		
Taking care of children	67.5	73.8
Playing with children	66.1	71.5
Talking with children	76.5	81.6
Taking children places	59.0	62.9
Percentage reporting daily positive interaction with children		
Praise children	73.1	78.3
Laugh with children	84.2	91.2*
Hug or kiss children	86.8	91.5
Percentage "completely satisfied" with children and family life		
How well children doing in life	31.4	55.6*
Amount of family time	20.4	27.0*
Percentage almost always aware of children's whereabouts[a]		
On weekend[a]	80.3	87.9*
After school[a]	83.2	86.8

Source: Authors' calculations from the 2000 National Survey of Parents.
a. Only asked of parents with children aged five through seventeen.
*Difference between employed and nonemployed mothers statistically significant at $p < 0.05$.

ferences in reports of praising or giving "hugs and kisses" to children—though laughter was in a bit shorter supply in the households of employed than nonemployed mothers, perhaps due to greater time pressures in these households.

Although average levels of satisfaction in how their children were doing were high for both employed (8.4 on the ten-point scale) and nonemployed (9.0 on the scale) mothers, employed mothers were significantly less likely to rate themselves as completely satisfied with how their children were doing in life than nonemployed mothers were (31 percent versus 56 percent, respectively). In terms of parental monitoring, high percentages of both groups (over 80 percent) claimed to always know their children's whereabouts, with a significantly greater percentage of nonemployed mothers (88 percent) than employed (80 percent) saying they always knew where their children were on weekends. No significant difference was found with respect to after-school hours.

Although these reports about parenting are overwhelmingly positive, regardless of a mother's employment status, there are some signs of greater stress in households with employed mothers—a little less laughter, a little less parental monitoring, a little less eating dinner as a family, and less satisfaction with how children are doing.

Summary and Conclusions

We have shown that, overall, parents' child care time has not decreased over the past few decades, and time spent on the daily care of children has actually increased or remained constant for all three parent groups: married fathers, married mothers, and single mothers. Diary time spent in interactive activities, such as teaching and playing, has virtually doubled for each of them. Although a higher percentage of fathers' time than mothers' is spent in interactive activities, fathers have also come a long way toward closing the gap between the amount of time they spend and the amount of time their wives spend on more routine or custodial care of their children.

Estimates that include secondary child care along with primary child care also suggest a significant increase in child care time from 1975 to 2000, although a less sharp increase than for only primary activity time. A large portion of the expansion in child care time between 1975 and 2000 is due to parents combining child care and leisure activities, indicating that either child care has become more oriented toward fun activities, or that parents are more frequently including children in their own leisure activities.

When all time spent with children is considered, there is again an increase for married parents between 1975 and 2000 but a decline for single mothers. This hints at a growing inequality in parental time between children in one-parent and two-parent families today than in the past. All else being equal, married and single mothers may spend similar amounts of time in direct child care, but single mothers have more difficulty spending as much total time. Also, all is rarely equal in the lives of married and single mothers, with married parents more likely than single parents to be college educated, to bear children relatively late in life, and to have higher financial resources (Casper and Bianchi 2002). As a consequence, children in married-couple families may be benefiting from having two parents, both of whom share several characteristics associated with high parental time investments. In contrast, children in single-mother families have day-to-day access to the time of only one parent who also has characteristics associated with lower parental investments.

Moreover, the strongest shifts in the cultural context of parenthood may have been for married, middle-class parents (Coltrane 1996; Hays 1996, Lareau 2003).

On the more subjective side, all parents report high levels of involvement in the activities of parenting, as well as high levels of care and affection for their children. Again, married mothers report somewhat higher frequencies of helping with homework and reading to children than single mothers or married fathers, but the differences are not large. On affective dimensions, such as enjoyment of different parenting tasks, single mothers rank higher than married mothers.

We began this chapter with the 1999 Council of Economic Advisers' estimate of a recent 22-hour decline in parental time in the home, and whether that meant that more maternal employment and single parenting had eroded the quantity and quality of parental investment in children. We conclude that the overwhelming evidence is that it has not, on average, although the growing inequality in that investment between single-parent and two-parent families is disturbing.

Our estimates of how much mothers' employment should have eroded time with children—if no behavioral or other changes had occurred—are almost as high as those of the Council of Economic Advisers. Other factors being equal, employed mothers spend 16 fewer hours per week with their children than nonemployed mothers. Their households are also characterized by a little less togetherness, for example, fewer dinners as a family, a little less monitoring of children's time and less satisfaction with how children are doing, and a little less laughter.

Yet, overall, mothers' child care activities did not decline over time and married mothers were averaging more total time with children in 2000 than earlier. We explain the contradiction by speculating that today's mothers are probably keenly aware of the conflict between paid work and the management of time with children. If we assume they realize that employment is going to cut them out of an average of 16 hours a week of time with their children, what choices do mothers make? As we saw in chapter 3, they curtail employment when they are financially able to do so. So, over the life course of children, the employment effect is muted because mothers either shift out of employment, or they decrease their paid work hours to spend more time with their children when children's needs are greatest.

Not only that, but our estimate of increased time with children associated with being a mother in 2000 versus 1975, combined with the increase in fathers' time with children despite little reduction in their market work, both point to behavioral shifts that privilege time with children over other activities. Our evidence on increased multitasking during free-time activities with child care time also suggests an increased willingness of parents to sacrifice their own adult-focused time to expand that with their children and their children's activities. That observation fits with ethnographic work on middle class childhoods by researchers at UCLA (Verrengia 2005) and as chronicled by Lareau (2003).

Why might parents do this more now than in the past? Does it make sense that parents can spend more time caring for their children today than at the height of the Baby Boom? If so, what would predispose parents to this behavior?

First, if parenting has become more voluntary, parents now have greater ability to time childbearing when it suits them. For an increasing segment of the population, then, parenthood is not something that "just happens." Rather it is something one decides to do because one wants the experience of parenting, with all that it entails—including the large amounts of time children require. Smaller family sizes somewhat reduce how daunting this task is, because it takes fewer years to rear one or two children to school-age than to do the same for three or four children, as was more typical in Baby Boom families.

Second, parents may accompany their children to extracurricular events, supervise play dates, and generally spend more time hovering over their children today because they are afraid not to. With longer distances to be traveled between home, school, and children's activities, and more traffic to be negotiated in covering these distances—coupled with heightened concerns about crime and child abuse (Best 1990; Kurz 2002; Warr and Ellison 2000)—parents are typically increasingly anxious about the safety of their children. Neighborhoods full of stay-at-home mothers with their children roaming freely from house to house, or yard to yard, in part reflect Baby Boomers' nostalgic memories of childhood in the past. Yet children today probably are accorded less unsupervised freedom of movement than in earlier years because parents fear that harm will come to their children if they are not with them. And for children living in poverty especially, these fears may be based in the realities of dangerous neighborhoods.

Third, as fertility declines, each child becomes in some sense "more precious" (Zelizer 1981), or more worthy of intensive investment (Gauthier, Smeeding, and Furstenberg 2004). As the level of affluence rises and parental educational attainment increases, expectations have probably increased about what children need and what children can accomplish if only they receive the proper parental inputs. Parents may feel increased cultural and normative pressure to provide large amounts of time to children to be considered good parents. The diary trends thus may reflect the parental response to increasing normative pressures, particularly pressures to be an involved father that may have intensified in recent decades, along with pressures for mothers to be more involved—despite being stretched for time because of more market work or more solo parenting.

Large investments in child rearing, then, just like large investments in market work, take time. Yet, the question remains: if not less time on child care, what are working mothers and single parents giving up? This "what gives" question is the topic of the next chapter. Specifically, what isn't getting done in American family households? What price do American parents seem willing to pay for a more child-focused existence in which market work and single parenting also figure more prominently than in the past?

= Chapter 5 =

Housework, Leisure, Personal Care, Relationships: "What Gives" in Busy Families?

FOR MOTHERS to spend more time in child care (as well as in market work) since 1965, something has had "to give." For example, many observers expect that the shift to more paid work has caused mothers to find fewer hours for precious sleep. Others surmise that to do it all, today's mothers have had to give up free time.

Yet the data in this chapter show that neither of these obvious trade-offs—for sleep or for leisure—account for much change in mothers' lives, on average. Less sleep and less leisure do distinguish employed from nonemployed mothers' lives, however. The data also show that married fathers' lives have shifted in important, though less dramatic, ways. For them, what gives is paid work and personal care to allow for their increased child care and housework time.

As noted in chapter 2, time-diary data allow us to get at three important aspects of how the lives of mothers and fathers may have changed to allow them similar or increased time in child care: reduced time in other primary activities, increased child-oriented secondary activities that accompany these main activities, and increased time with children, perhaps instead of with friends and other adults, even when parents engage in adult-oriented activities.

Changes in Primary Activities

In terms of the 168 weekly hours of primary activities for both married and single parents between 1965 and 2000, figure 5.1 shows the changes in the four most general categories of time: paid work, family care, personal care (including sleep), and free time activities. Appendix tables 5A.1 and 5A.2 provide more detailed time-use categories and appendix table 5A.3 details the type of activities clustered under each category.

Figure 5.1 Cumulative Time Use for Parents

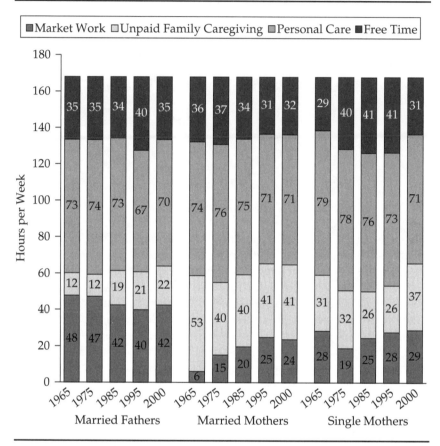

Source: Authors' calculations from the 1965–66 Americans' Use of Time Study; the 1975–76 Time Use in Economic and Social Accounts; 1985 Americans' Use of Time; the 1995 Electric Power Research Institute (EPRI) Study; and the combined file of the 1998–99 Family Interaction, Social Capital and Trends in Time Use Study and the 2000 National Survey of Parents.

Note: Estimates of personal care, unpaid family caregiving, and market work statistically significantly different between 1965 and 2000 among married fathers, $p < 0.05$. All estimates statistically different between 1975 and 2000 among married mothers, $p < 0.05$. Estimates of unpaid family caregiving and personal care statistically different between 1975 and 2000 among single mothers, $p < 0.05$.

Chapter 3 (table 3.4) showed that married mothers in 2000 spent almost 18 more hours per week on market work than in 1965, averaging 24 hours in 2000 versus only 6 in 1965. Given the zero-sum constraint of 168 hours in a week, this 18-hour increase in 2000 compared with 1965 was offset by about 12 fewer hours per week of unpaid family care at home, 2 fewer of personal care, and about 4 fewer of free-time pursuits. These changes are graphed in the middle panel of figure 5.1 and discussed in detail below.

Single mothers' lives shown in the third panel in figure 5.1 have changed less, with no change in weekly work hours, a 6-hour increase in family time (largely spent in increased child care), and a gain of 3 hours in leisure, offset by about an 8-hour decline in personal care. It is hard to know what to make of single mothers' reporting so much less personal care time (such as sleep or grooming, which do have a somewhat discretionary character), particularly given the small samples of single mothers in the earlier periods.

Married mothers and single mothers are more similar to each other today than in the past, as married mothers have shifted toward more paid and less unpaid work. Moreover, as noted in chapter 3, both single mothers and married mothers have a greater overall work burden in 2000, an increase of about 6 hours (from 59 to 65 hours per week).

For married fathers, the shift in categories of time use over the past half century is only half as great as for mothers—but it is still almost a 10-hour-per-week change. However, the first panel of figure 5.1 shows that it goes in the opposite direction from mothers—that is, toward more family care, including the approximately 4 hours more per week that fathers spend on child care (as discussed in chapter 4), plus the 5 additional hours per week of housework (discussed below).

Increased family time of fathers seems largely to come from declines in paid work and in personal care. Married fathers averaged 47.8 market work hours (work and its commute) in 1965, compared with 42.5 hours today, a statistically significant decline. However, their increased domestic work has more than compensated for this decline, such that married men's workload has also increased—from 60 hours per week in 1965 to 64 hours today, as noted in chapter 3.

Changes in Family Care

Chapter 4 illustrated that an important part of mothers' time—child care—has been steady or increasing. Thus, married mothers' 16-hour-per-week increase in paid work as a primary activity (an 18-hour increase when commuting is added) has not taken time from child care, on average.

But surprisingly, on average, paid work has not generally replaced sleep either, nor has it crowded out leisure to any great extent. Rather, today's mothers have shed a sizable 13 weekly hours of core housework, a finding corroborated in the Middletown community studies of Caplow, Hicks, and Wattenberg (2001, 36–37).[1] In contrast, other family care in shopping and obtaining family services, such as adult medical appointments or repair services, has increased by about an hour.

Table 5.1 disaggregates housework into core or routine tasks and other types of housework. It also shows that the percentage of married mothers who reported any housework on the diary day dropped from almost 100 percent in 1965 to 91 percent in 2000 (top row in table 5.1).

How much this lost housework among married mothers represents cleaning that remains undone, now gets accomplished more efficiently, or is getting picked up by other people remains unclear. The drop in housework hours could mean that today's homes are less well-maintained than those of the past, especially given that homes are larger and thus have more areas to clean and organize. If standards for housework have dropped, which may be the case (Robinson and Milkie 1998), then having homes that are less clean and ordered, or clothes that are more wrinkled, is not a cause for concern.

Another possibility is that homes are just as clean and home-cooked meals are just as appetizing, but that mothers are doing proportionately less of the work. For example, there may be more outside or hired help or more take-home foods. Additionally, mothers may be more efficient today, particularly with the aid of technologies such as microwave ovens, dishwashers, and permanent press clothing that have made some housework tasks easier to perform. These technologies may allow more multitasking of housework activities, as indicated by the increase in housework hours reported as a secondary activity (figure 5.2). Earlier research suggests that all of these factors may have substituted for the greater amount of housework that women in the past accomplished (Robinson and Milkie 1998; Bianchi et al. 2000).

Married mothers seem to have swapped paid work for housework almost hour for hour. In other words, their 16-hour increase in paid work is almost completely made up by the 15 fewer hours in the unpaid work of household labor. However, because their paid work is almost exclusively outside the home, their overall accessibility to children has probably declined. That makes their increased interaction time with children even more remarkable.

Single-mothers' housework profile looks quite different from that of married mothers. We find no decrease in housework, with their 17 hours per week of housework in 2000 being almost the same as reported in 1965. So, although single mothers in the 1960s did only half the amount of housework that married mothers did, married mothers have reduced their housework so much that today they do almost as little housework as single mothers. As with married mothers, there is a decrease in the daily percentage of single mothers who report doing housework on the diary day, from 90 to 84 percent. Similar to married mothers, single mothers counter a decline in core housework somewhat by shopping and obtaining services 1.7 more hours per week in 2000 than in 1965.

Table 5.1 Trends in Parents' Housework, Hours per Week

	Married Fathers					Married Mothers					Single Mothers				
	1965	1975	1985	1995	2000	1965	1975	1985	1995	2000	1965	1975	1985	1995	2000
Percentage reporting housework	54.4	43.0	71.5	60.1	69.4*	99.6	97.6	95.3	89.6	91.2*	90.1	91.5	90.9	70.6	83.8
Total hours in primary housework activities	4.4	5.6	10.7	10.9	9.7*	34.5	25.2	22.5	21.6	19.4*	16.8	19.0	14.4	12.7	16.8
Core housework	1.4	1.6	4.1	3.6	4.6*	31.3	22.8	19.2	17.4	15.6*	15.6	18.2	12.6	9.4	13.9
Cooking meals	0.6	0.8	1.8	1.4	2.1*	10.9	9.4	8.1	6.5	5.8*	5.0	7.8	5.5	2.5	5.2
Meal cleanup	0.3	0.2	0.4	0.1	0.4	5.1	2.9	2.1	1.0	1.3*	2.7	2.1	1.4	0.3	1.1*
Housecleaning	0.3	0.5	1.5	1.7	1.8*	8.7	6.3	6.1	7.2	5.1*	4.2	5.9	3.7	5.2	4.4
Laundry and ironing	0.2	0.1	0.3	0.4	0.3	6.6	4.2	2.9	2.7	3.4*	3.7	2.4	2.1	1.4	3.3
Other housework hours	3.0	3.9	6.6	7.3	5.1	3.2	2.4	3.3	4.2	3.8*	1.2	0.8	1.8	3.3	2.9
Outdoor chores	0.6	1.0	1.4	2.8	2.0*	0.3	0.5	0.4	0.7	0.8*	0.2	0.2	0.2	0.8	0.4
Repairs	1.6	2.0	2.4	2.4	1.7	0.5	0.8	0.5	0.9	0.9	0.0	0.2	0.4	0.2	0.4
Garden and animal care	0.2	0.2	0.9	0.6	0.4	0.6	0.4	0.7	0.6	0.7	0.1	0.1	0.4	0.2	0.6
Bills, other financial	0.5	0.6	2.0	1.5	1.1	1.9	0.6	1.6	2.0	1.5	0.9	0.3	0.7	2.1	1.4
Sample size (N)	(326)	(239)	(583)	(133)	(550)	(358)	(278)	(673)	(198)	(700)	(59)	(91)	(230)	(109)	(299)

Source: Authors' calculations from the 1965–66 Americans' Use of Time Study; the 1975–76 Time Use in Economic and Social Accounts; 1985 Americans' Use of Time; the 1995 Electric Power Research Institute (EPRI) Study; and the combined file of the 1998–99 Family Interaction, Social Capital and Trends in Time Use Study and the 2000 National Survey of Parents.

*2000 estimates statistically different from 1965, p < 0.05.

Figure 5.2   Housework Reported as a Secondary Activity

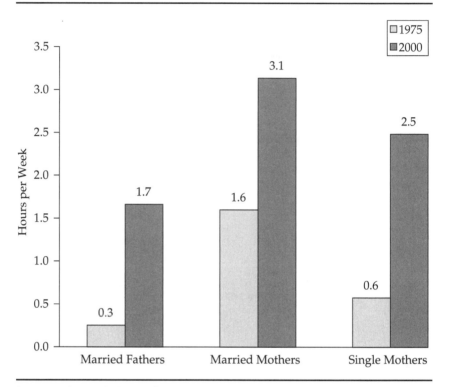

Source: Authors' calculations from 1975-76 Time Use in Economic and Social Accounts and the combined file of the 1998-99 Family Interaction, Social Capital and Trends in Time Use Study and the 2000 National Survey of Parents.
Note: 2000 estimates greater than 1975 estimates, $p < 0.05$.

We saw in chapter 4 how married fathers notably increased their child care hours. Fathers have also more than doubled their hours in housework, from about 4.5 hours in 1965 to almost 10 hours per week in 2000. Unlike child care, where the biggest increases for fathers occurred in the 1990s, fathers' housework time increased earlier—between 1965 and 1985—and has not changed appreciably since 1985. Including secondary time in housework adds an extra 1.7 hours per week to their family care in 2000 (shown in figure 5.2).

Some of the biggest increases in fathers' housework have been in the traditionally female tasks of cooking and cleaning. Fathers' hours preparing meals per week in 2000 was four times the minimal half hour figure in 1965; and they report more than six times as much house-cleaning (2 hours per week in 2000 compared with 20 minutes in 1965).

Traditionally masculine types of housework have also increased, but not as much, particularly in the form of more outdoor chores and bill paying—two chores that may now require more attention and time as housing lots have become larger and finances more complex. Time shopping for goods and obtaining household services has remained steady for fathers at about 5 hours per week (see appendix table 5A.2).

Changes in Personal Care

Television commercials often portray harried mothers as exhausted and pining for sleep. The numerous magazine articles, showing how mothers can make more time for themselves, suggest that they are more stretched for time than ever. Although certainly some mothers have had to squeeze out a great deal of personal (or free) time as they seek to balance paid work with family life, our time-diary data show that personal care in the form of sleeping, grooming, and eating has not changed much, at least on average. As shown in table 5.2, married mothers in 1965 spent about 9 hours per week eating, 55 hours sleeping and 10 hours grooming—compared with about 8 hours eating, 55 hours sleeping, and 9 hours grooming in 2000. For single mothers, the reduction in their sleep hours to 55 hours a week make them look almost exactly like married mothers, and married fathers for that matter; their meal times have declined slightly, but their grooming time remains steady.

Fathers' time in personal care is fairly similar across time, with declines in time spent eating of about 2.5 hours per week since 1965 (from 10.6 to about 8 hours), probably due to more fast food, eating while commuting in cars, or lunching at one's work desk. Like mothers, fathers still average about the same number of hours per week of sleep as they did in the 1960s, but spend almost a half hour less per week on grooming.

Changes in Free Time Activities

Table 5.3 provides a closer look at the trends in parental free-time activities, documenting first for married mothers a decline in free time from 36 hours per week in 1965 to 32 hours today. Although significant, this decline is not nearly as drastic as the declines in housework. For single mothers, reports of free-time hours were actually much higher in the 1975 through 1995 diaries, but in 2000 were only slightly higher than in 1965—31 hours in 2000 compared to 29 hours per week in 1965.

Changes have occurred in how free time is spent, however. Consistent with Putnam's (2000) thesis about the decline in community engagement, married mothers' time in organizations and in visiting with others has dropped significantly, with an hour less time in organizational activities

Table 5.2   Trends in Personal Care Activities of Parents, Hours per Week

Activity	1965	1975	1985	1995	2000
Married fathers					
Total	73.4	74.1	72.9	66.7	69.5*
Sleep	54.7	56.1	54.5	53.4	54.2
Meal	10.6	10.4	7.2	5.9	7.9*
Grooming	8.0	7.6	11.2	7.5	7.5
Sample size (N)	(326)	(239)	(583)	(133)	(550)
Married mothers					
Total	73.6	75.8	74.5	71.2	71.5*
Sleep	54.8	57.9	56.3	57.2	54.8
Meal	9.0	9.0	6.7	5.3	7.8*
Grooming	9.8	8.9	11.5	8.7	8.9
Sample size (N)	(358)	(278)	(673)	(198)	(700)
Single mothers					
Total	79.4	77.6	76.0	73.1	70.9*
Sleep	59.4	59.8	56.3	59.1	54.5*
Meal	8.5	7.9	5.5	4.1	6.3*
Grooming	11.5	10.0	14.2	9.9	10.2
Sample size (N)	(59)	(91)	(230)	(109)	(299)

Source: Authors' calculations from the 1965–66 Americans' Use of Time Study; the 1975–76 Time Use in Economic and Social Accounts; 1985 Americans' Use of Time; the 1995 Electric Power Research Institute (EPRI) Study; and the combined file of the 1998-99 Family Interaction, Social Capital and Trends in Time Use Study and the 2000 National Survey of Parents.
*2000 estimates statistically different from 1965, $p < 0.05$.

and 2.9 hours less visiting in others' homes. These married mothers in 2000 also show declines in reading of 2 hours per week and on hobbies of 1.3 hours. By contrast, their time in fitness activities has increased, and time in religious activities and listening to music has remained stable. Dwarfing all other uses of free time at all time points, however, is television viewing, which includes videos in 2000—being a steady 11 hours per week and similar to 1965. Because of small sample sizes, estimates for single mothers are unstable over the years, and therefore the only activity to show a statistically significant decline among single mothers is time spent attending events, which dropped from 4 to 1.4 hours per week.

Married fathers' leisure activities show only minor changes. Their overall free time has remained almost constant at 35 hours per week, with only one year (1995) showing unusual deviation from the overall pattern.[2] Similar to married mothers, their time visiting in friends' and relatives' homes and in reading has declined. As with mothers, fathers' television time remains the dominant leisure activity by far, consuming

Table 5.3   Trends in Parents' Free-Time Activities, Hours per Week

Activity	Married Fathers					Married Mothers					Single Mothers				
	1965	1975	1985	1995	2000	1965	1975	1985	1995	2000	1965	1975	1985	1995	2000
Total	34.5	34.7	33.7	40.5	34.5	35.7	37.1	34.1	31.3	31.7*	29.4	39.6	41.5	41.5	31.4
Education	1.0	1.2	0.5	1.6	3.1*	0.5	0.6	0.8	2.5	2.2*	1.7	3.3	3.5	3.5	2.5
Religion	1.1	1.3	0.8	0.6	1.6	1.2	2.6	1.6	0.7	1.3	0.7	1.3	2.0	0.8	1.2
Organizations	1.1	1.1	1.1	0.4	0.8	1.5	2.2	1.1	0.8	0.6*	0.5	1.0	0.7	0.3	0.8
Event	0.6	0.4	0.8	1.1	1.4*	0.7	0.9	0.9	1.8	1.4*	4.0	0.5	0.9	2.1	1.4*
Visiting	7.7	6.1	4.8	6.6	4.7*	9.3	6.4	5.7	5.1	6.4*	7.1	8.0	7.4	10.6	5.4
Fitness	1.4	1.7	2.5	7.2	2.3	0.5	1.0	1.5	1.7	1.4*	0.7	0.2	1.2	1.5	1.4
Hobby	1.3	2.2	2.4	4.1	1.6	3.0	3.0	2.7	1.1	1.7*	1.0	2.6	1.8	1.3	1.5
Television	13.6	14.9	14.9	13.9	14.2	10.5	13.4	12.9	11.1	11.2	9.3	16.1	16.1	15.7	12.3
Reading	4.0	2.7	2.4	2.0	1.1*	3.8	2.9	2.5	2.6	1.5*	1.2	1.8	1.7	1.0	1.3
Stereo	0.7	0.4	0.3	0.1	0.1*	0.3	0.2	0.2	0.0	0.1	0.6	0.9	0.6	0.0	0.3
Communication	2.0	2.5	3.3	2.9	3.7*	4.3	3.8	4.3	3.9	4.0	2.6	3.9	5.5	4.7	3.4
Sample size (N)	(326)	(239)	(583)	(133)	(550)	(358)	(278)	(673)	(198)	(700)	(59)	(91)	(230)	(109)	(299)

Source: Authors' calculations from the 1965–66 Americans' Use of Time Study; the 1975–76 Time Use in Economic and Social Accounts; 1985 Americans' Use of Time; the 1995 Electric Power Research (EPRI) Study; and the combined file of the 1998–99 Family Interaction, Social Capital and Trends in Time Use Study and the 2000 National Survey of Parents.
*2000 estimates statistically different from 1965, p < 0.05.

about 14 hours per week in 2000, much as in 1965. In essence, married fathers' time in leisure is somewhat greater than married mothers, but their patterns of change mirror those for married mothers in table 5.3.

In Summary

Mothers' time, particularly married mothers, has changed most since 1965, with an apparent trade-off of unpaid housework for paid work, a shift that has left their time with children intact. They also have a bit less free time, but report the same amount of sleep as in 1965. Single mothers have also increased their child care time a bit, with this time coming from personal care, but their housework and paid work have remained relatively stable.

How much fathers' lives have changed depend on one's point of view. Compared to their fathers' generation, married fathers today are spending more hours in family care—both child care (as discussed in chapter 4), and housework (as detailed in this chapter). That has been offset by less time in paid work and personal care. Changes for married fathers have not been as dramatic as for married mothers.

Moving Beyond Zero-Sum Measures: Increased "Time Deepening" via Secondary Activities

These shifts in primary activities tell only part of the story of social change, given that parents can try to gain time in their 24-hour days by multitasking—doing more activities at once to fit everything into their lives. Some evidence of this in the increase in child care combined with other activities was found in chapter 4 and in figure 5.2 with respect to housework.

Here we examine the amount of time spent in two activities at once, in an attempt to determine whether multitasking may have increased. Including secondary time does double count time, but perhaps allows a fuller picture of how families have changed. Thus an important way to examine whether parents have in essence sped up their daily lives is to look at the nature of multitasking.

The 1975 and 2000 diary data allow us to examine whether respondents report more secondary activities today. That is, when parents detail their day by each main activity, do more of them also report doing something else at the same time?

Table 5.4 shows that among all three groups—married fathers, married mothers, and single mothers—multitasking greatly increased over the last quarter of the twentieth-century. The first row shows time in multitasking in which work, family care, or personal care is the primary activ-

Table 5.4   Changes in Parent Multitasking, Hours per Week

	1975	2000	Change Hours	Change Percent
Married fathers				
Multitasking (excluding all primary free-time activities)	3.7	8.7*	5.0	134
Multitasking (excluding time when both secondary and primary activities are free time)	30.4	59.4*	29.1	96
All multitasking (all time where a secondary activity is reported)	39.4	78.3*	39.0	99
Sample size (N)	(239)	(550)		
Married mothers				
Multitasking (excluding all primary free-time activities)	7.7	14.6*	6.9	89
Multitasking (excluding time when both secondary and primary activities are free time)	32.4	64.1*	31.7	98
All multitasking (all time where a secondary activity is reported)	41.8	80.6*	38.8	93
Sample size (N)	(278)	(700)		
Single mothers				
Multitasking (excluding all primary free-time activities)	6.2	12.6*	6.4	104
Multitasking (excluding time when both secondary and primary activities are free time)	30.1	62.1*	32.0	106
All multitasking (all time where a secondary activity is reported)	39.4	78.9*	39.5	100
Sample size (N)	(91)	(299)		

Source: Authors' calculations from 1975–76 Time Use in Economic and Social Accounts and the combined file of the 1998–99 Family Interaction, Social Capital and Trends in Time Use Study and the 2000 National Survey of Parents.
*2000 estimates greater than 1975 estimates, $p < 0.05$.

ity and some secondary activity was reported. The second measure includes primary free-time activities if the secondary activity is not also a free-time activity—in other words, excluding that which consists of two simultaneous leisure activities. Using this measure we find married fathers' hours of multitasking increased from about 30 to 59 hours per week (a gain of 96 percent), married mothers from 32 to 64 (a 98-percent increase), and single mothers from 30 to 62 hours per week (a 106-percent increase). This is a gain of more than 6 hours per day, and when considering it in terms of waking hours only, about half of today's parents' time is spent doing two or more activities simultaneously.

When looking at all multitasking (including engaging in two leisure activities at once), we see that it has virtually doubled for all groups—with about 5.5 hours per day (or almost 40 hours per week) more now. For married fathers, the increase is from 39 to 78 hours per week, for married mothers from 42 to 81 hours, and for single mothers, from about 39 to 79 hours. One could argue that doing two leisure activities, one component of the measure called all multitasking, is not really multitasking; however it does describe a busier or more complex life style of packing more things into one's days. Such a shift may alter the look and the feel of family life for today's parents.

We were concerned that the increase in multitasking might be methodological, that in 2000, the computer-assisted telephone interview (CATI) process may have encouraged more consistent prompting of secondary activities than the personal and non-CATI interviews in 1975. The first wave of the 1975 collection involved a lengthy personal interview, though subsequent waves were shorter and by telephone. Although the prompt for secondary activities is similar across the years, the computer-assisted interview may have increased the likelihood that more respondents reported secondary activities, given that the computer automatically prompts the interviewer to ask about secondary activities when the respondent reports a lengthy primary activity. Further, the personal interview during the first wave of 1975 was lengthy and interviewers may therefore not have been as careful in detecting secondary activities, versus when they administered the telephone interviews in subsequent waves.

We compared multitasking reports in the third wave of the 1975 data collection, in which interviews were conducted over the telephone, hence the survey method was more comparable to 2000. Appendix table 5A.4 compares multitasking estimates between 1975 and 2000 using a subsample of the third wave in 1975. There is remarkable consistency across the 1975 estimates. There is no way to fully ensure that the increase in multitasking over time is not a methodological aberration. However, despite the fact that some of the increased 2000 reports of multitasking may be due to the increased probing of secondary activities, sizable increases remain in reports of multitasking between the 1975 third wave and the 2000 reports.

Uncontaminated Leisure or Quality Time

In a creative use of time-diary evidence from Australia, Bittman and Wajcman (2000) recently argued that the overall amount of free time captured in time diaries may not adequately portray the quality of leisure experiences. They note that leisure activities can be more or less contaminated by simultaneous activities that are not as enjoyable, such as folding laundry while watching a video. Even when two individuals have the same total number of hours of free time, the experience of leisure may be more fragmented for some than for others. Finally, leisure spent only with adults may be qualitatively different from that spent with children. The authors measured each concept using their detailed Australian time-diary data to locate significant gender differences in each behavior.

The theme of fragmentation of leisure is a common one among feminist scholars of leisure (Deem 1996, 6; Wimbush and Talbot 1988, 11). The notion is that women's leisure time is often chopped up into many small parcels during the day, and this means that they can never fully relax. If all one has is 10 minutes here and there, between chauffeuring children to and from lessons or sports activities in the after-school hours, that does not qualify as refreshing free time. To assess whether fragmented free time has increased over time, we examine the number of distinct free-time episodes on the diary day, as well as the length of the longest episode of leisure. To measure the contamination of leisure by other tasks, we assess how often a free-time activity occurs without the distraction of another nonleisure activity. Pure free time thus refers to periods when the primary activity reported is a free-time activity and no secondary activity is reported, or when the secondary activity is also a free-time activity.

One can further assess this pure leisure by examining the with whom data, focusing on whether the activity is spent only with adults or alone—or with children present. Adult leisure is conceptualized as a type of free time qualitatively different from that spent in the company of children (Mattingly and Bianchi 2003). One can also assess the amount of free time when a mother or father is alone (that is, the only adult) with children. Free time spent alone with children is time that is likely to be qualitatively different than time with children when other adults are present, because of the limited range of activities in which it is appropriate and feasible to engage when one is alone with children (especially very young children).

One caveat about labeling free time with children as contaminated free time is that diary and other studies show high levels of enjoyment of time with children. For example, using 1985 time-use data, Robinson (1993, 47) found that people greatly enjoyed playing with children and talking or reading to children, ranking these activities 8.8 and 8.6, respectively, on a ten-point enjoyment scale. Many parents cherish free time spent with their children, and we have noted the high enjoyment levels of activities involving children in the previous chapter.

Table 5.5 compares these various measures of the quality of free-time activities for married fathers, married mothers, and single mothers, using

Table 5.5   Trends in Parents' Free Time

	1975	2000
Married fathers		
Total (hours per week)	34.7	34.6
Fragmentation (average per day)		
Number of episodes	5.0	4.0*
Longest episode (hours)	2.2	2.4
Contamination (hours per week)		
Pure free time	30.1	29.1
Adult free time	20.6	18.3
Free time alone with children	2.1	3.8*
Sample size (N)	(239)	(550)
Married mothers		
Total (hours per week)	37.2	31.8
Fragmentation (average per day)		
Number of episodes	6.4	4.2*
Longest episode (hours)	2.1	2.2
Contamination (hours per week)		
Pure free time	32.9	25.8*
Adult free time	21.1	14.8*
Free time alone with children	5.0	7.4*
Sample size (N)	(278)	(700)
Single mothers		
Total (hours per week)	39.6	31.9
Fragmentation (average per day)		
Number of episodes	5.6	3.9*
Longest episode (hours)	2.4	2.2
Contamination (hours per week)		
Pure free time	34.4	26.5*
Adult free time	20.5	17.4
Free time alone with children	12.3	9.9
Sample size (N)	(91)	(299)

Source: Authors' calculations from the 1975–76 Time Use in Economic and Social Accounts and the combined file of the 1998–99 Family Interaction, Social Capital and Trends in Time Use Study and the 2000 National Survey of Parents.
*2000 estimates statistically different from 1975, $p < 0.05$.

diary data from 1975 and 2000 (again, mainly because they are the only studies containing the requisite full diary reports to calculate the various measures of fragmentation and contamination of leisure activities). Among married mothers, there has been a decrease in the number of episodes of leisure per day, along with the total amount of free time. Because the longest episode of free time is similar at both time points, there is no strong evidence that leisure has become more fragmented for married mothers.

The contamination measures, however, do suggest a possible erosion in the quality of free-time experiences. Pure free time, that is free time uncontaminated by secondary activities (such as housework, child care, or grooming), declined fairly substantially—from about 33 to 26 hours a week for married mothers. Adult child-free time shows a significant decline as well. Conversely, free time alone with children increased.

For single mothers, the total amount of free time, along with the number of free-time episodes per day, declined between 1975 and 2000. The longest episode indicator also suggests a possible decrease in the quality of leisure. As for married mothers, pure free time (free time uncontaminated by nonleisure activities) has declined.

When we examine trends in the quality of married fathers' free time, there is little indication of change over the decades. Although the number of episodes of leisure per day has declined (as for mothers), pure free time and adult free time (perhaps the most refreshing kind of leisure) did not change much for fathers. Fathers have increased their leisure time spent alone with their children, that is, without the children's mother or any other adult present.

In sum, mothers and fathers appear to have greatly deepened their time through multitasking over the past decades, which indicates a faster or more complex pace of life today. When we consider the quality of leisure more explicitly using these new measures, it appears that the quality of married and single mothers' leisure may have declined by some measures. Married fathers' leisure experiences seem more stable.

Deepening Time for Children by Reducing Time with Others

There is another way that parents (especially mothers) may have deepened time over the decades—that is, made time for children despite increases in paid work and other obligations. They could be spending less time with other people in their lives. Thus, another question we can address using the with whom component of the diary data concerns the significant people with whom mothers and fathers do spend time.

Table 5.6   Trends in Parents' Time with Spouse, Hours per Week

	1975	2000	Percent Change 1975 to 2000
Spouse only			
All married parents	12.4	9.1[a]	−26
Married mothers	11.8	8.6[a]	−27
Married fathers	13.0	9.6[a]	−26
Any time with spouse			
All married parents	35.4	28.4[ac]	−20
Married mothers	35.6	26.8[a]	−25
Married fathers	35.3	30.9[a]	−12

Source: Authors' calculations from the 1975–76 Time Use in Economic and Social Accounts and the combined file of the 1998–99 Family Interaction, Social Capital and Trends in Time Use Study and the 2000 National Survey of Parents.
a. 1975 to 2000 within gender difference statistically significant, $p < 0.05$.
b. Gender difference in 1975 statistically significant, $p < 0.05$.
c. Gender difference in 2000 statistically significant, $p < 0.05$.

Perhaps, for example, the modern employed mother may make up for a felt lack of shared time with her preschooler by including that child in her leisure activities or by choosing a child-friendly leisure activity (like going to a park) rather than having an adult dinner with friends. Perhaps married mothers and fathers can tag team paid work or errands, with one parent coming home to be with children as the other heads out the door. Although this ensures that children have adequate parental time, it also means that spouses rarely encounter each other during the day. Perhaps, as Putnam (2000) suggested, what today's mothers have given up are commitments that in the past put them in contact with others in the neighborhood school, church, or community center. We now look at time spent with spouses, friends, extended family, and in civic pursuits in order to assess a potentially complex way that parents' lives may have changed.

Trends in Time with One's Spouse

Table 5.6 shows trends in parents' time with their spouse. We again have the full diary data to exploit for only 1975 and 2000. In terms of time with spouse alone, both married mothers and fathers report significantly less time together, a decline from 12 hours per week in 1975 to 9 hours in 2000 (a 26-percent drop). In terms of spending any time with one's spouse, which includes when others are present or not, the figures are 35 hours in 1975 versus 28 hours in 2000 (a 20-percent drop).[3]

Table 5.7   Trends in Parents' Time with Friends and Relatives,
             Hours per Week

	1975	2000	Percent Change
Married fathers	10.1	9.7	−3
Married mothers	11.6[a]	10.6[a]	−9
Single mothers	19.3[b]	14.4[b]	−25

Source: Authors' calculations from the 1975–76 Time Use in Economic and Social Accounts and the combined file of the 1998–99 Family Interaction, Social Capital and Trends in Time Use Study and the National Survey of Parents.
a. Estimates for married mothers significantly different from single mothers, $p < 0.05$.
b. Estimates for married fathers significantly different from single mothers, $p < 0.05$.

Trends in Time with Friends and Extended Family

Do mothers and fathers spend less time with other family members, friends, or other individuals in their community? We saw earlier that primary activity time spent in visiting with other family members and friends in their homes has declined. However, primary activity time spent visiting is quite limited and does not take into account the with whom codes available for any activity, such as housework or leisure activities, other than visiting.

If one looks at total time with friends and relatives, the estimates suggest relative stability for married parents but a decline for single mothers. Table 5.7 shows that married mothers and fathers spent about 10 hours a week with friends and relatives in 2000, rather similar to 1975. Single mothers' time with friends and relatives has declined by 25 percent, from 19 to 14 hours a week.

Trends in Time in Social Leisure and Civic Pursuits

Another aspect of changing leisure time with others is provided in table 5.8, where we use the categorization developed by Liana Sayer (2001), as outlined in appendix table 5A.5. Free-time activities are grouped into those that promote community, or that reflect organizational or civic commitment. Social leisure activities with friends or family include socializing, eating meals, attending movies, pursuing hobbies, or engaging in other recreation, and they provide another perspective on time spent with others. Active but solitary leisure and passive leisure pursuits (a large component of which is television viewing) are also shown.

Using this categorization of leisure activity, married fathers engaged in 17 weekly hours of social leisure in 1975, compared with about 15 hours

Table 5.8   **Changes in Civic, Social, Active and Passive Leisure Activities**

	Hours per Week		Percentage Reporting	
	1975	2000	1975	2000
Married fathers				
Social leisure	16.9	15.2[b]	97.8	89.5[ab]
Civic leisure	2.1[b]	2.0	14.4[b]	12.5
Active leisure	2.8	1.7[ab]	23.6	18.4
Passive leisure	3.7	3.2	48.7	33.4[a]
Watching television	14.9	14.2[b]	77.2	78.2
Sample size (N)	(239)	(550)		
Married mothers				
Social leisure	18.2	18.1[c]	96.7	93.6[c]
Civic leisure	4.0[c]	1.6[a]	26.7[c]	11.3[a]
Active leisure	2.3	1.1[ac]	26.8	15.3[a]
Passive leisure	4.1	3.1	49.5	36.2[a]
Watching television	13.4	11.2[a]	77.4	64.8[a]
Sample size (N)	(278)	(700)		
Single mothers				
Social leisure	15.6	13.6	93.3[d]	83.3[ad]
Civic leisure	1.8	1.3	16.5	8.6[a]
Active leisure	2.1	2.0	23.6	23.2
Passive leisure	5.1	3.2[a]	42.4	33.5
Watching television	16.1	12.3	73.4	63.7[d]
Sample size (N)	(91)	(299)		

Source: Authors' calculations from the 1975–76 Time Use in Economic and Social Accounts and the combined file of the 1998–99 Family Interaction, Social Capital and Trends in Time Use Study and the 2000 National Survey of Parents.
a. Within gender difference statistically significant, $p < 0.05$
b. Estimates for married fathers statistically significantly different from married mothers, $p < 0.05$.
c. Estimates for married mothers statistically significantly different from single mothers, $p < 0.05$.
d. Estimates for married fathers statistically significantly different from single mothers, $p < 0.05$.

today. Married mothers spent 18 hours per week in social leisure in 1975, virtually the same amount as today. Social leisure has declined some for single mothers, from 15 hours in 1975 to 13 hours today.

There has also been a decline in the proportion of diary keepers reporting any social activity on the diary day. For example, where 93 percent of single mothers in 1975 reported some form of social leisure on the diary day, only 83 percent did so in 2000 (see table 5.8). For married mothers, the change was smaller, from 97 to 94 percent. For married fathers, however, the decline was from 98 to 90 percent. Although these levels remain high, perhaps socializing has become more constrained, given the somewhat fewer days per week that parents in 2000 reported it than those in 1975 did.

Time in civic leisure may be important, not only for parents, but also in terms of developing bonds of trust among community members, and in building social capital for children (see Sayer 2001). For married fathers, the already low number of hours in civic pursuits remained steady at about 2 hours per week, with 14 percent of the sample reporting this in 1975 and 13 percent in 2000. For married mothers, there is a large decline, from about 4 to 1.5 hours per week—and from 27 percent reporting to about 11 percent. For single mothers, there is about a half hour decline (from 1.8 to 1.3 hours per week), along with a drop from 17 percent to only 9 percent reporting this kind of activity.

In sum, there may be fewer instances each week of interacting with spouses for married mothers and fathers. There seems to be the same amount of time spent together with family and friends for married mothers and fathers, in contrast to a decrease for single mothers. Among married mothers, there is a large decline in civic time. Because this is the group that most changed their position vis-à-vis the home, it makes sense that they now look much more like married fathers and single mothers in terms of the time spent in civic activities per week.

Understanding Changes: Employed and Nonemployed Mothers in the Two Eras

Two trends form the conundrum of this chapter: the large shift of mothers into paid work in the face of stable or increasing maternal time in child care. A direct comparison of employed and nonemployed mothers' time in various activities fills in the picture of what gives to allow mothers to find time for both paid work and child care. Table 5.9 provides this comparison, showing differences in housework, sleep, and various free-time activities of both employed and nonemployed mothers in 1975 and 2000. Appendix table 5A.6 shows estimates of all time uses for employed and nonemployed mothers in 1975 and 2000.

Mothers trade housework for paid work, as noted at the outset of this chapter, with employed mothers averaging 8 fewer hours per week of housework than nonemployed mothers in 2000. Housework has dropped dramatically overall for all mothers, largely because more mothers are now employed and employed mothers do much less housework than their nonemployed counterparts. Nonemployed mothers in 2000 also

Table 5.9   Differences in Activities of Employed and Nonemployed Mothers, Hours per Week

	1975	2000	Combined
Housework			
Employed mothers' hours	17.1[a]	16.1[ab]	16.3[a]
Nonemployed mothers' hours	28.9[a]	24.6[ab]	26.4
Difference (unadjusted)	−11.8	−8.5	10.1
Difference (OLS adjusted)	−11.9***	−7.8***	−9.0***
Year (=2000) (OLS estimate)	—	—	2.1***
Sleep			
Employed mothers' hours	56.7[a]	53.4[ab]	54.0[a]
Nonemployed mothers' hours	59.7[a]	57.8[ab]	58.6
Difference (unadjusted)	−3.0	−4.4	−4.5
Difference (OLS adjusted)	−2.2	−4.6***	−3.8***
Year (=2000)	—	—	−2.7**
Watching television			
Employed mothers' hours	10.3[a]	9.6[ab]	9.7[a]
Nonemployed mothers' hours	17.1[a]	16.2[ab]	16.6
Difference (unadjusted)	−6.8	−6.6	−6.9
Difference (OLS adjusted)	−6.5***	−7.3***	−7.1***
Year (=2000)	—	—	0.6***
Total free time			
Employed mothers' hours	29.6[a]	27.7[ab]	28.0[a]
Nonemployed mothers' hours	44.3[a]	41.0[ab]	42.4
Difference (unadjusted)	−14.7	−13.3	−14.3
Difference (OLS adjusted)	−15.6***	−14.5***	−15.0***
Year (=2000)	—	—	−2.3
"Pure" child free time			
Employed mothers' hours	17.2[a]	13.8[ab]	14.5[a]
Nonemployed mothers' hours	24.0[a]	19.8[ab]	21.6
Difference (unadjusted)	−6.8	−6.0	−7.1
Difference (OLS adjusted)	−7.9***	−8.6***	−8.5***
Year (=2000)	—	—	−3.9***
Sample size (N)	(369)	(999)	(1,368)

Source: Authors' calculations from the 1975–76 Time Use in Economic and Social Accounts and the combined file of the 1998–99 Family Interaction, Social Capital and Trends in Time Use Study and the 2000 National Survey of Parents.
Note: OLS regression is used to produce an estimate of the employment difference net of associations of time engaged in the specific activity with number of children, children under age 6, educational attainment, age, marital status. The interaction of year and employment was never statistically significant. Year changes estimated by OLS regressions with concatenated 1975 and 2000 data.
a. Employed and nonemployed statistically significantly different at $p < 0.05$.
b. 1975 and 2000 statistically significantly different at $p < 0.05$.
***p-value < .001, **p-value < .01, *p-value < .05.

appear to do less housework than their counterparts in 1975. All mothers, like women in general, seem to be shedding housework.

Employed mothers also adjust other facets of their lives, averaging 3 or 4 hours less sleep per week than nonemployed mothers and watching television almost 7 fewer hours per week.[4] Both in 1975 and 2000, there was a large difference in the amount of free time between the two groups of mothers, with employed mothers having 15 hours less discretionary time each week (see the estimate for the combined model). With the focus on what is arguably the most "refreshing" type of free time—adult only, pure free time not contaminated by doing family caregiving—we find that free time has decreased significantly for both employed and nonemployed mothers. Thus, employed and nonemployed mothers seem to keep their time with children high by more often incorporating children into their free-time activities, which is consistent with the decline in their pure child-free leisure hours. At the same time, employed mothers may be relatively more harried than their nonemployed counterparts, because they have significantly fewer pure free-time hours each week.

Table 5.10 shows that both nonemployed and employed mothers seem to have curtailed their hours of civic leisure, with employed mothers averaging almost 2 fewer hours per week in community activities, and with neither group averaging very many hours in this type of activity in 2000. Employed mothers also spend almost 3 fewer hours per week with friends and relatives. Married employed mothers also seem to be spending far less time in total with their spouse than in the past, resulting in an estimated 6 fewer hours per week with their spouse (in the combined models) than nonemployed mothers.

In sum, what mothers give up to finance employment but keep child care time relatively high is substantial. Employed mothers experience time deficits in an array of activities. Employed mothers spend less time on housework, sleep fewer hours per week, and have much less discretionary time. In addition, they have less time with their spouse, family, and friends.

Recall from chapter 3 that the employed mother averages a 71-hour work week, compared with the average 52-hour work week for the nonemployed mother. That employed mothers have so much less overall free time raises concerns about the quality of their down time (and consequent health and well-being) as they try to balance paid work, child care, and nonmarket work. Further, the finding that employment restricts mothers' participation in civic and social pursuits raises more global concerns about how the quality of civic and social organizations is affected, or perhaps diminished, by the demands placed on employed mothers' time.

Table 5.10   Differences in Civic and Family Activities of Employed and Nonemployed Mothers, Hours per Week

	1975	2000	Combined
Civic leisure			
Employed mothers' hours	2.4[a]	1.1[ab]	1.3[a]
Nonemployed mothers' hours	4.2[a]	2.6[ab]	3.3
Difference (unadjusted)	−1.8	−1.5	−1.9
Difference (OLS adjusted)	−1.6	−1.7*	−1.7*
Year (=2000) (OLS estimate)	—	—	−1.5*
Time with friends and relatives			
Employed mothers' hours	11.7	11.1	11.2[a]
Nonemployed mothers' hours	15.0	13.2	14.0
Difference (unadjusted)	−3.3	−2.1	−2.7
Difference (OLS adjusted)	−5.0*	−1.5	−2.6*
Year (=2000)	—	—	−2.0
Time alone with spouse			
Employed mothers' hours	11.3	8.0	8.6[a]
Nonemployed mothers' hours	12.2	9.9	10.8
Difference (unadjusted)	−0.9	−1.9	−2.2
Difference (OLS adjusted)	−1.7	−2.6*	−2.2*
Year (=2000)	—	—	−2.8*
Any time with spouse			
Employed mothers' hours	35.1	24.0[a]	26.2[a]
Nonemployed mothers' hours	35.8	32.8[a]	34.1
Difference (unadjusted)	−0.7	−8.8	−7.9
Difference (OLS adjusted)	0.1	−9.4*	−6.0*
Year (=2000)	—	—	−7.4*
Sample size (N)	(369)	(999)	(1,368)

Source: Authors' calculations from the 1975–76 Time Use in Economic and Social Accounts and the combined file of the 1998–99 Family Interaction, Social Capital and Trends in Time Use Study and the 2000 National Survey of Parents.

Note: OLS regression is used to produce an estimate of the employment difference net of associations of time engaged in the specific activity with number of children, children under age six, educational attainment, age, marital status. The interaction of year and employment was never statistically significant. Year changes estimated by OLS regressions with concatenated 1975 and 2000 data.

a. Employed and nonemployed statistically significantly different at $p < 0.05$.

b. 1975 and 2000 statistically significantly different at $p < 0.05$.

*$p < 0.05$.

Summary and Conclusions

As mothers have increased their attachment to the labor force and have done more parenting alone, what has changed? The number of hours spent on core housework as a primary activity each week has decreased almost 15 hours among married mothers, on average. Single mothers' housework activities have not changed all that much, probably because single mothers have always done less housework to provide economically for their children. In many ways, married mothers' time allocations have become more similar to single mothers' across the decades.

For mothers, other subtler and smaller changes have taken place as well. Specifically, both married and single mothers today report more multitasking, and all mothers report less time in civic leisure pursuits. Among married mothers, less time is spent with their husbands. To some degree, these more subtle changes probably arise from married mothers' shift of work activities from unpaid work (largely in the home) to paid work outside the home. In their movement into the workplace, married mothers are increasingly positioned physically outside their home and neighborhood for more hours per week than in the past.

As employment becomes widespread for mothers, those who are not employed at any given point in time become a more select group. Many trends characterize both groups—for example, the decline in housework and civic engagement and the decline in time alone with a spouse. Yet nonemployed mothers may be better able to carve out time for themselves and make time for activities that include both parents (or perhaps the whole family), whereas employed mothers may be managing to keep more balls in the air by tag-teaming child care with their husbands (thus reducing their overall time with their spouse) and limiting the time they devote solely to adult-only leisure activities.

The way married fathers spend their time has changed as well, but in less dramatic ways. Fathers not only increased their child care time, but also now spend more hours per week on housework than before. This moderate turn toward family activities is paralleled by some decline in their paid work activities and in personal care. Fathers also show an increase in multitasking and spend less time with their wives than in the past.

As noted, the story about family time combines both continuities in parents' lives along with some important changes. Married mothers' increased paid work has pulled them from other activities, mainly unpaid work, but also from time in their communities. Although it has not pulled them away from children to any large degree (at least not in terms of average interaction time as shown in chapter 4), it may be reducing the time they have to refresh and rejuvenate.

The question of how today's mothers feel about their time—with children, with their spouse and for themselves—as well as how they feel about balancing and tradeoffs thus becomes an intriguing one. We suspect that even though mothers objectively may average the same amounts of time interacting with their children, they may feel more strained in comparison to the full-time homemaker mothers of years past. Perhaps this is due to rising cultural standards, to mothers' relative lack of accessibility to family members (not captured by the diary data), and to the speeding up of daily activities in the form of multitasking.

Fathers also seem to be at a crossroads. Cultural standards for fathers' involvement in family life have increased, potentially increasing their time pressure. Yet chapter 4 showed that today's fathers are spending notably more time with children, at least in comparison with previous time points. This may make men feel that they are doing a better job of balancing work and family than their fathers did, making it interesting to know more about fathers' feelings about time in contemporary U.S. society. After a short digression into joint parental time provided by an examination of the weekly diaries in the next chapter, we turn to the topic of feelings about time in chapter 7.

Chapter 6

Gender Equality, Role Specialization, and "The Second Shift": What Do Weekly Diaries Show?

ARLIE HOCHSCHILD (1989) has chronicled the long work days of mothers and the resulting strains in their relationships with their husbands. Working women, who devoted many hours to paid work, came home only to log in many more hours of unpaid work in the form of cooking dinner, meeting children's needs, doing laundry, and the like. Hochschild documented how the women she interviewed faced the equivalent of a second job when they returned to the home after work. The existence of this arduous second shift raises the question of whether women's movement into the labor force has been liberating or has instead further shackled them to endless hours of drudgery, to the point of exhaustion.

The claim in the second shift literature, particularly that on housework, is that the current situation is less fair to women than men. Women still do twice as much housework and child care as men, as we have shown. Qualitative research shows that women also do more of the work to connect family members to extended kin (DiLeonardo 1987). Although men have increased their time in domestic work, this has not been enough to counterbalance women's increased presence in the marketplace. Hence, it is argued, as long as women feel more responsible than men for the smooth functioning of the family, they will continue to bear a disproportionate burden of the work in families (Hays 1996: Williams 2000).

One of the difficulties with the more quantitative assessments of the second shift, especially on housework, is that unpaid domestic work is considered in relative isolation from paid work. This is particularly problematic when assessing the total workloads of individuals and gender inequalities in meeting those workloads. Families need both the income that is provided from the first shift and the caregiving and housework that constitutes the second shift for employed persons. Ideally, one would like to study the time both women and men allot to market and nonmarket activities that benefit the family, to better understand both how burdensome these responsibilities are in terms of time and whether responsibilities for family maintenance are unequally shared by men and women, particularly mothers and fathers.

Here we use our weekly time diaries gathered from dual-earner households to take a fresh look at gendered workloads, including the second shift in middle-class families. We look at married couples to assess gender differences in time use over an entire week and examine the patterning of work across the week. Second, we investigate the correlates of total workloads of mothers, fathers—and, most important, the intra-couple gap in weekly workloads. By so doing, we provide perspective both on how busy middle-class, dual-earner parents are and how the second shift of family caregiving is shared in these families.

Moreover, having information from both parents allows us to assess how correlated the time allocations of mothers and fathers are. In the past, a specialization ("separate spheres") argument dominated the time allocation literature, especially in economics. Mothers specialized in the home, fathers in the market. Specialization seems to be giving way to much more similar time allocations of mothers and fathers, although it certainly has not disappeared, as we have discussed. Correlations of activity time between mothers and fathers suggest where parents do similar things for the family, where they differ, and perhaps where one spouse's time allocation influences the other's behavior.

The correlation in mothers' and fathers' time in child care also has implications for inequality across families—some children may be getting a great deal of parental time from both mothers and fathers, and others relatively little from either or both. We examine inequality in parent-child time across families and identify which parental activities are more or less associated with child care time. The weekly diaries provide an independent and more holistic way of estimating how equal the weekly workloads of mothers and fathers are, and allow us to assess parallel gender differentiation apparent in market work, child care, housework, personal care, and free time.

The Gender Gap in Weekly Workloads in Middle-Class Working Families

Table 6.1 compares the gender division of labor in time use among all married parents, shown in the first panel. For dual-earner, middle-class married couples, the second panel highlights the subsample of parents from our one-day diary collections comparable to those selected to keep weekly diaries (dual-earners with at least some college education). By multiplying their daily reports by seven, we obtain weekly time-use estimates for comparison to the sample that actually kept weekly diaries. Estimates obtained from the weekly diaries are shown in the third panel of table 6.1, one which shows average total workloads when paid and unpaid work are combined—as well as the gender differentiation of the component activities of market work, unpaid work (and its three components of housework, child care, and shopping), and includes estimates for the remaining uses of time, namely that spent in personal care and free-time activities. Averages are shown for both mothers and fathers, as is the gap in average hours between mothers and fathers, and (finally) the percentage of the combined hours done by fathers.[1]

Among all parents (as discussed in chapter 3), the average total workload is almost equal, with married mothers averaging 65 hours and fathers 64 hours per week. These equal overall workloads are found despite marked gender difference in paid versus unpaid work, with fathers performing 34 percent of housework and 33 percent of child care, in contrast to their 64 percent of market work. In hourly terms, mothers averaged 19 fewer weekly hours of market work than fathers, but 13 hours more of housework and shopping and 6 hours more of child care.

In their one-day diaries, dual-earner, middle-class parents seem busier than all married parents, with mothers averaging total workloads of 71 hours per week and fathers averaging 67 hours (49 percent of the family's total workload). The figures derived from the weekly diaries indicate workloads to be relatively equal for mothers and fathers, but the figures for total workloads of mothers in the weekly diaries are 8 hours lower than the estimates from single-day diaries (63 hours per week) and similar to the one-day estimates for all married parents. Mothers in the weekly diary sample reported a little less market work, shopping, and child care (only about 75 percent of the average child care in one-day diaries multiplied by seven). Again, total workloads reported in the weekly diaries are similar for mothers and fathers, with fathers' 65 work hours per week averaging about 51 percent of the family's total workload. Gender specialization of fathers in market work and mothers in housework and child care are similar to the diary figures for all parents, with fathers doing about 60 percent of the paid work and mothers doing more than 60 percent of the unpaid work in the home.

One major concern with the sole use of daily diaries has been the synthetic nature of the extrapolated weekly estimates—that is, weekly figures constructed from different individuals aggregated across the days of the week. The suggestion here is that the results of the weekly diaries

Table 6.1   Married Parents' Average Hours Per Week in Activities, 2000

| | All Married Parents | | | |
| | All One-Day Diaries | | | |
	Mother	Father	Gender Gap	Father as Percentage of Total
Total paid + unpaid work	64.9	64.0	0.9	50
Total paid work	23.8	42.5*	−18.7	64
Total unpaid work	41.1	21.5*	19.6	34
Housework	19.4	9.7*	9.7	33
Child care	12.9	6.5*	6.4	33
Shopping	8.8	5.3*	3.3	38
Personal care	71.5	69.5	1.9	49
Free time	31.7	34.5*	−2.8	52
Sample size (N)	(700)	(550)		

Source: Authors' calculations from the 2000 Sloan Weekly Diary Study and the combined file of the 1998–99 Family Interaction, Social Capital and Trends in Time Use Study, and the 2000 National Survey of Parents.
*Gender differences statistically significant, $p < 0.05$.
a. Dual-earner defined as both spouses working at least ten hours per week; "middle class" defined as at least some college education.

are remarkably consistent with the results from the daily diary data. In both samples, total productive time is relatively equal for spouses, with market work, household work, and child care following the same gender divisions. The largest discrepancy is the higher estimated weekly workload of mothers in our one-day diaries (71 hours) versus weekly (63 hours) diary studies.

In most dual-earner, middle-class families (as in most dual-earner families in general), fathers are employed full-time. Hence, a major difference in weekly workloads may be between those families where both parents work full-time and those where mothers work part-time (to accommodate the family workload). Figure 6.1 uses the weekly diaries to graph the total workloads of mothers and fathers, and it compares the weekly workloads in families where both parents work full-time with those where the mother works part-time outside the home.

In middle-class families, when both the mother and the father work full-time, the combined total workload is high—averaging 135 hours a week. However, the combined total workload in families where the wife works part-time is also high, at 129 hours per week, largely because these mothers do more nonmarket work than mothers who work full time. However, when these middle-class mothers work part-time, their total work remains significantly less than that of their counterparts work-

| Dual-Earner, Middle-Class[a] Married Parents | | | | | | | |
| One-Day Diaries | | | | Weekly Diaries | | | |
Mother	Father	Gender Gap	Father as Percentage of Total	Mother	Father	Gender Gap	Father as Percentage of Total
71.1	67.3	3.8	49	62.7	64.5	−1.9	51
32.9	46.5*	−13.6	59	30.2	46.5	−16.3	61
38.2	20.8*	17.4	35	32.6	18.1	9.6	36
16.7	9.0*	7.8	35	16.4	9.5	7.6	37
12.4	6.6*	5.7	35	9.2	4.3	4.9	32
9.1	5.2*	3.9	36	7.0	4.3	2.7	38
68.7	69.4	−0.8	50	71.5	68.2	3.3	49
28.2	31.3	−3.1	53	33.8	35.3	−1.4	51
(331)	(280)			(427)	(427)		

ing full-time (60 hours per week versus 68 hours) and of fathers (69 hours per week versus 60 hours per week for mothers). Although it is not necessarily leisurely to be a mother employed part-time in a middle-class, dual-earner family—mothers still log 60 hours a week of paid and unpaid work, it is a considerably lighter workload than for fathers and mothers who are employed full-time. A final important comparison afforded by figure 6.1 is that among couples where both are employed full-time, there is remarkable gender equality in total workloads, with mothers averaging 68 hours per week compared with 67 hours for fathers.

The Weekly Patterns of Activity for Mothers and Fathers

Using the weekly diaries, figure 6.2 shows the primary time allocation (paid and unpaid) of work over the seven days of the week for mothers and fathers—the weekly rhythm of the work of parents. Much less paid work is undertaken on the weekend, whereas housework and shopping times increase for both parents. On weekdays, a considerably higher proportion of fathers' time is devoted to working for pay, and a relatively smaller proportion is spent in unpaid work activities. Hence the dissimilarity in what mothers and fathers do for families is greater

Figure 6.1   Average Total Workload of Married Middle-Class Parents

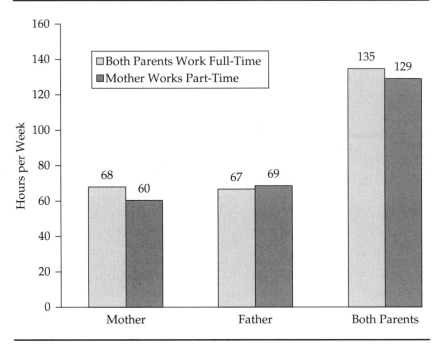

Source: Authors' calculations from the 2000 Sloan Weekly Diary Study.
Note: Mothers' workloads differ by mothers' employment status, $p < 0.05$.

during the work week than on the weekends, when total paid work effort drops for both mothers and fathers.

Perhaps most interesting is that when one counts both paid and unpaid work, fathers' work efforts are certainly no smaller than mothers' during the week. Indeed, fathers' workdays may be a little bit longer, especially on Fridays. On the weekends, mothers in our sample of middle-class employed parents may work a bit longer than fathers, especially on Sundays. The overall picture thus is one of clearly gender-differentiated tasks and day-of-week differentiated time allocations, but with basic balance in the length of the total workweek among fathers and mothers.

He Does, She Does

As noted, having weekly interconnected diaries of mothers and fathers within the same family makes new insights into the everyday trade-offs and dynamics of parental lifestyles possible. For example, do fathers

Figure 6.2   Work Hours of Married, Middle-Class, Dual-Earner Families

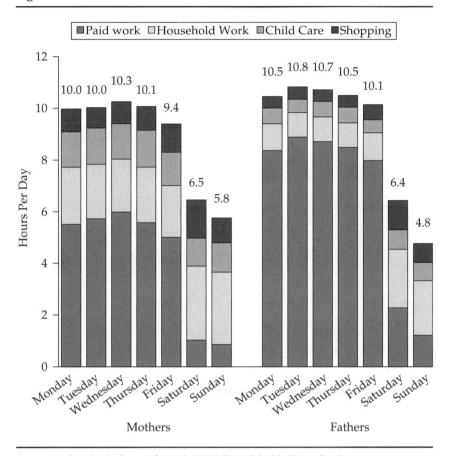

Source: Authors' calculations from the 2000 Sloan Weekly Diary Study.

perform more child care when mothers provide less, or are fathers' and mothers' time in child care positively correlated? Robinson and Godbey (1999) find in previous time-diary studies that people busy in one activity are more active in other related activities as well. Is this phenomenon also evident among married couples—are people busy in a given realm married to someone active in the same activities?

Table 6.2 shows correlations between mothers' and fathers' time in selected activities. It can be seen that all correlations for each activity (with the exception of paid market work) are indeed positive, meaning that the more time the mother spends on an activity the more time the father spends on that activity as well (and vice versa). Thus mothers

Table 6.2   Correlations of Mothers' and Fathers' Weekly Time in Activities

Paid work	−0.02
Housework	0.14*
Child care	0.50*
Shopping	0.33*
Grooming	0.31*
Eating	0.30*
Sleeping	0.29*
Education	0.03
Information technology, Internet use	0.16*
Religion	0.52*
Organizations	0.47*
Visiting	0.58*
Fitness	0.50*
Hobbies	0.36*
Television	0.37*
Reading	0.30*
Conversations	0.76*
Relaxing	0.39*
Travel	0.38*

Source: Authors' calculations from the 2000 Sloan Weekly Diary Study.
*p < .05.

who do more housework, child care, and shopping tend to be married to men who also spend more time in these activities. Mothers who spend more hours in personal care activities, including eating and sleeping, are married to husbands who also spend more time in these activities.[2] Why is market work not significantly correlated in these middle-class families? For one, the variance is restricted because only spouses who both work some hours are included. Second, fathers' paid work hours in these families vary little—95 percent work full-time hours. However, the paid work of a spouse is correlated with other activities.

An examination of more detailed subcategories of activities (table 6.2) shows positive correlations of .50 (or higher) for fathers and mothers apparently jointly engaged in selected leisure activities (household conversations and fitness activities) and in religious activities. Spousal correlations of about .30 and above are found for time spent shopping, in personal care, eating, sleeping, in organizational activity, in recreation and hobbies, watching television, reading, relaxing, and traveling.

Perhaps the most prominent and important correlation of this type in table 6.2 for the purposes of this book is the .50 correlation found for child care. That means that the more attention children receive from one parent, the more they receive from the other. Rather than parents trading off time with children to make up for that not given by the other parent, then, they seem to contribute their time to their children in concert.

That strong relation might be thought to be simply a function of the more child care that is needed in families with younger children or with more children. However, the correlations remain above .40 when calculated separately for families with one, two, and three or more children. Although the joint mother-father contribution is lower (r = .34) among families with preschool children, it remains a strong and statistically significant correlation.[3]

Although less prominent, the correlation (r = .14) between mothers' and fathers' housework time is also intriguing because the correlation is still positive, meaning again that the more one spouse does the more the other does—perhaps here to achieve a higher standard of cleanliness or organization in the household. A more detailed examination of the components of this overall housework figure tells that story more clearly, because cleaning and repair activity are positively correlated at the same level (r = .14 and above) with other organization-related or management-related housework. In contrast, cooking, meal clean-up, and laundry seem more solo activities, ones in which whether one spouse does it has no bearing on (is uncorrelated with) whether the other does it as well. Grocery shopping is a solo activity, whereas shopping for other goods (or being at the mall) is more often a joint endeavor.

Table 6.3 shows the correlation of mothers' and fathers' time in paid work with their time in other activities. For example, the weekly paid work hours of fathers correlates negatively (r = −.37) with the weekly hours he spends doing housework. Among mothers, the negative correlation is even larger (r = −.50). Mothers' paid work hours are also significantly and negatively correlated with their child care hours (r = −.37), but the correlation is not as large as for housework.

Table 6.4 shows the correlations of a spouse's paid work hours with mothers' and fathers' time in a range of activities. In the first column, we see that the paid work hours of a father are significantly and positively correlated (r = .19) with the child care hours of the mother. The longer the father works, the more child care the mother does. A mother's work hours, on the other hand, are not significantly correlated with a father's child care time (table 6.4, column 2).

In general, paid work time for either the mother or the father tends to be unrelated to any more housework, shopping, or personal care time by the other. Nor do long work hours by one spouse relate to less (or more) paid work by the other. Indeed, the only significant correlates with mothers' longer paid work hours for fathers is the greater

Table 6.3   Correlations of Parents' Paid Work Hours with Their Time in Other Activities

	Paid Work Hours with	
	Mothers' Activities	Fathers' Activities
Paid work	1.00	1.00
Housework	−.50*	−.37*
Child care	−.37*	−.10
Shopping	−.31*	−.29*
Personal care	−.30*	−.28*
Eating	−.13*	−.14*
Sleeping	−.21*	−.17*
Education	−.22*	−.15*
Information technology	−.20*	−.17*
Religion	−.08	−.09
Organizations	−.13*	−.19*
Visiting	−.05	−.09
Fitness	−.20*	−.18*
Hobbies	−.28*	−.18*
Television	−.06	−.12
Reading	−.09	−.18*
Conversations	−.08	−.09
Relaxing	0.0	−.07

Source: Authors' calculations from the 2000 Weekly Diary Study.
* $p < .05$.

television viewing and sleeping, along with the less time spent in hobbies or exercise. Significantly less reading by mothers is found the longer the father works (table 6.3).

With regard to child care time and other activities of the other spouse shown in the second panel of table 6.4, the only significant correlations for more father care are more mother relaxation and less organizational activity or television watching. The more time the mother spends on child care, by contrast, the less the father does housework, shops, goes to church or other organizations, and the less he watches television.

Positive spillovers are also evident in the third panel of table 6.4 for the time-consuming but low-effort activity of television viewing. That means that couples appear to conspire to be more or less active, which has considerably greater effect on their overall time expenditures than other activities. Indeed, fathers' greater television time relates to less child care among mothers, whereas more television watching by mothers relates to significantly less child care among fathers.

Table 6.4   Correlations Between Married Mothers' and Fathers' Time

	Paid Work Hours of Spouse with		Child Care Hours of Spouse with		Television Hours of Spouse with	
	Mothers' Activities	Fathers' Activities	Mothers' Activities	Fathers' Activities	Mothers' Activities	Fathers' Activities
Paid work	−.02	−.02	−.04	.19*	.18	−.06
Housework	−.04	.07	−.04	−.14*	−.10	.00
Child care	.19*	−.03	.50*	.50*	−.14*	−.17*
Shopping	−.04	.01	−.08	−.11*	−.08	.02
Personal care	.00	.04	−.09	−.02	−.15*	−.02
Eating	.07	−.03	.01	.01	−.11*	−.01
Sleeping	−.03	.10*	−.08	−.01	.01	.00
Education	−.04	−.03	−.01	.00	.01	.00
Computer	−.07	.00	−.07	−.04	.00	.03
Religion	−.05	−.01	−.08	−.11*	−.11*	−.16*
Organizations	−.04	−.02	−.11*	−.16**	−.11*	−.12*
Visiting	.01	.03	−.04	−.04	.00	.03
Fitness	−.06	−.11*	.00	−.06	−.07	−.14*
Hobbies	−.07	−.18*	.02	.02	−.06	−.08
Television	.06	.18*	−.17*	−.14*	.37*	.37*
Reading	−.14*	.02	−.09	−.07	−.08	−.02
Conversations	−.07	−.06	.05	.04	−.07	−.07
Relaxing	.07	.01	.12*	.00	−.13*	−.06

Source: Authors' calculations based on the 2000 Sloan Weekly Diary Study.
*p < .05.

Summary and Conclusions

This chapter is the first use of American seven-day time diaries, rather than extrapolated daily diaries, to assess the gender gap in work. Particularly important is the replicated finding in both the weekly and daily diary studies that total productive time is roughly equal for mothers and fathers, with fathers doing about twice as much paid work and mothers doing about twice as much household work. Previous literature tends to focus on child care or housework only, stressing how women perform more than an equal share of these activities. However, focusing only on one form of work is not sufficient. Data on housework and child care lend support to claims about the second shift making women busier— but fathers are similarly busy once researchers include their paid work. In marriages in which mothers work part-time, the total workload of mothers is actually less than that of fathers.

When cross-checking the activity times of parents using the weekly diary study, the most noteworthy finding here is that children who have the most contact with one parent tend to have a high level of contact with the other as well. This is one of the strongest ways in which parents spend their time together, and holds no matter what the number or ages of the children or how long either spouse works.

There are other intriguing correlations with child care time that weekly data make possible, especially the finding that the more the father works (but not the mother), the greater the mother's time in child care (and the less she reads). On the other hand, the more the mother works, the more the husband sleeps or watches television. For both parents, the more child care, the less television viewing by either spouse, and the more her child care, the more he works (and the less he does housework, shops, goes to church or other organization activity, or watches television).

One final noteworthy finding is that even these ultra-busy parents still average about 33 hours of free time per week, (with fewer than 10 percent of couples having less than 20 hours per week, which is what most parents estimate they have). On the one hand, this is up to 10 hours less weekly free time than in the diaries of nonparents (Robinson and Godbey 1999). On the other hand, it suggests considerably more flexibility in arranging activities than most parents feel they have. It is to parents' feelings about time pressures and the quality of family life that we turn in the next chapter.

═══ Chapter 7 ═══

Feelings About Time: Parental Stress and Time Pressures

WE HAVE concentrated on the behavioral or activity component of time in working families—what parents report actually doing with their time. However, busy and overworked are also subjective classifications. How people feel about their time allocations—the meaning they give to their prioritization of activities— is also of great interest. We have become particularly fascinated with the apparent disconnect between what parents actually do with their time and how they judge the balance in their lives, much as Robinson and Godbey (1999) found for adults in general. We thus focus here on the subjective dimension of the time allocations we have documented in earlier chapters.

The cultural landscape of family life today is one that continues to be strongly shaped by gendered beliefs—that is, ideas about the ways in which men and women ought to behave and their expectations of how they should feel within families. Indeed, the cultural ideals surrounding motherhood and men's roles in families continue to influence decisions parents make about how to allocate their time and, more fundamentally, for what we will examine here: mothers' and fathers' feelings about the way they apportion that time.

Here we examine two major facets of the emotional texture of contemporary parents' lives, and, to the extent possible, assess how these parents' feelings have changed over time. First, we look at how parents feel about their time allocations to their children, their spouses, and themselves. We focus mainly on feelings about time spent with children because of the public lament about parents not spending enough. How do parents actually feel about the time they allocate to their children? Similarly, do they spend enough time with their spouse or on themselves? Related to this, how often do mothers and fathers experience feeling rushed? How often do they feel as if they are doing two things at once? For mothers, differences in all of these feelings are examined based on their employment status.

A second major facet regarding the parental experience is their more general assessment of their work and family lives. How do employed parents feel about the degree to which they have been able to balance work and family life? Have they had to make sacrifices in either paid work or family life to strike a comfortable balance?[1]

Time with Children in Twenty-First-Century America—The Power of Ideology

Do parents spend enough time with their children? The popular answer to this question is an emphatic "no." According to the 1990 General Social Survey, fully 85 percent of Americans agree or strongly agree with the statement that "parents today don't spend enough time with their children." Yet, as we discussed in chapter 4, if anything, parents spend more time interacting with children compared with earlier generations, not less.

Why might today's parents (paradoxically) feel that they don't spend enough time with their children? There are two key reasons. First, as we suggested in chapter 1, the cultural ideologies of intensive parenting may be even more prominent today. The belief is that larger quantities of parental time are not only morally right, but also critical to the proper development of the child. Second is the nostalgia for a mythical past—one in which family time is believed to have existed as relatively uncomplicated, freely chosen, and rejuvenating.

First, ideals about intensive mothering, involved fathering, and child-centeredness may cause parents to feel as if they do not have the time they need because these ideals prescribe that good parents spend large quantities of time with children—that children are priceless. Intensive mothering is a cultural ideal to which women are expected to sacrifice careers, leisure time, and whatever else is necessary to ensure that their children thrive.

Hays (1996) argues that the belief has become even more prominent today. Among both working-class and middle-class mothers, good mothering is defined in terms of being there for children. Paid caregivers cannot fully substitute for mothers' time because these substitutes do not provide enough love and commitment to the child. Many of Hays's respondents believed that even fathers' time did not adequately compensate for mothers' time, because fathers did not properly attend to children when left alone with them. This may contribute to mothers' feelings that the time they give to their children—especially when they are employed—is never enough.

The child becomes a central focus, with needs and desires constantly attended to, and much time is spent attempting to reason with and to understand his or her wants. The resulting effort required to respond to individual children is extraordinarily labor intensive—and most of this task is borne by mothers, even if they are employed full-time. Indeed, it is the mother who is ultimately held responsible for how children behave in the short run, and how they turn out in the long run. It may seem especially important that each child receives more intense devotion as family sizes become smaller, and the time investment seems more critical to parents who are increasingly concerned about high quality outcomes for their priceless children. A child-centered focus thus underlies the larger quantities of time that parents, particularly well-educated mothers, perceive as necessary to raising happy and successful children.

The dramatic social changes spurred by the feminist movement and by women moving into the labor force have affected fathers' behavior and attitudes as well. Fathers have become a familiar presence in labor and delivery rooms, taken up diapering and bathing young children, and joined in chauffeuring children. Fathers' behavior still lags behind changing ideals (LaRossa 1988; 1997; Townsend 2002). The relatively recent cultural ideal of involved fathering prescribes that fathers nurture their children on a day-to-day basis, regularly caring for and playing with them.

With data collected in our 1999 Omnibus Survey (described in appendix B), we can show how fathering ideals differ across cohorts. We asked three cohorts of adults—those born in the pre–World War II era, Baby Boomers, and Baby Busters—what the ideal division of labor was between mothers and fathers. As figure 7.1 illustrates, earlier cohorts of this national sample were much less likely than later cohorts to believe that fathers should share equally in caregiving. The figure clearly shows that caregiving—which requires large quantities of time with children—is something that has become relevant for modern fathers. Although fathers' breadwinning roles are still important—indeed assumed (Christiansen and Palkovitz 2001; Townsend 2002)—it is not enough for modern fathers to provide income to their children. They must contribute substantial amounts of time as well. What may make fathers feel time deficits with children, then, is that they work almost as many hours as they did in the past (see chapter 3 and Jacobs and Gerson 2004). However, there seem increasingly high demands for them to interact with their children on an intimate, day-to-day basis.

A second cultural ideology is important today—that of a nostalgia for a mythical family past. Although parents may be spending adequate amounts of time with children overall, what family members most desire is quality time, and that seems in shortest supply (Daly 2001). Cultural ideals of family life that dominate the popular media set high expectations for what should occur in the home (Shaw 1992; Daly 1996; Coontz 1992). Even those too young to have seen *Ozzie and Harriet* or *Leave it to Beaver* are familiar with them as benchmarks for what family time should be.

Figure 7.1   Percentage Who Believe that Both Parents Should be Equally Involved in Caregiving

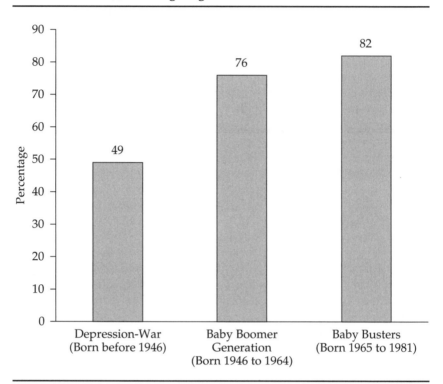

Source: Authors' calculations from the 1999 National Omnibus Survey, University of Maryland.
Note: Depression-War estimate statistically significantly different from Baby Boom and Baby Bust estimates, p < 0.05.

The images that have been projected into Americans' consciousness are therefore those of a sentimentalized and glorified past, in which families had mothers available, not only to mend clothes and provide lunches, but also to offer advice or soothe children's difficulties with siblings and friends. Even though the father was at work, he still was around the house a great deal—the center of the family in many respects, and regularly involved in both the work and play of parenting. Of course, their children were well-behaved and wanted to spend time with their parents. When these television families gathered in their living rooms or at the dinner table, parent-child time was portrayed as leisurely, lively, purposeful, enjoyable, and rejuvenating to all involved. When the reality of their time with children is measured against this, it is no surprise that today's parents feel they come up short in important respects (Galinsky 1981; Daly 1996).

The reality of family time, then and now, is of course much more complex than idealized images that color the public's beliefs (Coontz 1992). Rather than leisurely, time with children is often hectic and rushed. Busy lives are interrupted by intrusions such as ringing telephones, televisions, and other technologies. Family members' differing schedules often make any time together "coming" or "going" time—small slices of the day spent preparing for the next activity (Daly 1996). Rather than purposeful, parents' time with children is often "default time," that is, time when family members are together only coincidently, involved in mundane tasks such as cleaning the home and preparing for school or work (Daly 1996). A great deal of time that both parents and children have free to spend together in purposeful activity is spent in front of the television set, an activity not considered by most to be especially enjoyable or worthwhile, and often resorted to as a default (Robinson and Godbey 1999). When parents and children engage in such default time together, it is not likely to be experienced as the kind of time that compares favorably with these ideals.

Thus, rather than the enjoyable warmth of a nostalgic past, family time is sometimes demanding and unpleasant. Whiny preschoolers, disinterested school-age children, and surly teenagers—as well as bickering siblings and argumentative parents—inhabit all homes at one time or another. Hochschild (1997) argues in her book *The Time Bind* that both employed mothers and fathers felt that they were not able to be with children as much as they liked. Yet it was at work where both professionals and nonprofessionals felt most relaxed and able to spend time freely. Home seemed like work, because home was often full of onerous chores and difficult relationships. Hence parents could escape to relative freedom of the workplace.

Hochschild's work has been criticized by some scholars for overstating the case for a cultural reversal of work and family priorities, findings receiving little empirical support using representative samples (Kielcolt 2003; Maume and Bellas 2001). Her sample was also unusual, one that worked one more day per week than the average worker, according to Jerry Jacobs and Kathleen Gerson (2004). Yet her book clearly struck a responsive chord in pointing to the sometimes unpleasant realities of family time. Parent-child time that is hectic, interrupted, coincidental, or negative may not feel like time positively spent, no matter the quantity. This is especially true when parents compare their days with children to a mythical gold standard of parent-child time from the past.

A great deal of anecdotal evidence from media interviews and stories vividly illustrates the time stresses of busy, overworked, and oversched-

Table 7.1   **Feelings about Husband's Time and Time for Oneself of Employed Dual-Earner Mothers**

	1977	1997
Feelings about time		
Percentage of employed mothers who wish their husbands would spend more time with their children	43.2	55.7*
Percentage of employed mothers who feel they have not enough time for themselves	63.8	80.2*
Work and family characteristics		
Average hours mothers work per week	37.4	41.4*
Average hours husbands work per week	47.3	48.0
Percentage of mothers who have children under age six	41.7	41.0
Percentage of mothers who have children under age thirteen	84.3	78.7
Sample size (N)	(125)	(431)

Source: Authors' calculations from the 1977 Quality of Employment Survey and 1997 National Study of Changing Workforce.
Note: Means and percentages are not weighted.
Difference between 1977 and 1997 significant, * $p < 0.05$.

uled families today, even if typical parents from then and now look similar in terms of interaction time with children. Ethnographic interviews with small (and nonrepresentative) samples of parents also illustrate parents' perceived time bind (Daly 2001; Hays 1996)—with many parents saying that they want to spend more time with their families but find it difficult to do so in today's fast-paced world. Yet parents' feelings about time with children have been largely ignored because there is little hard data available from representative samples of parents.

Although we do not have data on how parents feel about their time with children at earlier points in history, there are trend data on feelings about one's spouse's time with children. Both the 1977 Quality of Employment Survey and the 1997 National Study of the Changing Workforce survey asked married employed mothers, "Do you wish your husband would spend more time (taking care of or) doing things with your child(ren), less time, or the same amount of time?" In 1997, 56 percent of employed mothers answered more time, compared with 43 percent in 1977, a statistically significant difference (see table 7.1).

What is interesting about table 7.1 is that the employed mothers sampled in the two years look similar on other characteristics. Whereas those in the 1997 sample estimated that they worked 4 hours more per week than those in 1977, mothers in each era had husbands who worked the

Table 7.2   Percentage of Parents Reporting "Too Little Time"
with Children

	Youngest Child	Oldest Child	Oldest and Youngest
All parents	47.6	57.7	42.1
All fathers	54.8[a]	60.0	47.8[a]
All mothers	41.8	55.6	37.4
Married fathers	54.0[b]	59.5	46.8[b]
Married mothers	37.4[c]	52.6[c]	32.2[c]
Single mothers	51.8	64.0	49.1

Source: Authors' calculations from the 2000 National Survey of Parents.
a. Gender difference statistically significant, p < 0.05.
b. Estimates for married fathers significantly different from married mothers, p < 0.05.
c. Estimates for married mothers significantly different from single mothers, p < 0.05.

same number of hours, and had children of roughly the same age. Thus the increased desire for more fathers' time with children reported by employed women in 1997 may reflect higher standards for fathers' involvement, or change in the ways that mothers experience family time.

We included questions about how parents feel about the amount of time they spend with their children in our 2000 National Survey of Parents (NSP).[2] Table 7.2 presents the percentage of parents who feel too little time with their youngest (or only) child (column 1), too little time with their oldest child (column 2), and too little time with both (column 3). Overall, 48 percent report too little time with their youngest child, 58 percent too little with their oldest child, and 42 percent too little with both. Although not shown here, the vast majority of parents who did not say they had too little time reported that the time was about right. Only about 5 percent reported too much time.

The 2000 NSP included a variety of measures about the quantity of time parents spend with children, as discussed in chapter 4. Questions asked respondents to estimate how many hours per week they spent in one-on-one time with their youngest child and how many nights they ate dinner as a family.

Each of these measures indeed is correlated significantly with feelings of inadequate time with children (see table 7.3). Parents who spend more total time and more one-on-one time with their children, as well as those who manage more daily meals together, are less likely to feel they do not spend enough time with their children. The quality time measure (one-on-one time with the youngest child) appears to be most closely associated with parents' assessments of feeling too little time with that child; however all three measures are highly correlated (at the p < .0001 level).

Table 7.3   Correlations of Quantity and Quality of Time with Children

	Too Little with All	Too Little with Youngest	Too Little with Oldest
All time with children (from diary in hours per week)	−0.19*	−0.17*	−0.12*
One-on-one time with youngest or only child each week (hours per week)	−0.23*	−0.28*	NA
Eating meals together (days per week)	−0.12*	−0.13*	−0.11*

Source: Authors' calculations from the 2000 National Survey of Parents.
*p < 0.05.

Gender and Feelings About Family and Work Life

Clearly, some parents today have less time with children and feel more "time poor" than others. Do mothers and fathers feel differently about their time spent with children, spouses, and by themselves, and in the work-family balance they have struck? A "gender perspective" (Ferree 1990) can help us to think about any differences in the contours of mothers' and fathers' feelings about time. This approach focuses on institutional barriers to women's equality across work and family life, and on cultural meanings, especially those surrounding motherhood that emphasize the all-giving nature of mothers to their children and families.

Do mothers and fathers who are employed full-time, and who spend similar amounts of time with their offspring, have the same feelings about spending too little time with children? Researchers who expect that women will spend more of their energy and time on children and families would say "no"—mothers will feel differently from fathers.

However, another perspective is a structural role perspective, which sees mothers and fathers as having similar feelings when they are similarly situated. Therefore, to understand feelings better, we examine the bivariate relationship between gender and feelings, and then examine how gender relates to parents' feelings about time with children—independent of the actual amounts of time spent at jobs or with children. This allows us to see if any gender effect remains, suggesting continued differences in the cultural expectations about parenting for mothers versus fathers.

How Mothers and Fathers Feel About Child Care Time

In prior research by Ellen Galinsky (1999) and by Joy Reeves and Robert Szafran (1996), fathers have reported more time strain with children than mothers. Although that is likely because fathers are working more hours outside the home for pay, and therefore spending less time with children, these demographic factors were not taken into account in the earlier studies. As shown in table 7.2, our data indicate that 54 percent of married fathers compared with 37 percent of married mothers and 52 percent of single mothers report spending too little time with their youngest child. More strain is reported for the oldest child than for the youngest: some 60 percent of married fathers, 53 percent of married mothers, and 64 percent of single mothers say that their time with their oldest child is not enough. That compares with 47 percent of married fathers, 32 percent of married mothers, and 49 percent of single mothers who reported too little time with both children. Although married fathers are different from married mothers, single mothers feel the worst about the time they allocate to their children. This may be due to their higher likelihood of being employed. Among employed mothers, almost half (47 percent) feel that they spend too little time with all children, but only 18 percent of nonemployed mothers report this.

Employment becomes relevant in understanding gender differences as well. Once we adjust for the actual time parents spend with children, and for their number of work hours and other background characteristics, we find that fathers do not feel more time strain with their children than mothers (Milkie et al. 2004; Nomaguchi, Milkie, and Bianchi 2005). Fathers' expression of too little time with children, then, becomes largely a function of their longer employment hours. Although married mothers and fathers feel similarly, single mothers feel significantly more strained than other groups even after controlling for employment.

In sum, although parent-child time has remained steady or increased over the years, almost half of American parents continue to feel they spend too little time with their children. Although fathers are more likely to think this way, once we adjust for work hours, actual time spent with children, and other factors, it is mothers (particularly single mothers) who feel it. As the gender perspective suggests, mothers are more accountable to being with children, which may put an especially acute strain on single mothers. Of course, those fathers not living with their children, who are not part of our sample, are likely to feel strong time strains as well (Furstenberg 1995; Hamer 2001).

Figure 7.2   Percentage Reporting "Too Little Time" with Spouse in 2000

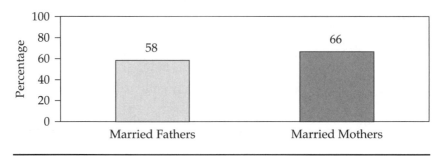

Source: Authors' calculations from the 2000 National Survey of Parents.
Note: Estimate for married mothers greater than married fathers, p < 0.05.

Gender and Feelings About Time with One's Spouse

We might expect that mothers and fathers today feel a sense of time strain within marriage—that busy lives intersecting over matters of housework, children's problems, and other demands might make parents wish for more relaxed time with each other. Of course, this assumes that the marriage is in a relatively healthy state. In marriages that are fragile, partners may be content with low levels of interaction.

One might expect that, even at the same level of time together, mothers might feel more of a time deficit with their husband than the reverse. First, mothers traditionally are expected to be responsible for the family's (and the husband's) well-being and for ensuring that he is well-attended, so that a woman might consider it her responsibility to arrange relaxation time with her husband. Second, she may want more time with a husband than he does with her, because wives desire more shared intimacy and see its development occurring through interaction—much as women seek time with friends to increase intimacy with them (Gager and Sanchez 2003).

When we examine our data for married parents (see figure 7.2), we find that mothers more than fathers do feel that they have too little time with their spouse—66 percent of mothers versus 58 percent of fathers. However, there are no significant differences between employed and nonemployed mothers' feelings. After controls for time with spouse from the diary data, among other background factors, we find that mothers still are significantly more likely to report too little time with their spouse (Milkie et al. 2004). The findings thus fit with the gender perspective in that women feel more pressing standards than men regarding "couple time."

Gender and Feelings About Time for Oneself

Time for oneself could mean time alone or time at one's favorite activities, such as visiting friends or attending sports events. According to a gender perspective, at the same levels of time allocation to families, work, or leisure, mothers more than fathers should feel as if they have too little time for themselves. This may be because women are the managers of children and husbands, and feel as if they can never escape the demands of family life—which are not neat and scheduled, but often prove disruptive, unexpected, and unending. Additionally, they may have less power within marriage to excuse themselves from family responsibilities to have time for themselves. Another possibility, though, is that fathers may experience more strain if their feelings of entitlement to free time is higher. As shown in chapter 5, the fact that fathers' free time is less likely to involve time alone with children suggests that fathers may allow more time for themselves than mothers do. At the same time, fathers may have higher standards than mothers about how much free time they should have (Nomaguchi, Milkie, and Bianchi 2005).

Our data from the National Survey of Parents (in figure 7.3) show very large differences between mothers and fathers in feelings of too little time for oneself. Some 57 percent of married fathers report this, but some 71 percent of married and 78 percent of single mothers do (see panel A of figure 7.3). Among the mothers (data not shown), we find a statistically significant difference between those who are employed (75 percent) and those who are not (68 percent).

What happens if we examine the diary time mothers and fathers spend on leisure, or in time alone? Although neither of these measures may be exactly equivalent to time for oneself, they are related. Surprisingly, the strong gender difference remains even when we account for fathers' greater leisure time, or for their time spent alone (data not shown).

This difference between mothers and fathers can be examined another way. A small but significant minority of fathers (12 percent) report feeling too much time for themselves, compared with only 3 and 4 percent of married and single mothers, respectively (data not shown). Analysis not shown here indicates that fathers reporting too much time have less education, fewer young children, and less time with their children than those reporting that the time they have for themselves is about right.

Gender and the Experience of Daily Time

Two questions examined how parents feel about the day-to-day experience of time. The first asked the extent to which parents feel rushed and

Figure 7.3   Parent Reports of Time Pressures in 2000

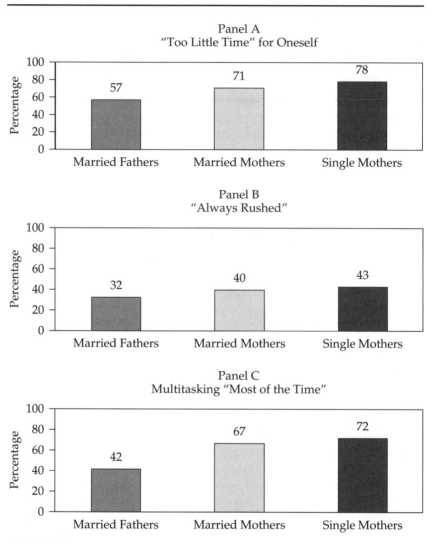

Source: Authors' calculations from 2000 National Survey of Parents.
Note: Gender differences statistically significant for all estimates, p < 0.05. Panel A, single mother estimates greater than married mother estimates, p < 0.05.

the second how often parents find themselves doing more than one thing at a time.

Overall, 37 percent of parents in 2000 say they always feel rushed, compared to 35 percent in 1975 (Mattingly and Sayer 2006). Married men are the least likely to say this—32 percent of married fathers versus 40 percent of married mothers and 43 percent of single mothers (see panel B of figure 7.3). After controlling for employment, education, number and ages of children, among other factors, married fathers remain significantly less likely to feel always rushed than married mothers or single mothers. Even after adding the objective diary measures (the number of activities and secondary activities per day), a significant gender difference remains between married fathers and all mothers. In brief, fathers are simply not as likely to always feel rushed.

Mothers' employment makes a difference, as we would expect. Fully 46 percent of employed mothers versus only 29 percent of homemakers report always feeling rushed. And controlling for the background factors noted, employed mothers are more than twice as likely to report feeling rushed as homemakers (data not shown). It is employed mothers who are distinct from both homemakers and fathers in these feelings.

We saw in chapter 5 that the three groups—married fathers, married mothers, and single mothers—report similar diary hours of multitasking across the week, and that multitasking had increased significantly for all groups between 1975 and 2000. The question examined here concerns parents' subjective perceptions of how often they do more than one thing at a time.

Overall, in the 2000 NSP, 57 percent of parents said they multitask most of the time, with large gender differences despite similar gender reports on objective multitasking from the time diaries. Only 42 percent of married fathers, versus 67 percent of married mothers and 72 percent of single mothers, report multitasking most of the time (see panel C of figure 7.3). Interestingly, using the objective measure of multitasking from the time diary, as well as other controls for employment and age of children, this gender difference still remains quite strong.

This underscores the idea that the perceived quality of mothers' time is quite different from fathers'. Mothers may actually do two things at once at the same rates as fathers, but they feel as if they must almost constantly be on the move to keep the family afloat. Perhaps, even within the same primary activity, mothers move faster, or do things that do not get recorded in the time diaries as secondary activities (such as cleaning while answering questions from children or talking on the telephone).

We can also examine how employment makes a difference for mothers in terms of subjective multitasking. Some 70 percent of employed mothers versus 62 percent of nonemployed mothers report this, a statistically significant difference even after demographic and other controls are considered (data not shown). Perhaps what is most interesting here is that even homemaker mothers are much more likely than fathers to report multitasking all of the time.

That mothers are more likely to perceive that they do many things at once may relate to their status as the household manager—responsible for organizing most of family life (Peterson and Gerson 1992). Moreover, among employed mothers, doing everything cannot be leisurely either. This group is high in reported multitasking and rushing, and in feeling that they have little time for themselves, which probably stems from a sense of being responsible even when away from the home: making decisions in absentia about the household, planning for children's health and development, creating and maintaining ties to extended kin, and the like. In managing something as complex as children's lives and a home, it seems there is always something that needs to be taken care of—if not at a given moment, then sometime in the next day or so.

Moreover, being a household manager means keeping track of many things. As households become more affluent, they must increasingly commit time and energy to tasks such as finding and buying household goods, as well as cleaning, fixing, and arranging modern electronics and technology—tasks more likely to affect middle-class mothers. Yet working-class families may have just as many objects to buy, fix, or replace—even if the items may be of a different type or quality. Moreover, working-class families must also deal with tighter financial constraints. Women's active role in managing family members, their social schedules, and the technology in the house may be relatively unexplored research territory, but may also account for the large gender discrepancy between fathers' and mothers' feelings about needing more time for oneself, feeling rushed, and feeling like they do more than one thing at a time.

Feelings About Time for Paid Work Versus Family: The Longer Term Balance

Parents in the 2000 National Survey of Parents were also asked to step back from thinking about time in relation to a particular person or task, and to assess the overall allocations to work and family in a more general, long-term sense. Prior work on gender and the work-family balance suggests that although gender is clearly a factor in fathers and mothers choosing different paid work and family care options, both report similar levels of balance between work and family (Milkie and Peltola 1999). In other words, despite their different time allocations, mothers and fathers seem similarly satisfied with their current work-family arrangements. One limitation of this research, however, is that it usually excludes homemakers,

Figure 7.4   Balancing Work and Family Life in 2000

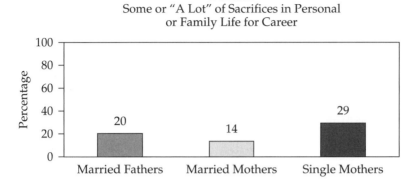

Panel A
Some or "A Lot" of Sacrifices in Personal
or Family Life for Career

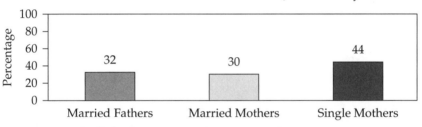

Panel B
"A Lot" of Sacrifices in Career or Job for Family

Source: Authors' calculations from the 2000 National Survey of Parents.
Note: Questions only asked of employed parents. Panel A, all groups statistically significantly different, p < 0.05. Panel B, single mother estimates greater than married father and married mother, p < 0.05.

thus leading to an incomplete picture of women who have already altered their career, job, or educational plans.

Among employed parents, 50 percent of married fathers, 52 percent of married mothers, and 48 percent of single mothers reported feeling very successful in balancing work and family life. In other words, close to half of all employed groups think they have achieved role balance. This holds true even after adjusting for work hours and other demographic factors (data not shown).

Although employed married fathers seem content with their current situation, they also report having made more sacrifices in their work and family lives than employed married mothers do. Panel A of figure 7.4 shows that 20 percent of employed married fathers, compared with

14 percent of employed married mothers, report making "a lot" of sacrifices in their personal or family life for the sake of their work life. What is interesting about the low percentage of employed married mothers who said that this is the case is that it would probably be even lower were non-employed married mothers included. Specifically, among the one-third of married mothers excluded because they are not currently employed, one would be very unlikely to find that their family has been given short shrift because most have left paid work for the sake of their families. Among employed single mothers, that figure rises to 29 percent reporting they have made a lot of sacrifices—which is more than double the 14 percent of employed married mothers and also significantly more than the 20 percent of married fathers. After multivariate adjustments, single mothers continue to feel they have made more family sacrifices, but the difference between married fathers and mothers disappears (data not shown).

Overall, higher percentages of parents report having made career or job sacrifices for family than making work sacrifices for the family, so that parents seem to be more able or willing to protect their family interests from work intrusions than the other way around. As shown in panel B of figure 7.4, about 32 percent of married fathers, 30 percent of married mothers, and 44 percent of single mothers report having made a lot of sacrifices in career or job for the sake of their personal or family life. Hence, again, single mothers appear more vulnerable in these long term assessments. However, if all married mothers in the sample were included (one-third of whom are not in the labor force), the percentage who say they made a lot of sacrifices would likely be higher. This is an important topic for future research.

Summary and Conclusions

Gender seems to operate in at least two important ways to affect parents' family and work lives. At the behavioral level, men and women make different decisions in allocating their time, based in part on choice and in part on institutional forces and cultural pressures. These differences have diminished in recent years, but mothers continue to adjust their schedules more than fathers do.

This chapter has discussed the ways in which gender operates at a second level of feelings about time allocations. The fact that women fit themselves to the needs of their family shows up in their feelings of time strain across different domains of work and family. Particularly among married mothers, we find more of them wanting more time for themselves than more time with children. This may be because they have, to a greater extent, adjusted to being there for children's needs and wants, rather than for themselves or their husbands.

Married fathers spend less time with children than mothers and feel more time shortages with children. However, after control for work hours and other factors, the group that feels the most time strained is single mothers. Mothers are also more likely to feel too little time with their spouse and for themselves. In the same way, they are much more likely to feel that their daily time is rushed and that they are multitasking. It is interesting that mothers and fathers tend to have different feelings about family and work life, not merely because they are in different work-family positions. They spend different amounts of time in paid work, in housework, and with children, and often have different feelings—even when their different time allocations are held constant. This suggests that cultural expectations about what mothers and fathers should do remain strong, with mothers feeling more of a need to put children and family first as they sacrifice their own need.

In terms of balancing time and energies across work and family (among a subsample of employed parents that excludes 5 percent of married fathers, 33 percent of married mothers, and 19 percent of single mothers who are not employed), married mothers appear the most content with their allocations, and single mothers the least. Single mothers are more likely than other groups to feel that they have made sacrifices both in family and personal life for work, and in their job for family. Thus, they feel especially strained—perhaps not surprisingly given their lack of another parent to help balance their dual commitments to work and family.

In sum, parents seem to give themselves over to rearing children to the extent possible, given other demands on their time and limited resources in some families. This is particularly true for single parents who more often feel that their efforts are not enough. Part of the "worth" of their often heroic efforts is the type of the childhood they can afford for their children. Hence, the activities of children are intriguing and important. We next examine some evidence about children's activities afforded by child time diaries.

Chapter 8

Children's Time Use: Too Busy or Not Busy Enough?

OUR DESCRIPTION of the changing American family in earlier chapters has almost entirely centered on adults. Although parents clearly play a major role in organizing and making decisions about family life, most observers would probably agree that from a very young age, children are also active participants in the rhythms of everyday family life. When they become teenagers, both their academic and extracurricular activities and their personalities are likely to influence how often, when, and where family time takes place (Lareau 2000). Yet the perspectives and activities of children tend to be overlooked in the mainstream literature on family (Thorne 1993; Skolnick 1991).

Contrasting Views of Childhood

There are two opposing streams of thought about American childhood in the literature. One is that American children have too much leisure time. They watch too much television, play too many video games, and do too little homework (Hofferth and Sandberg 2001b). In essence, children are not engaged enough in active and productive activities. Many of these arguments are fueled by data on children's achievement in science, commerce, and technological innovation in other countries. According to this view, children are not adequately prepared to compete in the global marketplace, which is why Americans are no longer unchallenged in business, the sciences and engineering (National Commission on Excellence in Education 1983; Salisbury and Lieberman 2003).

The second and contrasting view sees children as overscheduled—shuffled to and from activities and pressured to excel in academics with little down time to just "be a kid." Children in middle-class families often recite a litany of extracurricular activities and lessons in addition to their time spent in school (Lareau 2003). Many of these teenagers may also be juggling part-time jobs.

What is common to these two perspectives—that children engage in too much passive leisure and that they are overscheduled—is that both are pessimistic. As such, they may be an extension of the long historical trend of worrying about children. In the 1920s, the Boy Scouts of America and the National Committee for the Study of Juvenile Reading published studies of children's leisure that suggested that young people had too much leisure time on their hands that was not used constructively. The studies focused on the questionable moral standards in movies and magazines (Wartella and Mazzarella 1990). In the 1950s and following decades, a "moral panic" reemerged over how young people spent their leisure time, and over the influence of television and rock-and-roll music (Gilbert 1986). Concerns about movies, magazines, and rock-and-roll were in time replaced by anxiety over television viewing, video game playing, and Internet use (Wang, Bianchi, and Raley 2005).

As early as 1939, an associate of the Child Study Association of America bemoaned what it called the extinction of children's leisure time by the increase in scheduled and organized activities (Frank 1939, 389–93). These concerns are strikingly similar across the decades—suggesting that there will always be worries about children's use of time (see Corsaro 2003).

The competing perceptions of childhood may also arise from comparisons with the past. Reed Larson and Suman Verma (1999) suggest that the shift from industrial to postindustrial conditions, which was associated with increases in family wealth and universal education, redirected children's activities from repetitive labor to "new possibilities for learning and psychosocial development" (701). Children thus replaced the large chunk of time spent in household labor activities with time spent in schoolwork and media use (Larson 2001; Larson and Verma 1999). Thus, compared with the past, children may well spend more time both doing homework and watching television.

Children's Diary Activities

To explore how children's day-to-day lives have changed as a response to recent increases in maternal employment and single parenting, we review published estimates of children's time use acquired from time-diary data—as well as findings from the recent 2002 Panel Study of Income Dynamics Child Development Supplement (PSID-CDS), which contains time diaries of children age five to eighteen. These children were sampled both on a weekday and weekend during the 2002 school year. This analysis of the PSID-CDS is restricted to own, adoptive, or stepchildren of household heads or wives of household heads in which both a weekend and weekday diary are available.

Free Time

Children's free time has, then, historically come under a great deal of scrutiny. Do children engage in enough enrichment activities like reading and lessons on skill building? Is their free time too structured? Are children minding their health by engaging in physical activities? Although the answers to most of these questions are a matter of opinion (that is, how much enrichment is enough and how many structured activities are too much), the trends and levels in particular activities do provide some benchmarks to guide such debates.

Hofferth and Sandberg's (2001a) analysis of time expenditures of children age three to twelve is one of the few studies of how children's activities have changed over time. They found sports and art activities rose between 1981 and 1997 among children age three to twelve,[1] evidence of Sutton-Smith's (1994) depiction of a historical trend to supervise, control, and rationalize children's free time—in other words, to structure play time. This finding is also consistent with Lareau's (2003) analysis of middle-class families, which showed how these children are typically enrolled in several structured activities, often amounting to several lessons, practices, and games in the course of a week. Nationally, about half of children six to seventeen years old participate in structured extracurricular activities such as sports, clubs, and lessons, with teenagers age thirteen to fifteen years old spending the most time in such structured activities as lessons and competitive sports (Fields et al. 1994; Meeks and Mauldin 1990).

Table 8.1 shows further detail on particular free-time categories such as participation in organizations, structured sports activities and other time outdoors, art activities, hobbies, and time spent on home computer activities for sons and daughters age five to eighteen in the 2002 PSID-CDS (see appendix table 8A.1 for classification of activities). Overall, these children report spending just over 1 hour per week participating in organizational activities (like youth groups), about another hour attending events (like baseball games), about 3 hours in structured sports, and almost an hour in art activities.

Sons have 5 hours more free time than daughters, spending more time in sports, hobbies, and play activities. This finding is consistent with Hofferth and Sandberg's (2001a) analysis of children age three to twelve in the 1997 PSID-CDS. In 2002, we also find that younger children (age five to eleven) have about 5 hours less free time per week than older children (age twelve to eighteen), largely because they sleep more. In contrast, older children are more often engaged in structured activities such as sports, hobbies, and attending events.

Together, the structured and organized free-time activities still amount to less than the 8 hours a week on average that children spend playing.

Table 8.1   Children's Diary Time, Hours per Week, 2002

Activity	All	Ages Five to Eleven	Ages Twelve to Eighteen	Sons	Daughters
Total paid work	1.6	0.0	3.1*	1.3	1.9*
Total household work	6.0	5.3	6.7*	5.0	7.0*
Total day care	0.2	0.5	0.0*	0.2	0.3*
Total personal care	83.6	87.5	79.9*	82.5	84.6*
Sleep	68.2	71.7	65.0*	68.1	68.3
Meal	7.1	7.7	6.4*	7.1	7.1
Grooming	8.3	8.1	8.4	7.3	9.2*
Total education	35.2	35.6	34.9	35.4	35.1
School	31.2	32.5	30.0*	31.7	30.6
Homework	4.1	3.1	4.9*	3.7	4.4*
Total free time	40.6	38.3	42.7*	43.1	38.3*
Home computer activities	2.5	1.1	3.9*	2.6	2.4
Organizations	1.1	1.0	1.2	0.9	1.2
Religion	1.5	1.7	1.4	1.5	1.6
Events	1.0	0.7	1.3*	0.9	1.0
Visiting	2.8	2.3	3.3*	3.0	2.6
Sports	3.1	2.2	3.9*	3.9	2.3*
Outdoors	0.9	0.9	0.8	0.8	0.9
Hobby	0.1	0.0	0.1*	0.2	0.0*
Art activities	0.9	1.0	0.8*	0.8	1.0*
Playing	8.0	10.5	5.7*	10.2	5.9*
Television	14.5	13.9	15.0*	15.0	14.1
Reading	1.5	1.8	1.2*	1.4	1.6
Household conversations	0.5	0.4	0.5*	0.4	0.5*
Other passive leisure	2.3	0.8	3.7*	1.5	3.0*
NA	0.7	0.7	0.7	0.5	0.9*
Total	168.0	168.0	168.0	168.0	168.0
N	(2,280)	(1,151)	(1,129)	(1,137)	(1,143)

Source: Authors' calculations from the 2002 Panel Study of Income Dynamics Child Development Supplement (PSID-CDS).
Note: Includes own, adoptive, or stepchildren of household heads or wives of household heads.
*p-value < 0.05.

However, this varies markedly by age (Robinson and Bianchi 1997). When children are young, they average about 10.5 hours per week playing, which drops significantly to 5.7 hours for those in the twelve to eighteen age group. Older children compensate for this drop by watching more television, playing more computer games, engaging in more sports activities, and spending more time visiting friends. Although they spend more time in structured activities as they age, this still amounts to only a small proportion of their overall free time. Therefore, it appears children on average still spend more time in unstructured leisure activities than in structured ones—television being the major factor (Meeks and Mauldin 1990). However, the time children spend in structured activities may still feel like a great deal of time to parents who have more than one child engaged in such activities, who must chauffeur children to and from activities, and who are bound by the scheduling deadlines these activities impose on family life (Lareau, Weininger, and Bianchi 2005).

Television and Media Use

Among children's free-time activities, social observers seem most concerned about the levels of children's television viewing, although the same is argued about adults' free time (see Kubey and Csikszentmihalyi 1990). Whereas research on health effects shows a clear association with higher levels of obesity (Robinson 2001), the developmental effects of television are unclear (Larson and Verma 1999). The popular view is that watching television is not a desirable activity for children. Even if families disapprove of high levels of viewing, most homes nonetheless have multiple televisions. A sample of American urban and suburban young adolescents revealed the average family had 3.4 sets per household (Brown et al. 1990). Some parents may see television as a way to keep their children home: Reed Larson, Robert Kubey, and Joseph Colletti (1989) showed a positive correlation between television viewing and time spent with family—although there was a stronger positive association between children's time spent reading and family time.

Cross-sectional studies show television viewing peaks during the preadolescent and early adolescent years, from ten to fifteen (Bianchi and Robinson 1997; Larson, Kubey, and Colletti 1989; Larson 2001; Meeks and Mauldin 1990; Timmer, Eccles, and O'Brien 1985). It accounts for 25 percent of fifth and sixth graders' time on weekend mornings and almost 40 percent of their time on weekend evenings, with these percentages tapering off among older children (Larson, Kubey, and Colletti 1989).

Television viewing dominates children's free time, as it does for parents. In the 2002 PSID-CDS in table 8.1, television accounts for the largest chunk of children's free time, taking 14.5 hours per week (or more than 2 hours a day on average). The problem with estimates of television viewing, including those derived from time diaries, is that it is not always clear how actively these children were watching a television program—or if the television was simply in the background during dinnertime or other activities. Therefore, estimates of children's television viewing tend to be highly variable, from 8 to 20 hours per week (Larson and Verma 1999).

Besides television, children also spend time using interactive media such as computers, although at a much lower level than that of television viewing. Table 8.1 shows computer usage (excluding that related to homework) is around 2.5 hours per week among children. This figure rises significantly as children age: about 4 hours per week for children age twelve and over versus only about 1 hour for younger children. Hofferth and Sandberg (2001a) also report boys spend more time using computers than girls, although our estimates indicate no gender differences. The little time spent on the computer, relative to television viewing, may be explained by children's more limited access to computers, though some computer time may be captured under the homework categories.

Reading

The introduction of television and computer technologies, in addition to generally being viewed as undesirable activities for children, has also been blamed for children's decline in reading time. However, it is difficult to determine what children would be doing with their time in the absence of television. Aletha Huston et al. (1999) argue, for example, that television viewing simply displaced similar activities like attending movies and listening to the radio. A historical analysis of children's leisure time showed there has been a substantial decline in children's nonschool reading since the 1920s (Wartella and Mazzarella 1990). In 2002, estimates of reading for children age five to eighteen are around 1.5 hours per week on average. These numbers seem particularly low when compared with the substantial time spent watching television (14.5 hours per week) and using the computer (2.5 hours per week).

Educational Activities

The most substantial enrichment activity for children is attending and studying for school. As one would expect, many of their activities revolve around education, primarily time spent in class—31 hours plus an additional 4 hours per week during the school year doing homework (table 8.1). Daughters do slightly more homework (4.4 hours per week) than sons (3.7 hours per week), a finding consistent with most Experience Sampling Method (ESM) studies of time spent reading and doing schoolwork (Larson and Verma 1999).

The PSID-CDS overall estimates of time spent in education, however, are somewhat higher than other published estimates. For example, a review of studies of children's and adolescents' time use indicated that middle-school and high-school students average anywhere from 19 to 30 hours a week doing schoolwork—including both time spent in class as well as homework (Larson and Verma 1999, table 3)—or somewhat less than what is shown in table 8.1. Our sample focuses on the entire school-age population, and because the PSID-CDS is conducted only during the school year, summer months are not averaged in these figures. Hence, focusing on the group most likely to be enrolled in school full-time during the nonsummer months, we see that the average of about 35 hours per week children spend on their education is comparable to an adult's full-time work schedule. Moreover, this estimate excludes participation in extracurricular activities (such as sports practices, meets, music lessons, drama clubs, and the like) that often take place at schools in the hours before or after the regular school day. It is not clear whether these activities feel more like work or free time to the children involved in them, but some children pack many activities into their week during the school year in addition to their 31 hours of class time. This bolsters concerns about overscheduling.

Paid Work, Housework, and Child Care

In addition to school, some children also engage in paid work, do chores around the house, and provide care for other children in the household. The strongest gender divisions in time use for adults are found in the same categories, with adult women spending far more time in housework and child care and adult men spending more time in market work (see chapters 3, 4, and 5). The emergence of these gender differences in household work is reflected in our children's figures as well, with girls doing about 7 hours per week of housework, child care, and shopping compared to about 5 hours per week for boys. Most studies find girls doing more household work than boys (Bianchi and Robinson 1997, Sanchez and Gager 2004, Larson and Verma 1999, Robinson and Godbey 1999).

What is surprising about children's time use is how household work follows adult gender patterns, but market work does not. One might expect sons to be encouraged to prepare for their provider role early in life by getting a job, whereas daughters may be encouraged to do unpaid work around the house. However, the PSID data show little gender difference in paid work, and if anything daughters do more work for pay than sons (1.9 versus 1.3 hours per week). At the same time, one might still find daughters doing "pink collar" jobs such as babysitting, and sons doing more stereotypically masculine paid jobs such as mowing lawns.

Maternal Employment

Throughout this volume, we have encountered two upward trends that have greatly heightened public concerns about the adequacy of parental investments in children: maternal employment and single parenting. Table 8.2 examines how children's time expenditures in 2002 vary by their mothers' employment status. Table 8.3 compares children's schedules in two-parent and single-parent households.

The findings in table 8.2 are consistent with how one would expect children's time-use patterns to be associated with maternal employment. First, children in both types of households spend similar amounts of time in the main activities of doing household work and engaging in educational activities, a finding consistent with earlier research on younger children's time-use patterns (Bianchi and Robinson 1997; Hofferth and Sandberg 2001b). Second, the gaps in time-use patterns between children of nonemployed mothers and employed mothers are not large. For example, children with employed mothers spend slightly less time reading or being read to (1.4 hours per week) compared with children of nonemployed mothers (1.8 hours per week)—also consistent with the chapter 4 finding that employed mothers report reading to their child somewhat less frequently than nonemployed mothers. Children with employed mothers also spend less time eating than children with nonemployed mothers (6.9 compared with 7.6 hours per week), also consistent with the chapter 4 data on eating family meals. This may indicate that meals may be more rushed in households where mothers engage in paid work, though the differences only amount to a little over a half hour in the course of a week.

Children with employed mothers seem to make up these time deficits in reading and eating in the leisure areas of attending events, visiting, sports, outdoor activities, and hobbies. Employed mothers may schedule more events and activities for their children to overlap with their employment schedules. There also may be demographic and attitudinal differences between families, such that employed mothers place a higher value on entertainment and social activities. They also may have more income to spend on these activities. However, it is important not to overstate these generally small differences.

Single Mothers

Table 8.3 shows that the differences in children's time use between two-parent and single-mother families are also not dramatic. The largest difference is for television viewing, with children in two-parent families watching 14.2 hours per week compared with 15.8 hours per week for

Table 8.2   Differences in Children's Time Use by Maternal Employment Hours per Week, 2002

Activity	Children with Employed Mother	Children with Nonemployed Mother	Difference (Employed— Nonemployed)
Total paid work	1.5	1.8	−0.3
Total household work	6.0	5.9	0.1
Total day care	0.3	0.2	0.1
Total personal care	83.2	85.0	−1.8
Sleep	68.0	69.1*	−1.1
Meal	6.9	7.6*	−0.7
Grooming	8.3	8.3	0.0
Total education	35.1	35.5	−0.4
School	31.1	31.3	−0.2
Homework	4.0	4.2	−0.2
Total free time	41.1	38.9	2.1
Home computer activities	2.6	2.4	0.2
Organizations	1.0	1.3	−0.2
Religion	1.5	1.7	−0.2
Events	1.1	0.7*	0.4
Visiting	2.9	2.3	0.6
Sports	3.2	2.6*	0.6
Outdoors	0.9	0.6*	0.3
Hobby	0.1	0.0*	0.1
Art activities	0.9	0.9	0.0
Playing	8.0	8.2	−0.3
Television	14.7	13.7	1.1
Reading	1.4	1.8*	−0.3
Household conversations	0.5	0.5	0.0
Other passive leisure	2.3	2.3	0.0
NA	0.8	0.5	0.2
Total	168.0	168.0	
N	(1,853)	(427)	

Source: Author's calculations from the 2002 Panel Study of Income Dynamics Child Development Supplement (PSID-CDS).
Note: Maternal employment defined as working one or more hours per week. Includes own, adoptive, or stepchildren of household heads or wives of household heads.
*p-value < 0.05.

Table 8.3 Differences in Children's Time Use by Family Structure,
Hours per Week, 2002

Activity	Two-Parent Families	Single Mothers	Difference
Total paid work	1.7	1.3	0.4
Total household work	5.9	6.4	−0.5
Total day care	0.3	0.2	0.1
Total personal care	83.4	84.2*	−0.8
Sleep	68.0	69.2*	−1.2
Meal	7.2	6.7*	0.4
Grooming	8.3	8.3	−0.1
Total education	35.1	35.6	−0.5
School	31.0	32.0	−1.1
Homework	4.2	3.6*	0.6
Total free time	40.9	39.4*	1.6
Home computer activities	2.7	1.8*	0.9
Organizations	1.1	0.9	0.2
Religion	1.6	1.2*	0.5
Events	1.0	0.9	0.2
Visiting	2.8	2.9	−0.1
Sports	3.2	2.6*	0.6
Outdoors	0.9	0.9	0.0
Hobby	0.1	0.1	0.0
Art activities	1.0	0.6*	0.3
Playing	8.1	7.6	0.6
Television	14.2	15.8*	−1.6
Reading	1.5	1.2*	0.4
Household conversations	0.5	0.4	0.1
Other passive leisure	2.2	2.5	−0.3
NA	0.7	1.0	−0.3
Total	168.0	168.0	
N	(1,611)	(669)	

Source: Author's calculations from the 2002 Panel Study of Income Dynamics Child Development Supplement (PSID-CDS).
Note: Includes own, adoptive, or stepchildren of household heads or wives of household heads.
*p-value < 0.05.

children with single mothers, a difference that may be partly accounted for by greater time spent in enrichment activities, such as doing homework, reading, and art activities among children living with two parents. At the same time, children in two-parent households may be substituting some of their television time for recreational computer use—2.7 hours per week spent using the computer compared with 1.8 hours per week for children in single-mother families.

Much like the trends for maternal employment, the differences between children's schedules in two-parent and single-mother families are small. Given how dramatic the increases in maternal employment and single parenting have been, we might expect children's time-use patterns to diverge more. The lack of any major differences, at least among school-age children, suggests that regardless of employment or marital status, parents strive to raise children similarly with regard to time use.

Correlations Between Children's and Parents' Time Use

In addition to tabulating the differences in children's time use between two-parent and single-mother families, we can gain deeper insight into the lives of children in dual-earner households by examining our chapter 6 data from weekly diaries. Among these middle-class dual-earner parents and their children who kept weekly diaries, we can assess relationships between parents' and children's activities.

Children's participation in the key activities of fitness, reading, housework, and television viewing are highly and positively associated with their mother's participation (with the exception of school homework, given that few mothers do homework). For example, the more sports or fitness a child reports engaging in, the more his or her mother reports. Fathers' participation in these activities is also significant: their participation in fitness, reading, as well as housework activities is also positively correlated with their children's participation. However, the correlations between children's and father's activities are not as strong as those among mothers and children. Further, in the case of watching television, only the mothers' viewing habits correlate with child viewing.

Does this mean more active mothers encourage their children to be active, or do more active children run their mothers ragged? Although one cannot tell from a single time point, what does seem clear is that mothers are more likely than fathers to be in sync with their children's participation, possibly to push their children to engage in various activities, suggesting that it is primarily mothers who are the organizers of children's activities.

Beyond mothers' and fathers' participation in leisure and housework, the only other significant predictor of children's participation is age. Older

Table 8.4   Family Meals Together

	1975 Third Wave	2000
Average number of days per week family eats dinner together	5.0	4.6*
Percentage eating "main meal" together at least once a week	100	96
N	(400)	(1,172)

Source: Authors' calculations from the third wave of the 1975–76 Time Use in Economic and Social Accounts; and the 2000 National Survey of Parents.
Difference between 1975 and 2000 statistically significant, *p-value < .05.

children spend less time in fitness activities, watch more television, and do more housework.

Family Time

Children's time spent with family is difficult to assess because it can be conceptualized in various ways—ranging from pure family time, such as eating dinner together, when family members are presumably conversing, to more fluid activities, such as sitting around the television. Here members may be in and out of the room, answering the telephone, or doing homework with minimal direct interaction.

Studies suggest that families sit down to eat dinner together less frequently than in the past (Kinney, Dunn, and Hofferth 2000). This may be related to children's activities that conflict with the dinner hour or to tag-teaming parents who work evening shifts for child care reasons. Concerns about the high rate of childhood obesity have fueled the view that children may be eating more on the go and perhaps getting less nutritious meals. Whether eating together is associated with child obesity is unknown, and table 8.4 shows that eating the main meal together has declined only slightly between 1975 and 2000 (5.0 versus 4.6 meals per week respectively).

We also know from previous time-diary and ESM studies that time spent with family members varies significantly by children's age. Reed Larson and Maryse Richards's (1991) ESM study of children's companionship indicated that fifth graders spend close to half of their waking hours with their families, whereas ninth graders spend only one quarter of it. Even though time with family decreases with age, the amount of time talking with family members does not (Larson et al. 1996). When both teenagers and parents are away from home, they still check in with one another.

Middle adolescence is nonetheless a time when parental controls loosen and, perhaps more importantly, access to automobiles opens up opportunities for weekend plans outside the home. Most junior high school adolescents are not allowed to go out on their own at night, but Larson and Richards (1994) find that parents tend to give their high school children more freedom.

Children's Feelings About Their Time Use

The amount of time spent away from home increases in high school according to Larson et al.'s (1996, 39) beeper studies, the weekend in particular becomes a time for teenagers to "address needs and yearnings that school and other responsibilities prevent them from addressing during the week." Larson (1998) also reports that fifth- to eighth-grade children report feeling happier on weekends than on weekdays, and that this emotional differentiation widens as they transition to high school. What teenagers are doing on weekends that makes them happy has been characterized as both a partying and a romantic script. The first involves driving around and meeting up with friends, and the second includes dating or interactions with a romantic partner, both of which Larson (1998) found to be highly associated with feelings of enjoyment. At the same time, being out with friends on weekend evenings was associated with more risky behavior, such as substance abuse, delinquency, and sex—meaning that adolescents' independence at this time sometimes compromises their well-being.

The dark side of the weekend for teenagers is time spent alone (Larson 1998, 46). In contrast to adults, who may see time to oneself on a weekend evening as a luxury, given the high percentage of parents—especially mothers—who reported too little time for themselves in chapter 7, high school teenagers generally report negative feelings when they are alone on a Friday or Saturday night. Because teenagers see the weekend as a time when exciting things are supposed to be happening, being alone at that time may be particularly difficult and lonely for them (Larson 1998). Across their waking hours, including weekdays, these beeper studies show that high school students spend approximately 26 percent of their time alone, compared to between 17 and 25 percent in early adolescence (Larson and Richards 1991; Csikszentmihalyi and Larson 1984).

Turning the Tables: What Do Children Think About Their Parents?

Earlier chapters have described how much time parents spend with their children, how parents feel about the way they spend their time with their children, and how parents feel about how well their children are doing in life. Although we did not collect data on children's subjective assessments of time, Ellen Galinsky (1999) collected data from a national sample of 1,023 children in the third through twelfth grades in which she assessed children's feelings about their parents' time allocation. One of Galinsky's more surprising findings centered around answers to the question posed to both children and parents: "If you were granted one wish to change the way that your mother's/your father's work affects your life, what would that wish be?" Some 56 percent of parents anticipated that their children would want more time with their parents and for their parents to spend less time at work, yet only 10 percent of the children actually wanted more time with their mothers and only 16 percent wanted more time with their fathers. A far larger proportion, 34 percent, wished that their mothers would be less stressed and less tired, and 28 percent wished this about their fathers (Galinsky 1999).

In other words, the issues that are central to adults are not necessarily central to school-aged children. Moreover, Galinsky's (1999) study found nearly half of the children gave their mothers an A for spending time talking with them. From children's perspective, whether a parent is there when they need a parent is their main concern.

Galinsky's (1999) findings also indicate that both the amount and quality of parents' time matters to children. There is a strong association between the time children report spending with parents and how positively they report being parented. Larson and Richards's (1991) ESM study also assesses children's feelings about their time spent with family. They found that although this time diminishes as children age, their feelings toward their family do not. There is a slight decline in affective feelings for family in the sixth through eighth grades, but by ninth grade the subjective quality of their family time returns to the fifth grade level. Thus, though the nature of the parent-child relationship is changing—particularly in the amount of time they spend together—adolescents do not necessarily become so alienated from their parents that they enjoy their parents' company less.

Summary and Conclusions

This chapter highlighted the time-use trends and patterns of primarily school-aged children. Unlike adults who spend a great deal of time in paid and household work, children spend much of their waking hours in educational activities and free time. Children spend large amounts of their free time in unstructured play and watching television, yet little time reading, lending support to the argument that children squander their leisure time. On the other hand, the amount of time in household chores, part-time jobs, and extracurricular activities is substantial and has fueled the argument that children are overscheduled and their lives too programmed to be enjoyable.

Taken as a whole, the findings in this chapter underscore certain themes. First, children's time spent in household activities follow the same gendered patterns observed in earlier chapters among parents. Second, the differences between children's time in families with employed mothers and those with nonemployed mothers, as well as those between two-parent and single-mother families, remain relatively and reassuringly small. Third, family time is important and valuable to all members of the family, especially children, and even though the structures of families may be changing, the bonds that hold parents and children together remain strong.

Chapter 9

Multinational Patterns in Parental Time: How Unique Is the United States?

W E HAVE seen that the widespread hypothesis about parents spending less time with children is at odds with the picture of everyday family life that emerges from American time-diary surveys. Here we review parallel diary data from five other Western countries (three primarily English speaking) to see whether the results in previous chapters are unique to the United States. The basic results in chapters 4 and 5 are thus recapitulated for comparison with data from national-level diary studies of parents in Canada, the United Kingdom, France, and the Netherlands, as well as partial data from Australia.

Previous analyses by Philip Stone (1972) and Michael Bittman (2000) have indicated that many of the trends and predictors of child care found in the United States are found in other Western countries as well, and we largely replicate that conclusion in our analyses. In most of these countries, one also finds the trend for notably increased proportions of mothers working. We also examine multivariate regression results from these five countries about how parental child care time relates to paid employment levels, ages of children, numbers of children, marital status, education level, and parental age.

A main limitation of our analyses is that the diary child care figures from other countries come, for the most part, from primary activity reports, because information on secondary activities and social contact with children for most other countries is not available. Thus, it is again important to recognize that the primary activity times reported here represent lower bound estimates of time with children—as shown in chapter 4, primary activity times are less than a third of the time found when with whom questions are included in the diary. As shown in chapter 4, changes are less pronounced for these more expansive measures of time with children than for primary activities for the United States and Canada—the only countries collecting these data in our comparison. In

Canada, the with child times are actually 10 to 20 percent lower in 1998 than in previous surveys, unlike the U.S. increases found in chapter 4.

It is also important to note that there are rather different diary methods used in these other countries. Some diary studies used closed diaries with fixed-time intervals (rather than the open diaries in the United States). Some diaries are collected in person or by mail rather than by telephone, and differ in other ways as well. There are, moreover, differences in sample sizes and the frequency with which the surveys are conducted. These can lead to unwanted differences, not just across countries, but within the same country—as occurred in both Canada and Australia, where the earliest data collections were confined to single localities.[1]

Of particular cross-national interest in our analyses are the trends toward higher child care time among American fathers and mothers noted in chapter 4. One important factor to consider is the presence and number of children in the home, because that number has declined markedly in the United States since the 1960s. Another important factor is the high rate of employment among today's American mothers. However, when adjusted by regression analysis for family status and employment status, we have seen that the U.S. child care figures continue to be notably higher today for both mothers and fathers. Married fathers report almost 4 more hours of weekly child care in 2000 than in 1965 or 1985, married mothers 2 to 3 hours more, and unmarried mothers 4 to 6 more hours than in the past. Detailed figures indicate that this pattern holds for those with both preschool and older children. However, the most dramatic increase over the thirty-five years has been for fathers, who more than doubled their child care hours, as documented in chapter 4.

In the analyses that follow, the interest is in whether these upward trends are found in other countries, and whether the demographic predictors in the United States are found in other countries as well. We have the opportunity to examine, first, how important a role various parental demographic factors play in predicting higher child care time and, second, time-diary activity differences between parents and nonparents (and parents of preschoolers versus those with older children). The activity differences are intended to provide insights into how daily life changes as a result of becoming a parent.

Cross-National Trends in Child Care Time

Figures 9.1 and 9.2 graph trends in primary child care activities separately for mothers and for fathers in the United States and the five comparison countries. With some exceptions, the time trends slope upward. The increases for mothers in figure 9.1 are most visible for the United Kingdom since 1975, but also are persistent in Australia, the United

Figure 9.1   Trends in Mothers' Primary Activity Time Spent on Child Care in Six Countries

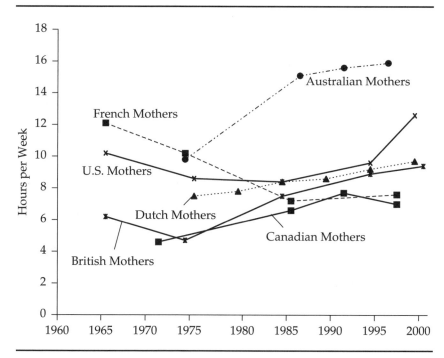

Source: Historical time-diary data, selected countries (see appendix C).

States, and Holland since the 1970s. For Canadian mothers, there is a slight decrease between 1992 and 1998, with the 1998 figure slightly higher than in 1986. The downward pattern for French mothers shows up as the glaring exception to the upward trends in figure 9.1.

The increases for fathers (in figure 9.2) are more clearly evident than for mothers (in figure 9.1). The most dramatic increases are found in the United Kingdom, the country with the least amount of parental involvement in the 1960s and 1970s. Again, the major exception to rather consistent upward trends in child care occurs in France, where fathers' time decreased in the 1970s and 1980s but has increased since 1986. Here again, then, the United States is not alone in having fathers who spend more time in child care.

Similar patterns of increased parental care are found in Anne Gauthier, Timothy Smeeding, and Frank Furstenberg's (2004) analysis of diary data from sixteen countries (which, like our analysis, also includes the United States, Canada, France, and Australia, but neither the Netherlands nor the

Figure 9.2   Trends in Fathers' Primary Activity Time Spent on Child Care in Six Countries

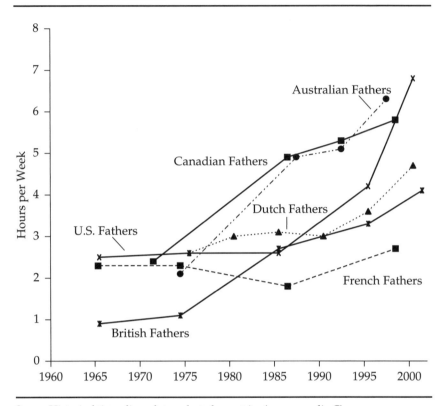

Source: Historical time-diary data, selected countries (see appendix C).

United Kingdom). These authors also conclude that the increase is found both among fathers and mothers, and that the ratio of fathers' time to mothers' time has increased over time (as implied in figures 9.1 and 9.2). They find that both employed and nonemployed mothers have increased their time in child care, with a greater increase among nonemployed mothers, who are presumed to prefer spending time with children. In his analysis of diary data from twenty countries (which overlap considerably with those in the Gauthier, Smeeding, and Furstenberg's 2004 analysis), Jonathan Gershuny (2000) also found a trend toward more child care internationally, but only since 1985, with decreases between the 1960s and the 1970s, as in the United States (see chapter 4). Something of a universal change in child care perceptions and norms would thus seem to be a trend, on which we speculate more at the end of this chapter.

Predictors of Child Care Time

Table 9.1 summarizes the importance of the main demographic factors in predicting child care time across countries. To reduce the complexity and size of the resulting tables, the table uses a summary scale running from 0 (no relationship) to ++++ for variables that predict double or more time with children between the included and omitted category after regression adjustment, with values +, ++, and +++ reflecting relationships of increasing difference between these extremes. Thus, in the case of the ++++ entry for U.S. mothers of preschool children, their activity time is more than 15 hours per week (after regression adjustment) compared with 7 hours for mothers of older children.[2]

For U.S. fathers, in contrast, the figures are 9 versus 4 hours for primary child care by those with preschoolers—compared with those with older children (and 31 versus 17 hours for "with child" time, also a ++++ pattern). In the United Kingdom, the corresponding figures for primary child care activity are 16 hours for mothers of preschool children versus 4 hours for mothers of older children, and 7 versus 4 hours for fathers, again both more than double even after multivariate regression adjustment. The clearest conclusion emerging from the data as presented in table 9.1 is that presence of preschool children is the strongest predictor of child care time in each country for both mothers and fathers, even after the other predictors are taken into account.

Several other conclusions to be drawn from table 9.1 seem to generalize across countries:

- The number of children often becomes an insignificant predictor once the age of the youngest child is taken into account.

- Employment is the other major demographic predictor of child care time, and exerts a significant influence even after other predictors are taken into account. Employment reduces child care time significantly for both mothers and fathers in all countries, except for fathers in the United States.

- Education is a consistent, but often insignificant, predictor of child care time after other factors are taken into account. This conclusion is somewhat counter to Liana Sayer, Anne Gauthier, and Frank Furstenberg's (2004) finding of significant education effects for mothers (but not fathers) in time diaries from the four countries they analyzed: Canada, Germany, Italy, and Norway, which vary widely in economic support and services for families. Sayer, Gauthier, and Furstenberg also indicate, however, that the relation of education to child care is not particularly strong after other predictors are taken

Table 9.1 Relationship Between Child Care Time and Selected Background Predictors[a]

	Mothers					Fathers				
	United States	Canada	United Kingdom	Netherlands	France	United States	Canada	United Kingdom	Netherlands	France
Number of children	+	+	NA	+	++	+	+	NA	+	0
Presence of preschool child	+++	++++	++++	++++	++++	++	+++	+++	++++	+++
Employment	--	---	---	--	--	-	--	--	---	-
Education	+	+	+	0	+	+	++	0	++	++
Marriage	+	0	-+	0	0	0	++	++	-	-
Over age forty-five	--	---	-	-	-	-	--	-	-	-

Source: Selected international time use data sets (see appendix C).

a. The analytic technique used is Multiple Classification Analysis (MCA) of Andrews, Morgan, Sonquist, and Klem (1973), which is ideally suited to time-diary data in terms of showing differences in time use after adjustment for other demographic predictors of child care time.

Note: Relationship strength: 0 = no relationship; +/- = positive/negative direction to the relationship, but not statistically significant at 0.05 level; ++/-- = significant positive/negative relationship; +++/--- = significant positive/negative relationship, 50% or higher figures; ++++/---- = significant differences more than double from low group to high group. NA indicates that data are not available.

Table 9.2   **Mean Weekly Hours of Child Care, Selected Countries**[a]

	Preschool Children	School Children	Ratio
Mothers			
United States	15	7	2.1
Canada	21	7	3.0
United Kingdom	16	4	4.0
Netherlands	20	6	3.3
France	16	4	4.0
Fathers			
United States	9	4	2.3
Canada	10	4	2.5
United Kingdom	7	2	3.5
Netherlands	9	3	3.0
France	6.5	2	3.3

Source: Selected international time use data sets (see appendix C).
a. The analytic technique used is Multiple Classification Analysis (MCA) of Andrews et al. (1973), which is ideally suited to time-diary data in terms of showing differences in time use after adjustment for other demographic predictors of child care time.

into account. Again, these corroborating results come from three countries not analyzed here, and these authors use a different set of predictor variables.

- Married parents—at least in the United States, United Kingdom, and Canada—spend more time with children than single parents, meaning that these children not only lose the most father time, but some mother time as well.

- Older (age forty-five and older) parents spend notably less time with their children than younger parents, after taking age of children into account. That is, it is not solely older children that account for older parents spending less time with children. Lower figures are also found, but to a much lesser extent, for young parents, those age eighteen to twenty-four.

The primary activity comparisons after regression adjustment for mothers with preschool versus older age children are shown in table 9.2. The ratio of time for those with young versus older children in the two North American countries (2.1 and 3.0) are lower than for the European countries (4.0, 3.3, and 4.0), and suggest that U.S. and Canadian parents spent comparatively more time with older children than their European counterparts. As with mothers, the North American fathers allocate their child care time somewhat more equally to older and younger children

Table 9.3   Mean Weekly Hours of Child Care for Employed and Nonemployed Mothers, Selected Countries[a]

	Employed Mothers	Nonemployed Mothers	Employed as a Percentage of Nonemployed
United States	9	15	60
Canada	9	16	56
United Kingdom	6.5	12.5	52
Netherlands	7	11	64
France	6	10	60

Source: Selected international time use data sets (see appendix C).
a. The analytic technique used is Multiple Classification Analysis (MCA) of Andrews et al. (1973), which is ideally suited to time-diary data in terms of showing differences in time use after adjustment for other demographic predictors of child care time.

than European fathers, who concentrate more time on very young children. Overall, however, the child care time figures cited are remarkably consistent across culturally unique countries using somewhat different methods of diary data collection.

In terms of employment status differences, the second most important predictor of child care time in the table 9.1 analyses, rather similar employment differentials are again evident in maternal time across countries. As shown in table 9.3, across countries, employed mothers average between 52 and 64 percent of the time nonemployed mothers spend in child care activities. The difference is greatest in the United Kingdom, where employed British mothers spend about 52 percent as much time, and smallest in the Netherlands, where employed Dutch mothers spend 64 percent as much. The comparable percentages are intermediate in the United States and France, where employed mothers averaged 60 percent of the child care time of their nonemployed counterparts, and in Canada, where the estimate is 56 percent.

The Activity Correlates (Consequences?) of Parenthood

Table 9.4 summarizes the cross-national findings about the correlates of six activities (paid work, housework, shopping, sleeping, television, and total free time) of parents versus nonparents after controls for four important demographic factors (employment, education, marital status, and age). These analyses suggest how daily life may change, or what activities might be bartered, as a result of becoming a parent.

Looking first at the activity differences by presence and number of children in table 9.4, we see first that having children means less free

Table 9.4   Presence and Strength of Relationship between Parenthood and Various Activities[a]

	Paid Work	Housework	Shopping	Sleep	Television	Free Time
Presence and number of children						
Mothers						
United States	--	++	0	-	-	-
Canada	0	+++	0	-	-	---
United Kingdom	--	++	+	-	-	--
Netherlands	-	++	+	-	-	--
France	-	+	0	0	-	--
Fathers						
United States	+	0	0	-	-	--
Canada	+	+	0	0	--	---
United Kingdom	0	+	+	0	-	--
Netherlands	0	--	0	0	-	--
France	0	0	0	0	0	0
Preschool age child						
Mothers						
United States	---	+	0	+	0	--
Canada	--	+	0	0	-	---
United Kingdom	-	++	+	-	-	---
Netherlands	---	0	-	0	0	--
France	---	0	-	0	-	-
Fathers						
United States	-	0	0	0	+	0
Canada	+	+	0	0	-	---
United Kingdom	0	+	+	0	0	--
Netherlands	+	+	-	0	0	--
France	0	0	0	0	0	0

Source: Selected international time use data sets (see appendix C).
a. The analytic technique used is Multiple Classification Analysis (MCA) of Andrews et al. (1973), which is ideally suited to time-diary data in terms of showing differences in time use after adjustment for other demographic predictors of child care time.
Relationship strength: 0 = no relationship; +/- = positive/negative direction to the relationship, but not statistically significant at 0.05 level; ++/-- = significant positive/negative relationship; +++/--- = significant positive/negative relationship, 50% or higher figures; ++++/---- = significant differences more than double from low group to high group.
NA indicates that data are not available.

time for women in all countries. The same is true for sleep, television watching, and paid work, although these differences are neither as large nor as consistent as for free time, and usually are not statistically significant. Some of this is accompanied by mothers' significantly greater time spent doing housework versus their childless counterparts. Shopping time is also somewhat higher among mothers than childless women in the United Kingdom and the Netherlands—but not in the United States or Canada. These differences also tend to be larger with more children in the household, but it is usually the presence of a child rather than the number of children that produces the biggest differences.

Fathers also have significantly less free time than those who are not fathers, and some of that is free time devoted to television viewing. Time devoted to shopping, sleeping, and housework is generally about the same for fathers as for those who are not fathers, though Dutch fathers actually do significantly less housework than childless men. Fathers in the United States and Canada also do slightly more paid work than childless men, which probably contributes to their lower free time, but that is not true in the Netherlands, France, or the United Kingdom.

Many of the same patterns are found for the presence of younger, preschool children versus older children, as shown in the lower panel of table 9.4. Mothers of younger children do less paid work and have notably less free time than mothers of older children. But their increased time on housework is not as prominent nor as consistent as is found in the comparison between those with and without children in the home. Differences in shopping, sleeping, and television watching are also neither as clear nor consistent as the declines in free time. Among fathers, those with preschoolers in the Netherlands and in Canada tend to work more hours, do slightly more housework, and (perhaps as a consequence) have less free time than fathers of older children. Differences in shopping, sleeping, and television times, however, are minimal, as they are for mothers of preschoolers.

Overall, then, table 9.4 suggests that having children mainly affects the amount of free time adults have, with television often becoming one casualty of parenthood. Paid work time drops most notably among mothers, especially if the child is preschool age. In some countries, paid work increases among fathers. Having a child means more housework for mothers, with the biggest differences between parents and nonparents rather than between parents with preschoolers and those with older children. Mothers in general also tend to get a little less sleep than their childless counterparts, but not those with preschool children—contrary to the stereotype of the continually ever-awakened new mother. Differences that come with being a mother are more pronounced than for being a father.

Cross-Time Trends in Other Activities

As noted, most countries also show a trend toward more paid work among mothers, mainly a function of more of them being in the workforce. In the Netherlands, there was almost a fourfold increase—from 3 to 12 hours—between 1975 and 2000. That and other factors have led to a dramatic and offsetting decrease in household work in most countries. However, time parents spend on sleep and other personal care activities tends to remain constant over time (data not shown).

The result, then, is little or no change across time in the amount of free time available to parents, though the trends do vary by country. There are modest increases in the United Kingdom and Canada, a notable decrease in the Netherlands, consistent with the increase in paid work among mothers—and in the United States between the 1980s and 1990s, primarily for mothers. Nor is an increase in television viewing the reason for the increase in free time in countries with an increase. Indeed, there have been overall declines in the television time of parents in Canada, the United Kingdom, and the Netherlands.

It is also important to note that some of these trends among parents are also generally found among nonparents in these countries as well. That is, it is not just mothers who are working more or doing less housework, but other women (nonmothers) as well.

Summary and Conclusions

Of the various trends and predictors of child care found in the United States that are also found in most other Western countries, the most important for this volume is the tendency for increased time in child care among parents, especially fathers and especially since the 1970s. The increases are most apparent for the United Kingdom (again since 1975), but they are evident in the United States and the Netherlands since the 1970s as well. There is also an increase in child care time among Canadian fathers (who consistently report far higher times than fathers in other countries), but a slight decrease in 1998 for Canadian mothers after an increase in 1992—although the 1998 figure is still slightly higher than in 1986. The downward pattern for French mothers and the curvilinear pattern—first down, then up—for French fathers since 1965 are notably out of sync with the general increases found in the other countries, both in our analyses here and in Gauthier, Smeeding, and Furstenberg (2004).

Although we cannot be sure why these overall increases occurred in the face of demographic trends that would predict decreases, such as increased maternal employment and more unmarried parents, a number of factors can be proposed in the American context. First, increased family planning measures and technology aimed at reducing unwanted pregnancies may mean that more of today's children are born to parents who have consciously decided to care for and invest time in them. Second, increased public attention to the incidence of child kidnapping and abuse, as well as a heightened awareness to the dangers children face in the absence of parents (latchkey children), may also motivate parents to keep a closer eye on their children, particularly when the children are young. Finally, norms about "good parents" who closely monitor their children's activities or who expose children to recreational activities and programs designed to prepare them for college or higher-quality work opportunities later in life may be a third factor related to increases in child care time.

Predictors of Time on Child Care

Turning to the major predictors of increased child care time within each country, the results again show considerable consistency across countries. The strongest predictor of increased child care for both mothers and fathers is presence of a preschool child, a factor producing differences that are barely affected even after the other demographic predictors are taken into account. Employment is the other major demographic predictor of decreased child care time, with married parents, middle-aged (versus younger or older) parents, and college-educated parents also showing higher than average child care times in their diaries. Interestingly, the number of children often becomes an insignificant predictor, particularly when the age of the child is taken into account. Although college education is also a predictor of more child care, it does not emerge from these analyses as important or consistent a predictor as Sayer, Gauthier, and Furstenberg (2004) found.

The cross-national findings about the correlates, or possibly consequences, of parenthood in terms of six activities (like paid work and free time) again show similar patterns across countries. Mothers in all countries have significantly less free time (including television viewing), and slightly less time as well for sleep and paid work than women without children. This is accompanied by the significantly greater times they spend doing housework, and shopping time also tends to be slightly higher among mothers than other women. Fathers also have significantly less free time than men who are not fathers, and some of that is free time devoted to television. Time devoted to shopping, sleeping, and housework are generally about the same, although Dutch fathers do significantly less housework than men who are not fathers. Fathers in the United States and Canada also do slightly more paid work, which probably contributes to their having less free time, but that is not true in other countries. Some of these same patterns are found when parents have preschool (versus older) children, although mothers with preschool children do not get less sleep—contrary to the stereotype.

One final conclusion is that these predictors tend to be stronger for mothers than for fathers, especially employment status among mothers of young children. This finding is a familiar one: a change in family factors is more likely to affect the time allocation of women than men.

= Chapter 10 =

Mothers' Time, Fathers' Time, and Gender Equal Parenting: What Do We Conclude?

T HE PRECEDING chapters contain three basic claims from our time-diary evidence. Each is novel and will likely be controversial.

First is that mothers are spending as much time interacting with their children today as forty years ago when they allocated far fewer hours to paid work. They do this by making children their top priority. They cut back market work when child care demands are highest, they privilege child care activities over other time expenditures (especially housework and time for themselves), and they include children in their leisure activities to maximize time with them. They absorb a higher workload despite a sense of not having enough time for their spouse and for themselves, always feeling rushed, and juggling more than one thing at a time. One important caveat to this conclusion is that we cannot show whether mothers are as accessible in the home as they were in the past, which may be part of why many mothers continue to feel that they do not spend enough time with their children despite their heavy investment in child rearing.

Second, we find fathers are doing more in the home, especially more child care, despite their continuing to devote large amounts of time to paid work. How do they manage this? Like mothers, they work long weeks. They seem willing to trade time in personal care, time alone, and maybe even some market work to expand what they do with their children. Moreover, they are increasingly taking on the responsibility for basic, routine aspects of caregiving—diaper changing, feeding, and the like—meaning they are not just participating in the easier or more enjoyable activities of child care. At the same time, many feel they do not spend enough time with their children.

Third, we find gender equality across mothers and fathers in overall workloads. If both market work and unpaid work count in what

169

constitutes what we think of as good parenting—and we argue both should be included—fathers and mothers contribute equally. This may be a controversial claim, given the vast literature that argues that it is mothers who bear the brunt of the increased family workload. In other words, fathers as well as mothers are burdened by a second shift.

There are several caveats to this claim of gender equality. First, mothers' greater subjective sense of time pressures may derive from their being the one who continues to orchestrate family life—a reality that is difficult to capture in time-diary data. Second, when children are reared outside a two-parent home, fathers are much less likely than mothers to shoulder the day-to-day responsibility of caregiving—that is, fathers remain more likely than mothers to drop the parental role altogether. At the same time, fathers who live with their children are working as much on behalf of their families as the mothers in those families. Third, women may not easily rebound from reducing paid work as they give their time over to unpaid labor. Lower pensions, forgone careers, and financial instability later in life (particularly in the case of divorce) can be a consequence of time away from full-time employment when children are young.

We began this volume by describing the subtle revolution in the latter half of the twentieth century in mothers' market work. This change reverberated throughout family life. We then proceeded to examine in great detail many of the consequences of this profound change. The time-diary evidence documents changes in family life that could not clearly be reflected in any earlier type of data collection. We have been particularly interested in time spent doing paid work but also in unpaid work for the household—the second shift of interest to family researchers. We have also examined changes in free-time activities that occur in families with children—time with others, not only children but also spouses, families and friends, and time in the community.

Our latest diary studies have been embedded in surveys that also ask respondents their feelings about various activities, including parental practices. These allow us to present a picture of not only the behavioral changes but also the subjective dimension of family life to place these changes in a clearer and broader context.

We began, in chapter 3, with the question of work hours: have they increased for parents and by how much? We used two data sources that covered the 1965 to 2000 period: the Current Population Survey (CPS) estimate data on work hours and our own time-diary data on both paid work hours and unpaid family caregiving and household work. Although the CPS data show an increase in maternal workloads, it is mainly in the percentage of mothers working for pay and the number of weeks worked per year, not in the weekly hours they worked. This reflects an increasing commitment of mothers to full-year market work. Because of the increase in weeks worked per year, estimated annual work hours doubled, from 444 to 1,172 hours between 1965 and 2000, when averaged across all mothers. Mothers' but not fathers' paid work hours remain sensitive to the age of their children, with most mothers working less than full-time, year-round when child care demands are greatest.

The CPS data show that parental workloads did increase, with combined paid work hours of mothers and fathers rising from 55 to 64 estimated weekly hours between 1965 and 2000 in households with married parents. The proportion of two-parent families working more than a combined 80-hour work week rose from 24 percent to 38 percent. Among all single mothers, average weekly paid work hours rose from 21 to 29 hours and from 33 to 36 hours among all single fathers.

Although time-diary figures that add paid and unpaid hours parallel the CPS trends, the diary increases in total workload are less dramatic. The diary figures suggest that today's parents are averaging a 9-hour work day, seven days a week. In 2000, mothers averaged about 6 more hours per week of (combined) paid and unpaid work than in 1965, and fathers averaged four more. Depending on one's perspective, this could be seen as a significant or an insignificant change. Where single parents and dual-earner families were already time constrained in 1965, a smaller proportion of all children were being raised in "busy" families in 1965 than today.

Given the evidence pointing to rising workloads among parents, our next question was what the implications were for the lives of busy parents. Perhaps the concern that most resonates with parents and policy makers is the fear that children may be shortchanged as parents' paid work commitments expand. The question examined in chapter 4 was thus what happened to parental time interacting with children, when so many more families now include two employed parents or only one parent.

Here, our answer will surprise many, as it did us. Overall, parents' primary child care time has not decreased over the past few decades: it has instead actually increased or remained constant for married fathers, married mothers, and single mothers. Focused time interacting with children—time spent teaching and playing with children—has increased for each of the three groups. Fathers are also providing an increasing share of the child care in the family, though still notably less than mothers.

More expansive measures of time estimates that include primary and secondary child care also suggest an increase in child care time between 1975 and 2000. With our most comprehensive measure—total time spent with children—we see an increase for married parents (but a slight decline for single mothers) between 1975 and 2000. One caveat is that, even with our most expansive time-diary measure, we still cannot track overall parental accessibility to children—that is, when a parent is available but not in the direct presence of a child. This type of maternal availability probably did decrease as mothers spent more time working away from rather than in the home. This makes the increase in mothers' focused time with children all the more remarkable, however.

A large portion of the expansion in child care time between 1975 and 2000 is possible because parents increasingly combine child care and leisure activities. Either child care has become more oriented toward enjoyable activities, or parents are more frequently including children in their own leisure pursuits. Parents report high levels of involvement in the activities of parenting and high levels of attention and affection for their children. Married mothers report that they help with homework and read to children more than single mothers (or married fathers) do, but the differences are not large. On affective dimensions, such as enjoyment of parenting tasks, single mothers actually rank higher than married mothers. Employed mothers also did not differ much from nonemployed mothers on our measures of parenting enjoyment.

We were then left with a puzzle: if mothers' paid workloads were increasing and couples' combined work hours were rising—but they were also expanding their attention to child care—what were parents doing less of? In chapter 5, we found that time doing housework was a major casualty of increased market work for married mothers. Although married fathers picked up some of that housework load between 1965 and 1985, married mothers shed far more hours than fathers picked up.

There were hints of other changes as well. Both married and single mothers today more often report multitasking or pursuing more than one activity at a time, and both married and single mothers report less time in civic leisure pursuits. Married mothers also spent less time with their husbands, and married fathers, like their spouses, recorded less time with their wives than in the past. Fathers seem to have traded some paid work and personal care to increase their time in family activities—both more housework and more child care. Fathers also showed an increase in multitasking.

The examination of paid work in chapter 3 and the assessment of child care, housework, and other free-time activities in chapters 4 and 5 suggest that mothers and fathers were becoming more similar in their time allocations. What about the claim that the overall workload in busy families falls disproportionately on the mother, particularly the employed mothers found in the literature on the second shift? Here, we turned to our weekly diary data in chapter 6, in which we had diaries from both parents in dual-earner families to corroborate a finding that emerged in our assessment of parental workloads in chapter 3. Although mothers did have a longer second shift of unpaid family work than fathers, fathers' longer hours in the first shift of paid work meant that the average total work week was amazingly similar to that of mothers. Even among full-time, dual-earner couples, mothers' total workload is virtually the same as fathers' (68 versus 67 hours per week). Data on housework and child care lend support to claims about the second shift making mothers busier—but fathers are equally busy if one includes their paid work.

When spouses' time expenditures were correlated with each other, a noteworthy finding was the relatively high correlation (0.50) between a mother's and a father's time in child care, suggesting that some children get a great deal of parental time and others relatively little. Child care is one of the strongest ways in which parents spend their time together, and it holds no matter what the number or ages of the children or how long either spouse works.

Moreover, even in our middle-class, dual-earner families who kept these weekly diaries, parents averaged more than 30 hours of free time per week. Fewer than 10 percent had less than 20 hours per week of free time. Parents have up to 10 fewer hours of free time than those who are not parents (Robinson and Godbey 1999), but seem to have more flexibility in arranging activities than they feel they have. The chapter 7 exploration of parents' feelings about time further documented that parents experience great time pressure—often feeling inadequate about the very thing to which they were devoting a large amount of time—their children!

Despite the diary reports suggesting that parents spend as much or more time with their children as ever, 40 to 60 percent still feel they spend too little. Married fathers spend less time with children, and more fathers than mothers report feelings of inadequate time. Controlling for hours of employment eliminates this gender difference. Mothers, on the other hand, are more likely to feel they spend too little time with their spouse, and to feel strongly about having too little time for themselves. Related to this, mothers are much more likely to feel that their daily time is rushed, and that they are juggling multiple activities. These gender differences hold even when mothers' and fathers' different time allocations are held constant.

As might be expected, employed mothers are especially likely to sense time deficits with their children and spouse and are also extremely likely to always feel rushed and to feel inadequate time for themselves. Here, married (employed) mothers are more content with their time allocation than single mothers. Single mothers are also more likely than other groups to feel that they have made sacrifices in family and personal life for work, and in their job for family. Thus it is the single mothers who stand out in many ways as feeling especially time constrained.

Although the bulk of our story is about parents' time use and time pressures, debates about the appropriate allocation of children's time also abound. Previous literature on children's time use has argued either that children have too much unstructured and unsupervised free time (particularly working-class and poor children) or the opposite, that children are overcontrolled and overprogrammed (particularly middle-class children).

In many ways, what is true for parents is also true for children—they are busy with school and extracurricular activities, yet their diaries also indicate many hours each week in free-time activities. Our collaborator Sara Raley's evidence in chapter 8 provides fuel for both sides of the debate. Although there are certain differences in the time expenditures of school-age children depending on their parents' employment statuses, these differences are surprisingly small. Among these school-age children, there appears to be more variation within single-parent households and within dual-earner households than there is between one-parent and two-parent households or between households where the mother is or is not employed.

Our weekly diaries also show how parents' behavior dovetails with their children's behavior. For example, mothers who engage in active leisure pursuits tend to have children who do the same. Television-watching parents have television-watching children, and so on. The data suggest a strong role-modeling aspect of parental time use and that parents also influence their children's behavior by structuring the family household and schedule both to elicit (or constrain) certain activities and to maintain stability and continuity in their children's lives.

Finally, our volume discusses international comparisons with the time-use diaries of our collaborators in other Western countries: Jonathan Gershuny of Great Britain, Michael Bittman of Australia, Andreas van den Broek of the Netherlands, Gilles Pronovost of Canada, and Laurent Lesnard and Alain Chenu of France. They document great similarity in parental uses of time in most of these countries, particularly time with children. That similarity is particularly striking given the widely differing family policy contexts of these countries, as well as the diary data collection methods they use. Thus the United States is not unique in showing both mothers' continued devotion to child rearing despite increased employment and fathers' more equal participation in the day-to-day rearing of children.

Finally, as we completed this volume, the much larger samples of time diaries with American parents collected as part of the new American Time Use Survey (ATUS) became available for 2003 and 2004. Our preliminary calculations with these new data suggest that the patterns we document in this volume—high levels of maternal and paternal time in child care and gender-equal total workloads—continue. Estimates from the 2003 ATUS across all domains of activities are remarkably consistent with the 2000 data point we end with in this volume (Bianchi, Wight, and Raley 2005; Bianchi, Raley, and Milkie 2006).

How Do We Make Sense of the Foregoing?

To understand the trends we have presented in this volume, we return to the arguments laid out at the outset. First, considering mothers, why would mothers embrace market work, yet go to such great lengths to protect their time with their children? Put differently, why do mothers choose (or get pushed into) something in-between—not full-scale market equality with men, but not the stay-at-home path that also solved work-family balance in the past, as indeed, it did so for many of their mothers or grandmothers?

As opportunities for women have expanded, being employed has become increasingly important to them. Employment provides resources but also meaning, a sense of worth, a definition of self and value, and a life outside the family. Moreover, many mothers cannot forgo employment, even if they wanted to, because their families rely on them as the sole breadwinner (as in many single-mother families). Two-parent families may need two breadwinners to make ends meet, either because the husband's earnings are low or because consumption standards are high in today's families. Wives' earnings provide important goods and services for the family.

But neither can women easily give over the caregiving of their family members (particularly their children) to others in a world where being a good mother requires intensive involvement in all aspects of their children's lives. If our interpretation is correct, the requirements for effective and good mothering have ratcheted upward at the very time when there are expanded opportunities for women to do other things with their time, such as devoting themselves to fulfilling jobs. The two competing pulls on mothers' time—one from the home, one from the marketplace—run parallel and add to societal ambivalence about maternal employment, an ambivalence that does not seem confined to the United States.

So how do mothers respond? They seek compromise in struggling for the elusive balance between work and family. They relinquish the goal of equality with men in the workplace, in favor of more hours at home when their children are young. They emerge at age forty or fifty with employment histories that are more marginal, more part-time, more episodic than men's. They let go of activities and goals that are not seen as precious as the time they spend with their children. They live with less pristine and more disorganized homes. They forgo time for themselves. They forgo time with their husband, hoping it won't erode the relationship in the long run. If employed, they expend less effort in organizational and community activities that they might otherwise do if only they had more time. They learn to live in a state of feeling time pressed—of feeling inadequate about the time they spend with their children, with their spouse, and on themselves. They do (or feel they do) many things at the same time, such as overseeing children's homework while making dinner and arranging for a home repair on the cordless phone. They adjust and readjust the work-family tradeoffs in their lives, picking up more hours of paid work as their children age, in an effort to gain more monetary resources and to create a successful and meaningful adult life.

What about fathers? Why have they been willing to put in more hours of child care, even as they continue to work long hours as their fathers did before them?

Fathers have had to adjust to a new family regime as well. First, they less often have the full-time services of a stay-at-home wife than in the past. This may relieve them of some of the financial pressure of being a sole provider for their household, but it also increases the expectation that they contribute to work in the home. Nor are they released from the perceived high level of investment required to produce happy, healthy, productive children. They feel pressure to maximize the income they provide their children—particularly if it helps purchase the culturally defined best care for children, namely, mother care. Second, they also seem to realize that family life is supposed to be an equal partnership and that they must invest their own time in nurturing precious children to adulthood. They increasingly want to be involved with their children, and they are married to women with high expectations for how involved a father should be in the home. At the same time, they also cannot easily relinquish their role as primary provider—their employment still defines the major way they become a good father and a good husband.

What, then, is the result with respect to gender equality in paid work and parenting? Are couples stuck in a new equilibrium where they are equal contributors to family well-being—one in which women's and men's time allocations to paid work and unpaid family caregiving is more similar than in the past, but where both mothers' and fathers' contributions to the family remain notably gender-specialized? Is the closest we will get to gender-similar parenting roles—where fathers average 64 percent of the market work hours and mothers 67 percent of the weekly hours of housework and child care? Or will there be further convergence in their time allocations?

The question of gender equality—and, even more so, gender equity or fairness in the division of family labor—is the most difficult to assess. Focusing on the trends assessed in previous chapters, our answer would be optimistic. Overall weekly workloads of mothers and fathers are similar, and the trend has been toward greater similarity over time, the result of mothers increasing their hours in paid work and fathers increasing their hours in unpaid work. At first it may seem as if only mothers were changing, by essentially reallocating their time away from housework to paid market work. However, fathers also responded by increasing their domestic hours, first in housework, and more recently in child care. Fathers' increased child care seems to have accelerated particularly in the 1990s, not only in the United States but elsewhere, and this perhaps bodes well for continued movement toward gender equality in both home and workplace.

On the other hand, if we focus on the current gaps in mothers' and fathers' time allocation to the home and the workplace, we are far less sanguine that gender equality is likely anytime soon. Mothers still shoulder twice as much child care and housework. Fathers still work much longer hours for pay. Mothers reduce their employment, sometimes quite dramatically, when they have preschoolers in the home. In contrast, fathers' employment is, for the most part, invariant by age of youngest child. It seems as if mothers worry most about adequate time for children whereas fathers remain focused on providing adequate money for their family.

Women and men are busy and, perhaps because time is at such a premium, fall into gender-specialized roles once a child arrives for at least two reasons. First, when couples try to decide about who should cut back on work, the gendered workplace structure encourages mothers to cut back because they are paid less and because family leaves are so incompatible with the demands of newborn care and breastfeeding. Second, given their own upbringing, in gender specialized homes, mothers may have been practicing traditionally female tasks and fathers so-called male tasks for a long time. When children are young, they may settle on a pattern of activities that becomes difficult to change or renegotiate when child care demands are no longer paramount. By then, everyone has grown accustomed to mothers who cook and run errands and to fathers who come home late from work. Children may learn what is appropriate by observing gender-specialized patterns in their parents, patterns that may then be recreated when they are adults.

What constitutes gender equality in the family and what the likely trends will be in the future is both difficult to portend and the source of much controversy. As we noted at the outset of this chapter, perhaps our most novel conclusion is that there already is a great deal of gender equality in parenting—at least as measured by total hours of work. This conclusion is at odds with much of the contemporary literature on the family, particularly the ongoing claim that there is a second shift that falls unfairly on women.

In part, whether one sees greater gender equality or greater gender inequity is a matter of emphasis. Considering only hours spent in the home, or on family work, the picture is one of unfairness to women, given that women do two-thirds of domestic work. If market work hours are more liberating or less onerous than nonmarket work hours,[1] women may be getting an unfair bargain in the family. Concentrating on current differences in who does unpaid work, and ignoring trends toward greater gender similarity in housework and child care, the claim that the second shift falls disproportionately on women is stronger.

If we assume that mothers are not choosing unpaid child care and housework over paid work—namely that men (or cultural and institutional factors) force women to specialize in the home when they would rather be pursing more equality in the market, then the second shift argument holds more sway. Moreover, if mothers' and fathers' time allocations miss the less visible "mental" work and stress of managing daily life that women perform much more often than men, there is even more gender inequity in the work weeks of parents. Clearly, thinking about gender equality in parenting more broadly to include single parents, mothers have an unfair load.

On the other hand, one could counter that paid work, not just unpaid work, can be stressful and onerous. Both paid work and unpaid family work are essential, and both require energy and often the ability to put the interests of others before one's own. It appears that fathers continue to feel a great deal of pressure to support their families through paid work, just as mothers feel a great deal of pressure to be ever available to their children and spouse. It becomes very difficult to disentangle how constrained the choices are for either fathers or mothers in a world where gender roles have become less rigid, but where powerful cultural prescriptions remain in place for what constitutes a good (or ideal) worker and a devoted mother or father and what investments are required to provide a good childhood for one's children.

Concluding Observations

Family life has changed dramatically over the last four decades as more women entered and remained in the paid workforce during their child-rearing years. Yet women did not abandon parenting, nor did they hand over their children to nannies and day care centers for extremely long hours each day. Rather, many of them worked part-time outside the home. They made valiant attempts to add market hours and to still maintain a high level of involvement in children's lives. What went by the wayside was what was easiest to drop, namely, housework. It is not clear how much families today would benefit from the 30-plus hours of housework that were required—or at least performed—by mothers of the Baby Boom in the 1960s.

Neither is it clear that nothing has been lost when so many more parents report multitasking, and so many feel inadequate about the time they spend with family members and on themselves. From the parents' subjective point of view, efforts to deepen time, to do more in a given hour than before, seem less than successful. It is perhaps not surprising there is so much attention in the popular press on how to simplify or how to take back one's life.

What is also not clear is how much of this fatigue and pressure of parenting is new and how much is a constant. Clearly, technological developments add to the sense of time pressure—paid work can interrupt family life and vice versa with great ease, given the availability of e-mail, cellular phones, and the Internet, particularly among the middle class. Technological developments may curtail the time needed for household tasks (microwave ovens being a case in point) yet they may also increase the likelihood of multitasking. The growth in services, readily available at all hours of the night and day, loosens the constraints on time but this may also add to the pressure to do more throughout the 24-hour day. Moreover, many workers who staff round-the-clock stores and businesses are parents struggling with their odd work schedules.

Why do parents feel such pressure? To some extent it is inevitable. In addition to the cultural pressures surrounding involved fathering and intensive mothering, parenting and paid work are structurally incompatible to some degree. Both demand full attention and thus are often at odds—especially when children are young and need intensive supervision, get sick often, or have school holidays and summer vacations. The patterns of childhood do not mesh neatly with the demands of the workplace, particularly in the United States where few public policies assist work and family balance. Accommodations are made to conflicts between children's needs and work schedules, but they are never perfect. Moreover, children's needs change constantly as they age. Family routines get established, only to shortly thereafter need to be reestablished around a new set of schedules and constraints. One may even wonder why rational people have children at all, given the work and uncertainty it takes to raise them.

Yet rearing children remains one of the most meaningful and rewarding investments of time that most adults feel they make in life (Robinson and Godbey 1999, appendix O). Thus, as people have fewer children, the commitment to the children they do have intensifies. The stakes become very high, as the pressure to rear the "perfect child" grows.

Should parents who read this volume conclude that they are spending enough time with their children and therefore simply relax? It is very difficult to know how much parental time with children is optimal, how much time mothers and fathers in fact need to parent to feel good about their performance as parents. If parents, especially mothers, always feel rushed or if they feel they are perpetually juggling many things at once, their (plentiful) parenting time may not yield very positive results either for them or their children. Moreover, their 30 hours of leisure a week, increasingly spent with children in tow, may also not feel very leisurely.

One of the greatest concerns in what we present in this volume is the series of differing results for single and married mothers. It suggests the possibility that there is growing heterogeneity in parents' ability to invest time in their children. The results for single mothers hint at greater inequality in parental time with children today than in the past, all else being equal. Married and single mothers may spend similar amounts of time in direct child care, but single mothers face more difficulty increasing their total time with children. Married parents are more likely than single parents to have a college education, to have children relatively late, and to have greater financial resources. In contrast, single mothers today are likely to have never married, to have less education, to have children relatively young, and to have fewer financial resources (Martin 2000). As a consequence, children in two-parent families may be benefiting from parents who both share a bundle of characteristics associated with high parental investments. In contrast, children in single-mother families not only have fewer financial resources but also have access to the time of only one parent whose characteristics are often associated with lower parental investments. Moreover, shifts in the cultural context of parenthood may have been strongest for married-couple, middle-class parents (Coltrane 1996; Hays 1996).

Despite the continued concerns about inequality between children in single-parent and two-parent families, and about parents' sense of time pressure, the actual behaviors described in our time-diary evidence paint a rather optimistic picture of family change. Families can undergo great change and still somehow protect that which seems most dear. Mothers are maintaining high levels of investment in child rearing, fathers are increasing theirs, so that mothers and fathers are increasingly sharing the demands of parenting. The transformation seems widespread, well under way, yet still evolving. Tracking that evolution—or revolution—in domestic roles of men, both those who live with their children and those who do not remains a top priority for future research. The revolution in mothers' paid work has not been without cost, but we are most impressed with family life's amazing resilience in the face of unprecedented social change.

Appendix A

Reliability and Validity of the Time-Diary Approach

THE TIME diary is a microbehavioral technique for collecting self-reports of an individual's complete daily behavior on an activity-by-activity basis. Individual respondents keep or report these accounts for a short, manageable period, such as a day or a week—usually across the full 24 hours of a single day. In that way, the technique capitalizes on the most attractive measurement properties of the time variable, namely the following:

- All daily activity is potentially recorded (including activities that occur in the early morning hours, when most people may be asleep). Thus, the diary accounts are by definition complete across the 1,440 minutes of the day.

- All 1,440 minutes of the day are equally distributed across respondents, thereby preserving the zero-sum property of time, one that allows various trade-offs between activities to be examined—that is, if time on one activity increases, it must be zeroed out by decreases in another.

- Respondents are allowed to use a time frame and an accounting variable they can both understand and access much the way they structure their daily life.

The open-ended nature of activity reporting means that the reports are automatically geared to detecting new and unanticipated activities (for example, the aerobic exercises of the 1970s, and after 1990 email and the Internet, VCR and DVD media, cell phones and other communications technologies) and to capturing all of how daily life might be spent.

Methodological Support for the Accuracy of Time Diaries

Two important properties of social science measures are reliability and validity. Reliability refers to the ability of a measurement instrument to provide consistent results from study to study or under different conditions—that is, do we get similar results using the same method? Validity refers to the ability of the instrument to provide accurate or valid data, in the sense that it agrees with estimates provided by other methods (such as observation or beepers).

Reliability

In the 1965 and 1975 studies, estimates from time diaries produced reliable and replicable results at the aggregate level. For example, Robinson (1977) found a .95 correlation between time-use patterns in the 1965 national time diaries (n = 1,244) and the aggregate figures for the single site of Jackson, Michigan (n = 788). Similar high correspondence was found for the American data and for time-diary data from Canada, in both 1971 and 1982 (Harvey and Elliot 1983).

Reliability was also noted using different diary approaches. Thus a correlation of .85 was found between time expenditure patterns in the 1965 U.S. Jackson time study using the tomorrow approach, and time expenditures for a random one-tenth of the sample, who also filled out a yesterday diary. In a later replication study in Jackson in 1973, an aggregate correlation of .88 was obtained (Robinson 1977).

Further support for the reliability of the diaries comes from the convergent results that were obtained from the telephone, mail-back, and personal interviews in the 1985 national study—and from the overall national results and those obtained in 1986 in Michigan, in 1987 and 1988 in California, and in 1986 and 1992 in Canada (Robinson and Godbey 1999).

Validity

Almost all diary studies depend on the self-report method rather than on observation. Like all verbal and nonverbal evidence, questions arise about the accuracy of the diaries. Several studies bear directly on the validity of the time diary, in the sense of there being an independent source or quasi-observer of reported behavior.

The first of these studies involved the low television-viewing figure from the 1965 time diaries relative to standard television rating-service figures. In a small-scale study (Bechtel, Achepohl, and Akers 1972), the television-viewing behavior of a sample of twenty households was monitored over a week's time with a video camera. The camera was mounted on top of the set, thus allowing the video camera and microphone to record all the behavior that took place in front of the television screen. The results indicated that both rating-service methods of television exposure (the Nielsen is audimeters and their viewing diaries) produced estimates of viewing that were 20 to 50 percent higher than primary or secondary viewing activities reported in time diaries or observed by the camera (Allen 1965).

Three more general validity studies provided further evidence of the validity of time-diary data. These examined the full range of activities, not just television viewing, and employed larger and more representative samples. A 1973 random sample of sixty residents of Ann Arbor and Jackson, Michigan, kept beepers for a one-day period and reported their activity whenever the beeper was activated (some thirty to forty times throughout the day). Averaged across all sixty respondents (and across waking hours of the day) the correlation of activity durations from the beeper and from the diaries was .81 for the Ann Arbor sample and .68 for the Jackson sample (Robinson 1985). In a second study, a telephone sample of 249 respondents interviewed as part of a 1973 national panel survey were asked to report their activities for a particular "random hour" during the previous day—with no hint from the interviewer about what they had previously reported for that hour in their diary. An overall correlation of .81 was found between the two aggregate sets of data—that is, between the activities reported in the random hours and in the diary entries for those same random hours (Robinson 1985). In a third study, Juster (1985) compared the with whom reports in the 1975 diaries of respondents with those of their spouses across the same day. Juster found more than 80 percent agreement between these independently obtained husband and wife diaries about the presence or absence of their spouse during daily activities. In a separate analysis of these 1975 data, Hill found a .92 correlation between time spent on various home energy-related activities and aggregate time-of-day patterns of energy use derived from utility meters.

More recently, one of the authors has conducted preliminary studies using the "shadow" technique with student samples. The students shadow someone they know across an 8-hour period of the waking day, recording all the things each person does during that observation period. The next day, that student then asks the shadowed person for an unrehearsed diary of the same activities. Although the samples so far have been very small and highly unrepresentative, and with some highly variable individual reporting, agreement at the aggregate level on most activities across the day is usually within plus or minus 10 percent.

Other studies suggest that attendance at religious services is overreported in traditional survey questions (Hadaway, Marler, and Chaves 1993; Presser and Stinson 1998). Methodological studies in other countries also attest to the basic generalizability of time-diary data (for example, Gershuny et al. 1986; Michelson 1978). Nonetheless, a definitive well-controlled study needs to be conducted to update and extend these results.

Do Busy People Fail to Answer the Diary?

One of the controversies surrounding time-diary data collections is whether busy individuals fail to respond to the diary. This is part of a larger debate about the reliability of estimates of time use from the diary and disputed claims about whether Americans are working more (for example, Schor 1991) or less (Robinson and Godbey 1999). There is a small methodological literature on this issue which includes comparisons with the Current Population Survey (CPS) (Jacobs 1998) and other diary studies (for example, Drago et al. 1998).

Gershuny (2000) has noted that participating in a time-diary survey requires more time and effort of respondents compared to participation in other types of surveys, and that time-diary surveys in general have higher nonresponse rates than other surveys on other topics. Nonresponse bias is consequently a potential problem because busy individuals may opt out of participation in a time-diary survey—especially one that requires completion of a weekly time diary as in chapter 6. However, based on a detailed comparison of participation rates in nineteen activities for individuals from a 1987 survey who elected to participate in a weekly time-diary survey, versus individuals who elected not to, Gershuny (2000) concludes that nonresponse was not associated with an individual's activity patterns, "in particular the general state of busyness or otherwise—of sampled individuals" (268).

In comparing our time-diary samples to CPS distributions on demographic background factors, there are higher response rates for better educated, employed individuals (actually, for busier people to the extent that employment and educational attainment are correlated with being busy!). In our analysis, we construct weights to correct for nonresponse bias and produce distributions on demographic variables that approximate the CPS distributions by age, sex, race, and education. With respect to the weekly diaries in chapter 6, activity estimates from the one-day diaries (taken times seven days) are compared to the weekly estimates we obtain from each of the three subsamples for the weekly diary collections. Initial examination suggests few significant differences between the more representative sample with the one-day accounting period and the samples who filled out weekly diaries.

= Appendix B =

Additional Data Sources

Earlier Diary Surveys

There are several time-diary surveys on which to make trend comparisons. In this monograph, we draw on four national time-diary studies conducted between 1965 and 1995. Each used the general approach outlined in chapter 2, though the interviewing mode moved from personal to telephone interview and from tomorrow diaries to yesterday diaries.

1965 U.S. Time-Use Study

As part of the 1965 multinational time use study, the Survey Research Center at the University of Michigan surveyed 1,244 adult respondents, age nineteen to sixty-five, who kept a single-day diary of activities (mainly in the fall of that year). Respondents in this 1965 survey completed tomorrow diaries, that is, respondents were visited by an interviewer who explained and left the diary to be filled out for the following day and who then returned on the day after the diary day to pick up the completed diary. All respondents living in rural areas and those living in households where no one was employed were excluded (Robinson 1977). Given the sample restrictions in 1965, we compared the 1965 parent characteristics with parent characteristics from the March 1965 Current Population Survey, and its sample of parents closely approximate U.S. parent population characteristics (Sayer, Bianchi, and Robinson 2004).

1975 U.S. Time-Use Survey

In 1975, the Survey Research Center, University of Michigan, surveyed 1,519 adult respondents, age eighteen and older, who kept diaries for a single day in the fall of that year (Robinson 1976); in addition, diaries were obtained from 887 spouses of these designated respondents to increase the sample size to 2,406 respondents. In 1975, respondents were initially contacted by personal interview, and a yesterday diary was completed during the interview. These respondents became part of a panel, who were subsequently reinterviewed in the winter, spring, and summer months of 1976. About 1,500 of the original 2,406 respondents remained in this four-wave panel. Some 677 of these respondents were interviewed a second time in 1981, again across all four seasons of the year (Juster and Stafford 1985). Because of the difference in activities between those who stayed or dropped out of the panel, we use only the original sample of respondents interviewed in the fall of 1975 for most of our trend analysis. In chapter 7, we draw on various subjective assessments ascertained in the third wave of the study, and we also use the third wave in our assessment of changes in multitasking in chapter 5. For comparability with other years, the spouse diaries are excluded from our analysis.

Because the sampling frame for the 1965 study was limited to respondents age nineteen to sixty-five (in families with at least one adult in the labor force and living in urban settings) to conform to the design of the larger 1965 Multinational Time-Use Study (Converse and Robinson 1980), we compared housework and child care estimates from parents in 1965 to a 1975 subsample of parents with characteristics that matched the 1965 sampling restrictions. Comparisons indicated that trends from 1965 to 1975 were the same, regardless of whether the 1975 subsample or the full 1975 sample was used as the comparison (Bianchi et al. 2000; Sayer 2001; Sayer, Bianchi, and Robinson 2004).

A comparison of the 1965 diary study with the March 1965 Current Population Survey also indicated that the sample closely approximates U.S. parent population characteristics (see Sayer, Bianchi, and Robinson 2004). In addition, Sayer (2001) examined men's and women's time in all activities for 1965, 1975, and a 1975 subsample of respondents who matched the 1965 sampling criteria. The differences between the 1975 subsample and total sample were small for these activities, which included market work, housework, child care, shopping, personal time, and free time. The overall trends between 1965 and 1975 are therefore similar regardless of whether the 1975 total sample or subsample is the basis of comparison (see Sayer 2001, table 5.3). To increase sample size, we use the total 1975 sample of respondent diaries in our analysis. To maintain comparability over time, we do not include diaries from spouses in our 1975 analysis sample because we have no spouse diaries in any year other than 1975.

1985 U.S. Time-Use Survey

In 1985, the Survey Research Center at the University of Maryland conducted a national study in which single-day diaries were collected from more than 5,300 respondents age twelve and older. This study employed the same basic open-ended diary approach as the 1965 and 1975 national studies. An important innovation in the 1985 study was the explicit attempt to spread the collection of diary days across the entire calendar year from January through December 1985.

The 1985 study included experimentation with mode of data collection. The main data for the 1985 study were collected by a mail-back method from a sample of Americans who were first contacted by telephone using the random-digit-dial (RDD) method of selecting telephone numbers. If the respondent agreed, diaries were then mailed out for each member of the participating household, age twelve or older, to complete for a particular day for the subsequent week. After respondents had completed their time diaries, they then mailed all the completed forms back for coding and analysis.

Some 3,340 diaries from 997 households were returned using this mail-out procedure during the twelve months of 1985. The other 1985 data included parallel diary data from 808 additional respondents interviewed in a separate personal interview sample in the summer and fall of 1985, and from an additional 1,210 yesterday diaries obtained by telephone as part of the initial contact for the mail-back diaries. Before combining diaries collected with different modes, we compared the mail-back, personal interview, and telephone samples of the 1985 study, and the analyses indicated combining the samples would not alter time trends reported in subsequent chapters, with the additional beneficial effect of augmenting the sample of parents for 1985.

U.S. Time-Diary Collections in the 1990s

Two time-diary studies were conducted by the University of Maryland's Survey Research Center by national random-digit-dial telephone procedures between September 1992 and December 1995. The combined study can be viewed as conducted in two phases: the first between 1992 and 1994, with 9,386 respondents of all ages; the second in 1995, with 1,200 respondents age eighteen and older.

All interviews in both phases used the retrospective diary (or yesterday) method, in which one respondent per household reported his or her activities for the previous day. A problem with the first larger survey is that pivotal questions about family status and income were not asked, so they are not used in this volume. The second phase of the study, conducted for the Electric Power Research Institute (EPRI), used virtually the same procedures as the first phase, except that it involved only 1,200 respondents and was conducted between January 1995 and December 1995. Specific new diary features and interviewer training were implemented to produce more detailed and numerous activity accounts. However, one limitation is that questions on secondary activity were not included. The response rate for the second phase of the study was 65 percent. We use these data selectively throughout our analyses.

Other Data Sources

We also draw on a number of other data sources, such as the family composition and labor force trends that are captured each March in the nation's labor-force survey—the Current Population Survey. We analyze questions on subjective feelings about time with children, spouse, and self that were included in our National Survey of Parents, but that were also included in the 2000 General Social Survey. We included questions on the gender division of parenting in a 1999 National Omnibus Survey conducted at the Survey Research Center of the University of Maryland. Questions from two surveys on the workforce had earlier been asked in the 1977 Quality of Employment and 1997 National Survey of Changing Workforce. Finally, we analyze children's time diaries from the Child Development Supplement of the Panel Study of Income Dynamics (PSID).

March Current Population Surveys, Selected Years

The Current Population Survey (CPS), a monthly household survey of roughly 60,000 households conducted by the U.S. Census Bureau, is nationally representative and designed to provide monthly official data on unemployment. In March of each year, an annual demographic supplement is collected to provide information on family living arrangements, income and poverty. We use selected years of the March CPS data that coincide with our time-diary collections to provide information on trends in family composition and to augment our examination of parents' paid work hours in chapter 3. March CPS data for the years in which all diary studies occur are also used to construct weights that adjust for nonresponse in the diary studies and that provide weighted samples to match U.S. population characteristics in these years. The CPS data files we use are distributed by the UNICON Corporation.

The 2000 General Social Survey

The 2000 General Social Survey (GSS), conducted by the National Opinion Research Center (NORC) at the University of Chicago (Davis and Smith 2000), interviewed a national probability sample of 2,817 adults age eighteen and older, with a response rate of 70 percent. We included questions on feelings of adequacy of time with children in the 2000 GSS in order to benchmark the chapter 7 questions in the 2000 National Survey of Parents. The GSS estimates are notably similar to those presented in chapter 7 and they are analyzed extensively in Milkie et al. (2004).

1999 Omnibus Survey

This Omnibus Survey was a national probability study of 1,001 adults conducted by Computer Assisted Telephone Interviews (CATI) in the spring of 1999 at the University of Maryland's Survey Research Center. Respondents were selected using random-digit dialing (RDD) of residential telephone numbers; within each sample household, the target respondent was selected at random from among all adults residing in the household. The response rate was 56 percent. The distributions of respondents' answers on key well-being variables were within a few percentage points of the distributions of respondents' answers to similar questions from the 1996 and 2000 General Social Survey, which had a 76- and 70-percent response rate respectively. We also included questions on the gender division of labor in parenting in the 1999 Omnibus Survey, as we presented in chapter 7 in figure 7.1 These data are analyzed more extensively in Milkie et al. (2002).

The 1977 Quality of Employment Survey

The 1977 Quality of Employment Survey (QES) was conducted by the Institute for Social Research at the University of Michigan with funding by several agencies of the U.S. Department of Labor (Quinn and Staines 1979). It conducted face-to-face interviews on a national probability sample of 1,515 employed American adults age sixteen and older who were working for pay for 20 or more hours per week in 1977, with a response rate of 79 percent. We present data from this survey in table 7.1.

The 1997 National Study of the Changing Workforce

Conducted by Louis Harris and Associates for the Families and Work Institute (Bond, Galinsky, and Swanberg 1998), the 1997 National Study of the Changing Workforce (NSCW) consists of a nationally representative sample of 3,551 employed American adults age eighteen or older. The interviews were conducted by CATI with a reported response rate of 95 percent. Data from this survey are shown in table 7.1, and parents' feelings of time pressure in dual-earner families are analyzed more extensively in Kei Nomaguchi, Melissa Milkie, and Suzanne Bianchi (2005).

Panel Study of Income Dynamics–Child Development Supplement, 2002

The 2002 Child Development Supplement (CDS-II) included a collection of 2,907 child (age five to eighteen) time diaries. This study was the second panel of children's diaries, first collected in 1997 when the children were twelve years old and younger. The CDS-I interviewed 2,394 families (88-percent response rate) who provided data on 3,563 children. The CDS-II successfully reinterviewed 2,021 of these families who still met data collection eligibility with a 91-percent response rate. The CDS is part of the Panel Study of Income Dynamics (PSID), a longitudinal study of a representative sample of U.S. individuals and their residential families. These data are analyzed in chapter 8.

═ Appendix C ═

Multinational Data

TO HELP us put our U.S. data in a broader context, we review data collected by researchers from Australia, the United Kingdom, the Netherlands, Canada, and France. They are similar multivariate programs designed to identify parallel trends and predictors of child care in each country, providing more detail than could be included in chapter 9. The results in each country are discussed under three sections in this appendix:

1. Time-use trends in parental uses of time within each country

2. How demographic factors, such as age and family composition, relate to child care among parents

3. Activity differences between parents and nonparents, presumed to provide some insight into how life changes for adults with children

The regression tables and calculations underlying these narratives can be found at http://webuse.umd.edu/rosetables.

These analyses use the Multiple Classification Analysis (MCA) program of Frank Andrews et al. (1973), which is part of the ANOVA software in SPSS. MCA is unique in providing average scores for each demographic category, before and after statistical adjustment for the other predictor (independent) variables. We have edited the contributions written by each country's time-use specialist to increase comparability across countries but have retained the insights that can only come from individual researchers living in each country.

Parental Trends and Predictors in the United Kingdom: 1961 to 2002

by Jonathan Gershuny, University of Essex

As in the United States, the overall changes in time-use patterns for parents are much the same as that for the working-age adult U.K. population in general.

190

Overall Trends for Parents

We see for men a small decrease in paid work, almost balanced by a small increase in their unpaid work. For women, we find the converse: an approximate doubling of paid work (albeit from a very low initial level of less than 11 hours per week), not quite balanced by a reduction overall in unpaid work.

Unpaid Work   When we look at the various different activities within the general unpaid work category, the patterns become slightly more complex. In the case of the general housework category (which includes cooking, cleaning, and do-it-yourself odd jobs), the rise in men's unpaid time seems to be concentrated in the 1975 to 1985 period. However, this reflects an overall decline in time devoted to odd jobs over the period: men's cooking and cleaning time has risen rather continuously over the last thirty years. By contrast, women's time devoted to odd-job activities has declined from about 5 hours per day in 1961 to 3 hours per day in 2002.

For the other unpaid work categories, however, we find rises in such work time for both men and women. Men's time devoted to shopping and associated domestic travel has risen from 0.2 hours in 1961 to 0.7 hours in 2001; women's, from 0.7 of an hour to 1.2 hours. Thus, a considerable convergence is represented here, but women still do two-thirds of the total.

One major reason for the overall dramatic increase in the United Kingdom is the change in the organization of retail service provision in the United Kingdom—from a full service to a self-service basis. This particular period has seen what Britains once considered the Americanization of shopping services. Instead of the once-ubiquitous corner stores at the end of most working-class residential streets and the specialist shops (bakers, butchers, fishmongers, grocers and the like) in the local high street, we have seen the spread of ever-larger supermarkets. The ever-larger in this context implies necessarily more average distance from the consumer, hence more shopping-related travel time, and larger and longer aisles (and more customers) that lead to more in-store walking and queuing time. The more recent trend for the emergence of in-store specialist shops—paralleling those same lost local bakers, butchers, and fishmongers, each with separate queuing systems in front of the main supermarket checkouts—further adding to the increase in shopping time.

Child Care   Among parents, men's time devoted to child care, as a primary activity, rose from about 1 to 4 hours per week, and women's rose from 6 to 11 hours—thus nearly doubling for mothers and quadrupling for fathers. At the same time, mothers still do more than twice as much parenting as fathers. This increase has a number of potential explanations.

1. A defensive response to growth in perceived dangers from road traffic or abusive adults.

2. A discretionary reflection of changing societal views of parental responsibility, deriving from child care specialists who advocate child-centered parenting and from economists who advocate the rewards of parental investment in their children's educational performance.

3. An increased parental desire simply to spend time with their children, which is made easier by the reduction in the totals of paid and core domestic work.

4. Changing definitions and intensity of housework; for example, earlier reported manual washing clothes may previously have in effect hidden child care activities, which were recorded in time diaries merely as secondary activities; these can now be reported as primary child care activities, because clothes washing using an automatic machine is more episodic across interspersed periods in which that child care activity would now be reported as a primary activity.

Personal Care   Sleep and other personal care time remain roughly constant over the forty-year period, with the small overall increase here reflecting growth in time devoted to personal grooming. Time spent eating at home has declined dramatically. Daily time devoted to meals alone or with other household members has pretty much been cut in half for both sexes, thus reflecting profound changes, both in dietary practices (smaller and less elaborate meals, eaten fewer times per day) and in the organization of household co-presence (a reduction in meals as an institution for family gathering—partially replaced by the collective watching of particular television programs). Moreover, the loss of within-household sociability at mealtimes is partly compensated for by a dramatic growth in eating out in pubs or restaurants—a parallel out-of-home sociable activity also often undertaken with other household members.

Free Time   With the paid-plus-unpaid work totals and personal care hardly changed, the residual of free time has also remained roughly unchanged. An overall increase in out-of-home leisure time has been compensated for by reductions in in-home reading and visiting friends (for men) and in time devoted to visits and hobbies (such as sewing) for women. Media-related time as a primary activity has actually declined for parents over the forty-year period, with the growth of television and video watching offset by reduced radio listening.

Predictors of Child Care Time

The effects of background variables on child care time are much as expected, with younger children (under age five) receiving more than three times more child care than older children, both before and after MCA adjustment. Full-time employed parents provide only about half the child care as nonemployed parents.

In line with the expectations of economists' human capital theories, more highly-educated parents provide 10 to 20 percent more child care than the less educated. Married (or cohabiting) parents provide 15 to 30 percent more child care than single parents do, after MCA adjustment for the other predictors. Younger parents provide more child care than older parents, in large part because their children are on average younger, as indicated in the MCA results. Nonetheless, parents over age forty-five still spend roughly 30 percent less time after children's age and other predictors are taken into account.

The other MCA-adjusted values are not substantially different from the unadjusted, indicating no serious interactions among the independent variables.

Parent-Nonparent Differences

Perhaps the most remarkable observation is the generally small effect that child care responsibilities have on the rest of parental activities during the week, once one controls for other variables using MCA. Many of the original, unadjusted differences between the parental categories for both men and women disappear after account is taken of covariance among the independent variables. For example, the apparent difference in the paid work time between parents and nonparents is plainly a result of association between age of parents and educational level—with younger first-time parents being less educated, less likely to be employed, and earning less. Dramatic differences between parents and nonparents are few, indicating that the effects of extra child care by parents seem pretty well compensated by alterations distributed across other activities.

Parental Trends and Time Use
in the Netherlands: 1975 to 2000

by Andries van den Broek, Social and Cultural Planning (SCP) Office of the Netherlands

At the time of the first "current" time-use study in 1975,[1] Dutch society was still largely characterized by the male breadwinner model. The degree of the traditional gender division between paid work and unpaid work at home in postwar Netherlands was probably unmatched in the Western world.

Overall Trends for Parents: Moving Away from a Gendered Division of Tasks

Many of the shifts in the use of time that occurred in the latter quarter of the twentieth century relate to this initial gender division of labor. This shift permeated society at two levels of sociological analysis. At the micro level, people lived in nuclear families, with the father earning the family income and the mother caring for the family at home. At the meso level, many societal arrangements were tuned in to this model, such as the school system, shopping hour schedules and the absence of child care facilities. By 1975, however, this traditional gender division was being challenged, as the 1960s finally arrived in the Netherlands.

Thus many of the trends in time since 1975, and tensions related to them, are a reaction to that strong division of labor between the sexes. Dutch time trends, then, may be more telling of where Dutch society came from, than of where it is moving.

Paid Work   The move away from a gendered division of tasks is clearly revealed in certain trends in parental time use.[2] The most dramatic change is the increase in paid work of mothers, which quadrupled from 3 hours per week in 1975 to 12 hours per week in 2000. In the meantime, fathers did not cut back their paid work, but increased it by 3 hours as well. Still, fathers do much more paid work than mothers (in 2000, 39 versus 14 hours per week). Today's Dutch household thus sells far more of its time to the labor market than it did twenty-five years ago.

Unpaid Work   Fathers have also begun to spend more time on tasks at home (up almost 6 hours per week between 1975 and 2000). In contrast, mothers started spending almost 5 hours less. Taken together, this results in a fairly steady input of time into caring for the family. Insofar as there was any overall change, it was in the direction of somewhat more rather than less, because the extra input by fathers outweighed the lesser input by mothers. Still, today's mothers do far more care of the household and the children than fathers do (in 2000, 35 versus 15 hours per week).

Two important subshifts occurred. First, both fathers and mothers increased their time spent on child care by more than 2 hours a week. Second, mothers showed an 8-hour drop in housework, a drop far bigger than the 3-hour gain contributed by fathers. Taken together, this indicates that the children did not suffer from the withdrawal of mothers. Tidying the house was reduced instead.

Personal Care   Notwithstanding certain fluctuations over the years, the time spent on personal care in 2000 was roughly the same as in 1975, both for fathers and mothers, much like trends found in other countries.

Free Time   The combined effect of fathers (as well as mothers) working more and of stable personal care time was less leisure for parents of both sexes. Free time of fathers was reduced by 8 hours per week, that of mothers by 4 hours. In 2000, as a result, the average Dutch father had fewer hours of free time per week than the average mother—the reverse of 1975.

Fathers appear to cut down on hobbies by 4 hours per week, reading by 2 to 3 hours, socializing by 2 hours, and home communication by 1 hour. Several other leisure pursuits also suffered, but to a lesser degree. Offsetting these scarcities, fathers increased their time spent watching television by 1 hour and using the computer and the Internet for 2 to 3 hours. Mothers also had to cut down on leisure, with a similar direction of change: less time on hobbies (a drop of 3 hours) and reading (2 hours), but an hour more time for both television and computer use (for leisure).

The alert reader may have observed that these pluses and minuses do not exactly cancel out. One reason is a decrease in undeclared time from 2.8 hours in 1975 to 1.4 hours in 2000, a category that includes occasional missing values as well as activities that were hard to classify—such as filling out the time diary.

Predictors of Child Care Among Parents

In predicting the weekly hours of child care of Dutch fathers and mothers, both striking similarities and distinct differences are evident. Starting with similarities, the presence of babies is a far stronger predictor of child care time than the number of children, both among fathers and mothers and both before and after MCA adjustment. In line with the traditionally gendered division of labor, however, this relation is much stronger among mothers than among fathers. Other similarities are that employment status differentiates, with full-time caretakers doing 50 percent or more child care. Marital status is not a significant predictor.

The other differences relate to differences by age and education. Controlling for other variables, child's age is unrelated to the child care time of fathers, but it is an important predictor of child care time of mothers. Even after MCA adjustment for age and number of children, child care time drops from 15 or more hours for mothers age 18 to 24 to about 7 hours for those age 45 to 64 (again age of child controlled). Conversely, educational attainment matters for fathers but not for mothers, with highly educated fathers putting in 50 percent more child care than those with less education.

Predictors of Six Activities Among Parents and Nonparents

Presence of preschool children is by far the most important predictor of paid work after MCA adjustment, and more so among women than among men. Babies also are associated with 6 hours less free time (but not less television) among mothers. Less free time and television time, as well as less sleep and (a little) less paid work, are found among mothers with more children; they also report increased housework.

Fathers of babies also report (7 hours) less free time after MCA adjustment, but no less time watching television or sleeping. They report about 2 more hours of paid work as well, but no more housework. Fathers with more children have 4 hours less free time and 2 to 3 hours less television, but also do 1 to 2 fewer hours of housework.

Trends in Child Care and Parenting in Canada: 1986 to 1998

by Gilles Pronovost, Université du Quebec, Quebec, Canada

Western families have experienced tremendous changes over the last century, particularly since the end of World War II. Some even claimed it marked the death of the family as a social institution.

Overall Trends for Parents

Among the most dramatic changes are the increased rates of divorce, the emergence of more single-parent families, new living arrangements, the rise of cohabitating among younger generations, and the reduction in the number of children, among others. On this subject, a most insightful analysis comes from Lynne Casper and Suzanne Bianchi (2002), who remind us of several positive changes—such as the increased level of schooling among parents, the new role of fathers, new intergenerational relationships, the decline of gender stereotypes, and the wide access of women to the job market. The least optimistic trend is the increased poverty among a significant number of American families (see also Milardo 2001).

In this context, one might wonder if family time and child time are declining. Undoubtedly, more people feel pressed by time or perceive that they work more than in the past. Surveys show that parents strongly support the idea that they should spend more time with their children, which leads to the assumption that they assume their child time is lower than expected.

Methodology

Statistics Canada completed its third time-budget study with 10,749 persons age fifteen years and older. Data were collected evenly across all months from February 1998 to January 1999 (Statistics Canada 1999). The agency had conducted two previous surveys in 1986 and 1992, using similar but not identical methodologies across the three surveys. The Canadian General Social Survey (GSS) is a continuing program with a single survey cycle each year. The target population for the GSS excludes residents of remote territories and institutions.

Trends in Canadian Parents' Use of Time   Canadian fathers decreased their weekly time at work (including travel) by 2 hours between 1986 and 1998, and mothers increased theirs by about 6 hours—due mainly to increased proportions of mothers who worked. The gender gap for paid work time is still strong, with employed fathers doing almost 10 hours more weekly paid work than employed mothers. However, among working mothers, the working week averaged about 75 percent that of working fathers in 1986 and that rose to 80 percent in 1998.

Among mothers, housework, including cooking time, remained about the same, but fathers increased their housework by 50 percent, or 4 hours a week. Men in 1998 did 60 percent of the housework of women compared to 38 percent in 1986 twelve years earlier. Shopping time decreased 10 to 15 percent for fathers and mothers, or close to an hour less per week. After some increase during the 1980s, child care decreased about an hour per week for mothers; there was a slow but steady increase for working fathers.

Whereas sleep time remained rather constant and about equal for mothers and fathers, grooming and other personal care time dropped 1 to 2 hours for fathers and closer to 4 hours among mothers.

The result is that total free time stayed rather constant across time, with mothers having 1 to 2 hours more free time per week, slowly approaching what fathers have. The age group that most clearly entered the so-called leisure society were retirees, whose total leisure time was 64 hours per week. That is close to 30 more hours than among the employed population age eighteen to sixty-four, and comparisons with France and Quebec show much the same pattern (Pronovost 2002).

Two other free-time patterns can be pointed out. The first deals with the increases in fitness and sociability over the previous decade. Contrary to the widely accepted assumption in Canada, people spend more time with others—in the range of about 1 hour more a week among mothers. The other pattern refers to the decline in the mass media consumption among both fathers and mothers. Until the 1980s, the increase in leisure time was mainly a function of more television watching. This is no longer the case, as a significant decline of 10 percent in viewing is found. In twelve years, the decline among the working population age eighteen to sixty-four is down from 47 percent to 40 percent of the total free time for fathers, and from 40 percent to 32 percent for mothers. What do people mainly do with this extra time? They socialize and engage more frequently in sport and fitness activities.

Trends in Child Care Time   Child care refers to the presence or absence of children in the family, including a small amount observed among grandmothers and grandfathers or among other members of the extended family. Since 1986, employed fathers have continuously increased their primary activity time for their children from 4.9 to 5.8 hours a week and employed mothers have reduced theirs to about 7 hours in 1998 (after an increase from 6.6 to 7.7 hours between 1986 and 1992). The result is a dramatic decrease in the gap between working men's and women's time on child care. The same increase followed by a decrease pattern also applies for nonworking mothers.

In other words, even if demographic data show a reduction of the mean number of children per family, this did not mean much of a decrease in time devoted to child care. However, one still observes less differentiation between working fathers and mothers, particularly if the mother is employed.

One significant factor, of course, is the presence of young children. Employed men and housewives spend twice as much time in child care when there are young children, and working mothers spend three times more. That is to say that the total time devoted to preschool children (five years old and younger) in Canada amounts to 11 hours a week for working fathers, 16 hours for working mothers, and 26 hours for nonworking mothers.

Many of the same trends and differences are found for total time spent with children, which is up to three times higher than primary activity time. Time spent with young children is almost double that for older children for both mothers and fathers. Consistent with primary activity time, the with-child data show enough of a decrease in 1998 that it is now lower in 1998 than in 1986 (after an increase between 1986 and 1992). This is counter to what is found in the American data.

With a measurement of family time as provided by the Statistics Canada data, that is, time spent with any member of the family, whatever the activity and without double counting, one can observe some decrease in family time between 1992 and 1998 (unfortunately with no comparable data for 1986). This family time does remain higher in families with young children, by 6 to 17 hours per week. Time with spouse shows the same pattern. About half of family time is spent with spouse and children together; the fathers spend about 65 percent of their family time with both, and mothers about 40 percent—meaning, of course, that mothers spend more of their family time alone with children. With respect to the activities involved, the family time of women is higher than for men with children only if some housework or child care is involved. These differences almost disappear during free time activities.

Associated Parental Background Variables

For both primary activity child care and time with child, the increase is not linear according to the number of children or their ages. The important breaking point is, obviously, between having or not having a preschooler—and having more than one, with the MCA showing a 7-hour difference in child care among mothers having two preschoolers versus just one, while the total number of children of any age makes only a 1-hour difference in having one or two. Child care time doubles in families with one preschooler, and it increases notably again with two of them, for both mothers and fathers. Although the total number of children of all ages does not show the same dramatic differences in time with a child, there is a notable increase from two to three or more children.

With respect to the other background variables, employment status appears to be the most significant predictor for the unemployed. After MCA adjustment, nonemployed women spent 5 hours more in child care and 8 hours more in time with a child compared with those who were employed. These differences are 3 and 10 hours, respectively, for nonworking fathers. Even if the increase is less dramatic, working part-time has more effect on child time for men than for women. These data again reflect the importance of child time among housewives.

Age is also a significant predictor, particularly being between the ages of eighteen and thirty-four, also of course reflecting the impact of having young children. As noted, child time is at its peak among young families, and is reduced significantly among older parents. In young families, child care is about 2 to 3 hours a week more among mothers (after MCA adjustment) and 4 to 5 hours more among fathers. Here again, one can observe a very interesting pattern in the increased role of men in child care. As in other countries, older (forty-five and up) parents spend dramatically less time caring for children, even after MCA adjustments for age and number of children.

The other background variables play a more minor role. College education adds just 1 hour a week of child care time for both men and women. A more complex situation is found for marital status, perhaps because of the mix of single and common-law married respondents in the 1998 survey (particularly among Quebecers, where a majority of young families now live in common law marriages). It may also be that some separated persons, formerly living in common law marriages, describe themselves as never married. One consequence is that we observe in Canada an increase in adjusted differences among single mothers in child care time, and notably higher time with children among those never married.

Canadian Parents Versus Nonparents in Uses of Time

Regarding work hours, having preschoolers, for mothers, shows a significant reduction in working hours of 4 to 6 hours less than other mothers after MCA adjustment. Fathers of preschoolers also report lower work hours after MCA adjustment, but more hours before adjustment. Number of children shows an interesting pattern, with women reducing their working time if there are three or more children in the family, men if there are two. If parents have one baby, however, both men and women show reductions of about four working hours; if they have two preschoolers, women will reduce work hours some 50 percent more. That probably means that with two children men tend to share some of the family load, but if there are three or more, men tend to increase their work time and women tend to stay at home.

Housework hours increase for mothers and fathers (but more consistently for mothers), with more and younger children. After MCA adjustment, only the 5 or more hours increase for women with three plus children stands out. Regarding sleep, outside of mothers with three or more children reporting 4 hours less sleep, no other differences by presence of children are significant. For television, having children or preschoolers is a significant predictor of lower viewing hours, particularly as the number of children increases. Finally, for overall free time, parents having more children or babies have less free time, though the original 7- to 13-hour differences are reduced to 3 to 5 hours after MCA adjustment for employment status and age.

Parental Trends and Predictors in France: 1965 to 1999

by Laurent Lesnard and Alain Chenu, Observatoire sociologique du changement (Sciences-po and CNRS) and CREST–Laboratoire de sociologie quantitative (INSEE) (France)

The overall changes in time-use patterns for French parents are very similar to those observed in the United States or the United Kingdom, with the dramatic exception of child care.

Overall Trends for Parents

As in the rest of the developed countries (Gershuny 2000), in France we find a gender convergence in paid and unpaid work time as well as in leisure. Television has also invaded French lives, almost doubling across more than three decades to reach 14 hours a week for men and 11.5 hours for women in 1999.

The gender convergence in paid work time is also dramatic. Not only did their labor force participation rate rise from 58 percent in 1975 to 80 percent in 2003, but French women age twenty-five to forty-nine also flooded the labor market, many holding full-time jobs while raising children (Maruani 2000). Indeed, the focus of the first two time-use French surveys, carried out by the French Institute of Demography (INED) in 1947 and 1958, was on women, because both workers and children were needed after World War II. Thus the main goal of these surveys was to help the French governments overcome the problems of combining motherhood and paid work for women. The social policies that followed provided strong public support for families: contrary to most developed countries, children are placed in special schools from the age of three, with long school opening hours.

France's family-friendly policies were not inspired by the gender egalitarian ideals prominent in Sweden, but were more mundane—in the service of increasing the birth rate—hence the public visibility of children. The policies have been, nonetheless, quite successful in terms of France's high fertility rate (for a developed country) that accompanied the high labor force participation rate of women. These fertility and economic development policies explain to a certain extent the dramatic decrease in the child care time of mothers that can be observed between 1965 and 1985. The link between welfare regimes and family time remains yet largely unknown, but Sally Pacholok and Anne Gauthier (2004) found a similar result for Sweden: Canadian mothers spend more time with their children than Swedish mothers. Strong public support of families helps parents to balance their daily lives. Contrary to liberal-oriented countries, children are not only a private matter and consequently, children are less central to couples' daily lives.

Child care time thus stopped falling in the 1980s, almost a decade after the turnarounds in the United States and the United Kingdom. This period has also been marked by the deregulation of part-time employment, until then highly regulated and very uncommon. Since then, women's part-time employment steadily increased to a 30 percent plateau. It is also the case that from the early 1980s single parenting increased—from 3 percent then to 7 percent by the end of the 1990s.

Structural factors thus explain only a part of these parental trends. An analysis for France—parallel to that of Sayer, Bianchi, and Robinson (2004) for the United States—would probably show considerable behavioral change. Otherwise, the increase observed between 1985 and 1998 would remain unexplained because part-time work is far from being always family friendly, especially when it is imposed by firms in search of flexibility. Moreover, father time has increased since the 1980s by 1 more hour per week, a highly significant increase given the earlier low parental involvement of French fathers. This increase is more pronounced for more educated fathers, whose work days were also substantially longer. Thus, although French parents can count on the public provision of quality child care facilities, they have increased the time they devote to their children.

Overall, then, fathers' paid work hours declined more than 10 hours between the 1960s and the 1980s, and mothers' work hours rose by 7. At the same time, fathers' housework and shopping time increased by 7 hours, and mothers' decreased by more than 7. Personal care rose by about 2 hours, mainly a result of longer meals. Free time also showed a slight increase, for men, within which the 80 to 90 percent increase (5 or more hours) in television viewing was offset by declines in reading, radio, visiting, and fitness activity. Whereas the child care time of French women was about 30 percent less in 1998 than in 1965, among fathers it was about 15 percent higher in 1998.

Thus the recent small rise in French mothers' time with children, combined with the increase in employment suggest that behavioral change has countered family change brought about by extensive public child care provisions (as earlier in the United States). Even if the decline in mothers' time with children has been more pronounced and lasted longer in France than in the United States or the United Kingdom, both public and parent support of children has increased in France—especially at-home support since the mid-1980s.

Predictors of Child Care Time

As in the United States, the crucial determinant of time spent with children is the presence and number of preschoolers (or children younger than three in the latest diary survey in France). Fathers spend 20 minutes a day with their children when there are no preschoolers, but almost 90 minutes when there are at least two preschoolers. The effect is unsurprisingly more pronounced for women at 54 and 193 minutes, respectively.

Education is also a significant predictor of parental time for mothers and fathers. More educated mothers spend 20 minutes more daily with their children than those with no completed secondary education. The increase is 10 minutes for fathers, also a significant figure given their lower daily parental investment. When controlling for other factors, part-time work does not make a big difference in mothers' time with children: only 8 minutes a day. Mothers who are not employed spend 40 minutes more a day with children than those who are employed full-time.

Parent-Nonparent Differences

In comparing parents with nonparents, much greater differences are found for mothers than for fathers. Mothers report not only far more housework than women without children, but have far less free time as well. With preschool children, there is not only dramatically less free time and paid work, but less housework as well. In contrast, the only significant difference for fathers is their increased child care, especially if the child is younger than three years old.

= Appendix D =

Tables

Table 3A.1 Labor Force Status of Parents in Households with Children Under Age Eighteen

	1965	1970	1975	1980	1985	1990	1995	2000
Total percentage	100.0	100.0	100.0	100.0	100.0	100.0	100.0	100.0
Two parents	90.3	87.4	82.4	78.4	75.2	73.6	70.6	69.7
Father sole earner	57.0	49.4	41.4	32.9	27.9	23.7	20.7	20.7
Mother sole earner	2.4	2.9	4.4	4.5	4.3	5.0	4.9	4.2
Dual earner	23.9	28.3	27.4	34.3	36.3	39.4	40.0	40.9
Neither	6.9	6.8	9.3	6.8	6.6	5.4	5.1	3.8
Single mother	8.8	11.1	15.4	18.6	20.7	21.6	23.4	23.4
Employed	4.4	5.5	7.5	10.3	11.2	12.5	13.8	16.1
Nonemployed	4.4	5.6	7.9	8.2	9.5	9.2	9.7	7.2
Single father	0.9	1.5	2.2	3.0	4.1	4.8	5.9	6.9
Employed	0.7	1.2	1.5	2.2	3.0	3.7	4.4	5.4
Nonemployed	0.2	0.4	0.7	0.8	1.1	1.2	1.4	1.5
Sample size (N)	(11,048)	(21,790)	(19,496)	(27,102)	(23,521)	(22,621)	(21,705)	(19,013)

Source: Authors' tabulations from the 1965, 1970, 1975, 1980, 1985, 1990, 1995, and 2000 March Current Population Surveys.
Note: Universe restricted to parents who are householders.

Table 3A.2 Joint Labor Market Status in Two-Parent Families with Children

	1970	1975	1980	1985	1990	1995	2000
With children under eighteen							
Total	100.0	100.0	100.0	100.0	100.0	100.0	100.0
Dual earner	34.3	35.3	46.1	50.7	55.8	58.6	60.8
Both full-time (35 or more hours)	18.8	18.5	25.3	28.7	32.3	33.0	37.0
Mother part-time, father full-time	13.2	14.0	17.2	18.2	19.3	20.2	19.1
Father part-time, mother full-time	1.2	1.5	1.7	2.1	2.3	2.9	2.6
Both part-time	1.1	1.4	2.0	1.7	1.9	2.5	2.2
Father sole earner	55.8	50.2	41.0	36.4	31.7	28.8	29.1
Mother sole earner	3.2	5.0	5.5	5.6	6.6	6.7	5.8
Neither	6.8	9.4	7.3	7.3	6.0	5.9	4.2
Sample size (N)	(16,130)	(13,728)	(18,384)	(15,765)	(15,257)	(14,315)	(12,215)
With children under six							
Total	100.0	100.0	100.0	100.0	100.0	100.0	100.0
Dual earner	24.7	26.6	37.4	43.9	49.2	53.6	53.8
Both full-time (35 or more)	12.1	13.0	19.2	23.4	26.6	28.5	30.5
Mother part-time, father full-time	10.8	11.3	15.2	17.0	18.7	20.2	19.1
Father part-time, mother full-time	0.9	1.0	1.2	2.0	2.0	2.4	2.1
Both part-time	0.9	1.3	1.7	1.6	1.9	2.5	2.1
Father sole earner	64.8	59.7	51.0	44.0	39.1	35.3	37.3
Mother sole earner	1.8	4.0	3.9	4.8	5.3	5.1	4.6
Neither	8.7	9.7	7.8	7.3	6.4	6.0	4.2
Sample size (N)	(6,914)	(5,590)	(7,422)	(6,909)	(6,834)	(6,192)	(5,109)

Source: Authors' tabulations from the 1970, 1975, 1980, 1985, 1990, 1995, and 2000 March Current Population Surveys.
Note: Universe restricted to all couples who are householders between the ages of twenty-five and fifty-four.

Table 3A.3 Joint Labor Market Hours in Families with Children Under Age Eighteen

	1965	1970	1975	1980	1985	1990	1995	2000
Two-parent families								
Mean joint hours	52.1	53.3	51.3	56.0	58.4	61.1	62.4	64.4
Father's hours	41.7	41.1	38.2	39.0	39.4	39.8	39.9	41.0
Mother's hours	10.4	12.2	13.1	17.0	19.0	21.4	22.5	23.4
Percentage 80 or more hours per week	18.2	20.2	19.5	26.0	30.0	33.7	35.2	38.3
Percentage 100 or more hours per week	3.6	3.5	3.7	4.9	5.8	7.1	7.9	7.8
Dual earner (percentage)	28.0	34.3	35.3	46.1	50.7	55.8	59.0	60.8
Mean joint hours	80.0	78.3	77.2	77.7	78.8	79.6	80.0	80.5
Father's hours	46.2	45.8	44.8	44.9	45.2	45.6	45.7	45.5
Mother's hours	33.7	32.5	32.4	32.8	33.6	34.1	34.2	35.1
Percentage 80 or more hours per week	59.5	54.9	52.1	54.5	57.3	59.4	58.9	62.1
Percentage 100 or more hours per week	13.0	10.3	10.4	10.6	11.4	12.8	13.5	12.9
Father sole earner (percentage)	62.5	55.8	50.2	41.0	36.4	31.7	28.8	29.1
Father's hours	46.1	45.5	44.4	44.5	45.2	45.3	45.6	45.6
Percentage 40 or more hours per week	89.9	88.5	86.0	87.3	88.1	88.7	84.4	86.8
Percentage 50 or more hours per week	29.7	29.3	27.2	28.0	31.8	33.8	35.7	36.4
Sample size (N)	(8,524)	(16,130)	(13,728)	(18,384)	(15,765)	(15,257)	(14,315)	(12,215)

(Table continues on p. 208.)

Table 3A.3 Joint Labor Market Hours in Families with Children Under Age Eighteen (*continued*)

	1965	1970	1975	1980	1985	1990	1995	2000
Total single mothers								
Mean hours	19.0	20.0	19.1	23.4	22.9	24.9	24.3	28.5
Percentage 40 or more hours per week	33.2	33.4	31.1	40.2	38.8	43.2	39.2	47.5
Percentage 50 or more hours per week	4.2	4.4	3.1	5.6	6.2	8.4	8.1	8.6
Sample size (N)	(858)	(1,854)	(2,279)	(3,816)	(3,737)	(3,840)	(3,971)	(3,418)
Total single fathers								
Mean hours	34.9	39.8	34.1	35.2	34.4	36.1	34.5	35.9
Percentage 40 or more hours per week	69.8	79.0	64.9	65.8	66.2	69.9	65.2	67.1
Percentage 50 or more hours per week	25.1	24.2	19.1	20.5	21.8	20.8	18.5	23.0
Sample size (N) (220) (303)	(587)	(750)	(846)	(1,005)	(1,060)			

Source: Authors' tabulations from the 1965, 1970, 1975, 1980, 1985, 1990, 1995, and 2000 March Current Population Surveys.
Note: Universe restricted to all parents who are householders between the ages of twenty-five and fifty-four.

Table 4A.1   Parents' Enjoyment of Various Activities

	Married Fathers		Married Mothers	
	Third Wave		Third Wave	
	1975	2000	1975	2000
Average rating of activity				
Taking care of children	9.2	9.0	8.5	9.3*
N	(152)	(407)	(136)	(505)
Playing with children	8.3	9.0*	8.5	9.2*
N	(149)	(407)	(135)	(498)
Talking with children	9.4	9.2*	8.9	9.6*
N	(155)	(408)	(138)	(505)
Taking children places	8.9	8.8	8.8	8.9
N	(155)	(407)	(137)	(505)
Percentage rating parenting activity a 10				
Taking care of children	63.8	50.6*	43.4	64.0*
N	(152)	(407)	(136)	(505)
Playing with children	47.7	55.8	45.9	65.3*
N	(149)	(407)	(135)	(498)
Talking with children	68.4	58.6*	52.9	77.0*
N	(155)	(408)	(138)	(505)
Taking children places	63.2	54.1*	54.7	52.3
N	(155)	(407)	(137)	(505)

Source: Authors' calculations from the third wave of the 1975–76 Time Use in Economic and Social Accounts and the 2000 National Survey of Parents.
Note: Rating of 10 on a 10-point scale means parents "enjoy a great deal."
*Difference between 2000 and 1975 statistically significant at p < 0.05.

Table 5A.1   Time Use Trends of Mothers, Hours per Week

Activity	All Mothers					Married					Single				
	1965	1975	1985	1995	2000	1965	1975	1985	1995	2000	1965	1975	1985	1995	2000
Total paid work	9.3	16.1	20.9	25.7	25.3	6.0	15.2	19.7	24.9	23.8	28.4	18.9	24.5	27.7	28.9
Work	8.4	14.9	18.8	23.4	22.8	5.5	14.1	17.8	22.7	21.4	25.5	17.2	21.9	25.1	26.1
Commute	0.9	1.2	2.1	2.3	2.5	0.5	1.1	1.9	2.2	2.4	2.9	1.7	2.6	2.6	2.8
Family care	49.5	37.9	36.2	36.0	39.8	52.7	39.9	39.7	40.5	41.1	30.8	31.9	25.8	25.8	36.7
Housework	31.9	23.6	20.4	18.9	18.6	34.5	25.2	22.5	21.6	19.4	16.8	19.0	14.4	12.7	16.8
Child care	10.2	8.6	8.4	9.6	12.6	10.6	8.8	9.3	11.0	12.9	7.5	8.0	5.8	6.4	11.8
Shopping-services	7.4	5.6	7.3	7.5	8.6	7.6	5.9	7.9	7.9	8.8	6.5	4.9	5.5	6.6	8.2
Personal care	74.4	76.3	74.9	71.8	71.3	73.6	75.8	74.5	71.2	71.5	79.4	77.6	76.0	73.1	70.9
Sleep	55.4	58.4	56.3	57.8	54.7	54.8	57.9	56.3	57.2	54.8	59.4	59.8	56.3	59.1	54.5
Meal	8.9	8.7	6.4	4.9	7.3	9.0	9.0	6.7	5.3	7.8	8.5	7.9	5.5	4.1	6.3
Grooming	10.1	9.2	12.2	9.0	9.3	9.8	8.9	11.5	8.7	8.9	11.5	10.0	14.2	9.9	10.2
Total free time	34.8	37.7	36.0	34.4	31.6	35.7	37.1	34.1	31.3	31.7	29.4	39.6	41.5	41.5	31.4
Education	0.7	1.2	1.5	2.8	2.3	0.5	0.6	0.8	2.5	2.2	1.7	3.3	3.5	3.5	2.5
Religion	1.1	2.3	1.7	0.7	1.3	1.2	2.6	1.6	0.7	1.3	0.7	1.3	2.0	0.8	1.2

Organizations	1.4	1.9	1.0	0.7	0.6	1.5	2.2	1.1	0.8	0.6	0.5	1.0	0.7	0.3	0.8
Event	1.2	0.8	0.9	1.9	1.4	0.7	0.9	0.9	1.8	1.4	4.0	0.5	0.9	2.1	1.4
Visiting	9.0	6.8	6.2	6.8	6.1	9.3	6.4	5.7	5.1	6.4	7.1	8.0	7.4	10.6	5.4
Fitness	0.6	0.8	1.4	1.6	1.4	0.5	1.0	1.5	1.7	1.4	0.7	0.2	1.2	1.5	1.4
Hobby	2.8	2.9	2.4	1.2	1.6	3.0	3.0	2.7	1.1	1.7	1.0	2.6	1.8	1.3	1.5
Television	10.3	14.1	13.7	12.5	11.5	10.5	13.4	12.9	11.1	11.2	9.3	16.1	16.1	15.7	12.3
Reading	3.4	2.6	2.3	2.1	1.4	3.8	2.9	2.5	2.6	1.5	1.2	1.8	1.7	1.0	1.3
Stereo	0.3	0.4	0.3	0.0	0.2	0.3	0.2	0.2	0.0	0.1	0.6	0.9	0.6	0.0	0.3
Communication	4.0	3.9	4.6	4.1	3.8	4.3	3.8	4.3	3.9	4.0	2.6	3.9	5.5	4.7	3.4
Total	168.0	168.0	168.0	168.0	168.0	168.0	168.0	168.0	168.0	168.0	168.0	168.0	168.0	168.0	168.0
Sample size (N)	(417)	(369)	(903)	(307)	(999)	(358)	(278)	(673)	(198)	(700)	(59)	(91)	(230)	(109)	(299)

Source: Authors' calculations from the 1965–66 Americans' Use of Time Study; the 1975–76 Time Use in Economic and Social Accounts; 1985 Americans' Use of Time; the 1995 Electric Power Research Institute (EPRI) Study; and the combined file of the 1998–99 Family Interaction, Social Capital and Trends in Time Use Study and the 2000 National Survey of Parents.

Table 5A.2 Time Use Trends of Fathers, Hours per Week

Activity	All Fathers					Married					Single				
	1965	1975	1985	1995	2000	1965	1975	1985	1995	2000	1965	1975	1985	1995	2000
Total paid work	46.4	45.4	39.8	39.5	41.8	47.8	47.2	42.5	39.8	42.5	31.8	15.4	24.9	38.4	36.7
Work	42.0	41.4	35.7	35.1	37.0	43.3	43.1	38.1	35.1	37.5	29.2	12.6	22.7	35.3	33.3
Commute	4.3	4.0	4.1	4.4	4.8	4.5	4.1	4.4	4.8	5.0	2.6	2.8	2.3	3.1	3.4
Family care	11.9	12.3	17.8	18.7	21.9	12.3	12.0	18.9	20.9	21.5	8.3	16.2	11.6	11.9	25.1
Housework	4.4	6.0	10.2	10.2	10.0	4.4	5.6	10.7	10.9	9.7	4.6	12.5	7.1	8.0	12.4
Child care	2.5	2.6	2.6	4.2	6.8	2.6	2.7	3.0	5.0	6.5	1.7	1.5	0.5	1.8	9.2
Shopping-services	5.1	3.7	5.0	4.3	5.1	5.3	3.8	5.2	5.0	5.3	2.1	2.2	3.9	2.1	3.5
Personal care	74.7	74.7	73.5	67.0	69.3	73.4	74.1	72.9	66.7	69.5	88.8	85.1	76.7	67.7	67.2
Sleep	55.7	56.7	55.1	53.0	53.8	54.7	56.1	54.5	53.4	54.2	66.2	66.1	58.6	51.9	51.0
Meal	10.5	10.5	6.9	6.5	7.8	10.6	10.4	7.2	5.9	7.9	9.4	12.1	5.4	8.3	7.3
Grooming	8.5	7.6	11.4	7.5	7.6	8.0	7.6	11.2	7.5	7.5	13.2	6.9	12.8	7.5	8.8
Total free time	35.0	35.7	36.9	42.9	35.0	34.5	34.7	33.7	40.5	34.5	39.1	51.3	54.7	50.0	39.1
Education	1.2	1.2	1.6	2.2	3.1	1.0	1.2	0.5	1.6	3.1	2.9	1.7	8.1	4.0	3.1
Religion	1.2	1.3	0.8	0.5	1.5	1.1	1.3	0.8	0.6	1.6	1.9	0.4	1.0	0.4	0.7

Organizations	1.0	1.0	1.0	0.5	0.9	1.1	1.1	1.1	0.4	0.8	0.4	0.1	0.8	0.8	1.0
Event	0.8	0.7	1.0	1.5	1.4	0.6	0.4	0.8	1.1	1.4	1.8	6.3	1.7	2.7	1.0
Visiting	8.2	6.7	6.1	7.2	4.8	7.7	6.1	4.8	6.6	4.7	13.9	15.1	13.5	9.0	6.2
Fitness	1.3	2.0	2.9	7.1	2.4	1.4	1.7	2.5	7.2	2.3	0.1	6.6	5.2	6.9	3.1
Hobby	1.2	2.4	2.3	3.9	1.7	1.3	2.2	2.4	4.1	1.6	0.0	5.3	1.7	3.2	2.4
Television	13.4	14.7	15.0	15.0	14.5	13.6	14.9	14.9	13.9	14.2	10.4	11.1	15.7	18.4	16.8
Reading	4.2	2.7	2.2	1.8	1.1	4.0	2.7	2.4	2.0	1.1	5.7	1.5	1.2	1.4	1.2
Stereo	0.6	0.4	0.5	0.1	0.2	0.7	0.4	0.3	0.1	0.1	0.0	0.4	1.2	0.1	0.7
Communication	2.0	2.5	3.5	2.9	3.6	2.0	2.5	3.3	2.9	3.7	1.9	2.7	4.7	3.2	2.8
Total	168.0	168.0	168.0	168.0	168.0	168.0	168.0	168.0	168.0	168.0	168.0	168.0	168.0	168.0	168.0
Sample size (N)	(343)	(251)	(693)	(180)	(632)	(326)	(239)	(583)	(133)	(550)	(17)	(12)	(110)	(47)	(82)

Source: Authors' calculations from the 1965–66 Americans' Use of Time Study; the 1975–76 Time Use in Economic and Social Accounts; 1985 Americans' Use of Time; the 1995 Electric Power Research Institute (EPRI) Study; and the combined file of the 1998–99 Family Interaction, Social Capital and Trends in Time Use Study and the 2000 National Survey of Parents.

Table 5A.3 Activity Classification

Work
Total work time, without commute. Includes:
Time spent on main job
Time spent on unemployment
Time spent on travel during work
Time spent on second job
Time spent on breaks at work
Commute
Time spent on travel to and from work
Total work
Total work, commute and education

Housework
Total time doing housework. Includes:
Time spent on food preparation
Time spent on food clean-up
Time spent on cleaning house
Time spent on outdoor cleaning
Time spent on clothes care
Time spent on car repair and maintenance (by respondent)
Time spent on other repair (done by the respondent)
Time spent on plant care
Time spent on animal care
Time spent on other household work

Child care
Total child care. Includes:
Time spent on baby care
Time spent on child care
Time spent on helping and teaching
Time spent on talking and reading
Time spent on indoor playing
Time spent on medical for child
Time spent on other child care

Shopping-services
Total shopping and using services. Includes:
Time spent on shopping for food
Time spent on shopping for clothes and household items
Time spent on personal care services
Time spent at medical appointment
Time spent on government and financial services
Time spent on car repair services
Time spent on other repair services
Time spent on other services
Time spent on errands
Time spent on travel related to obtaining goods and services

Family
Sum of Housework, Child care, and Shopping

Sleep
Time spent sleeping or napping

Meal
Eating, Includes:
Time spent eating
Time spent on meals or snacks at work

Grooming
Time spent on showering and bathing
Time spent on medical care
Time spent on help and care
Time spent on personal hygiene and grooming
Time spent on resting
Time spent on dressing
Time spent on other private activities
Time spent on travel related to personal care

Personal care
Sum of Sleep, Meal, and Grooming

Education

Total education time. Includes:
- Time spent attending full-time school
- Time spent on other classes
- Time spent on other education
- Time spent on email
- Time spent on homework
- Time spent using library
- Time spent using the internet
- Time spent playing PC or video games
- Time spent on other PC use
- Time spent on education related travel

Religion
- Time spent with religious groups
- Time spent on religious practices (weddings)

Organizations
- Time spent at professional and union organizations
- Time spent at special interest organizations
- Time spent at political and civic organizations
- Time spent at volunteer and helping organizations
- Time spent at fraternal organizations
- Time spent at child, youth or family organizations
- Time spent at other organizations
- Time spent on travel related to organizations

Event
- Time spent on entertainment
- Time spent on movies and videos
- Time spent at theater
- Time spent at museums or art

Visiting
- Time spent on visiting and social activities
- Time spent at parties and other social activities
- Time spent at bars and lounges
- Time spent on travel related to social activities

Fitness
- Time spent on active sports
- Time spent outdoors
- Time spent on walking or hiking

Hobby
- Time spent on exercise
- Time spent on hobbies
- Time spent on domestic craft
- Time spent on doing art
- Time spent on music, drama or dance
- Time spent on games
- Time spent on travel related to recreation

Television
- Time spent watching Television

Reading
- Time spent reading books
- Time spent reading magazines
- Time spent reading newspaper

Stereo
- Time spent listening to radio
- Time spent listening to records and tapes

Communication
- Time spent in household conversation
- Time spent thinking and relaxing
- Time spent on travel related to passive leisure

Total free
- Sum of Education, Religion, Organizations, Events, Visiting, Fitness, Hobby, Television, Reading, Stereo, and Communication

Source: Authors' derivation (Szalai 1972).

Table 5A.4   Hours per Week Multitasking

	1975	1975 First Wave[a]	1975 Third Wave	2000
	Married Fathers			
Multitasking (excluding all primary freetime activities)	3.7	4.1	3.8	8.7[c]
Multitasking (excluding time when both secondary and primary activities are free time)	30.4	30.9	36.7[b]	59.4[c]
All multitasking (all time where a secondary activity is reported)	39.4	40.2	55.9[b]	78.3[c]
Sample size (N)	(239)	(164)	(162)	(550)
	Married Mothers			
Multitasking (excluding all primary freetime activities)	7.7	7.5	8.5	14.6[c]
Multitasking (excluding time when both secondary and primary activities are free time)	32.4	33.9	41.6[b]	64.1[c]
All multitasking (all time where a secondary activity is reported)	41.8	43.2	59.3[b]	80.6[c]
Sample size (N)	(278)	(199)	(192)	(700)
	Single Mothers			
Multitasking (excluding all primary freetime activities)	6.2	6.8	6.3	12.6[c]
Multitasking (excluding time when both secondary and primary activities are free time)	30.1	33.2	34.7	62.1[c]
All multitasking (all time where a secondary activity is reported)	39.4	44.1	54.7[b]	78.9[c]
Sample size (N)	(91)	(55)	(53)	(299)

Source: Authors' calculations from the first and third wave of the 1975–76 Time Use in Economic and Social Accounts and the combined file of the 1998–99 Family Interaction, Social Capital and Trends in Time Use Study and the 2000 National Survey of Parents.
a. Only respondents who stayed through third wave.
b. First wave of 1975 (all first wave respondents) differs from 2000, $p < 0.05$.
c. Third wave of 1975 differs from 2000, $p < 0.05$.

Table 5A.5   Leisure Activity Classification

Category	Activity
Social leisure	Socializing with friends and neighbors
	Eating meals with friends and neighbors
	Attending sports and other events with friends or family
	Attending movies and videos with friends or family
	Attending the theater or museum with friends or family
	Attending parties with friends or family
	Going to bars and lounges with friends or family
	Engaging in outdoor recreation with friends or family
	Exercising with friends or family
	Doing hobbies with friends or family
	Doing domestic crafts with friends or family
	Performing music, drama and dance with friends or family
	Playing games with friends or family
	Engaging in other recreation with friends or family
	Having conversations with friends or family
	Letter writing
Civic leisure	Professional or union participation
	Political or civic group participation
	Volunteer group participation
	Religious participation
	Other group participation
Active leisure	Exercising alone
	Doing hobbies alone
	Doing domestic crafts alone
	Performing or making art alone
	Performing music, drama or dance alone
	Playing games alone
	Engaging in other recreation alone
Passive leisure	Listening to the radio, records, or tapes
	Watching television
	Reading books, magazines, newspapers
	Thinking or relaxing

Source: Sayer (2001).

Table 5A.6   Mothers' Hours Per Week Spent in Primary Activities

	1975			2000		
	All	Employed	Non-employed	All	Employed	Non-employed
Total paid work + family care	54.0	63.3	46.5	65.1	70.7	51.8[abc]
Total paid work	16.1	35.9	0.1	25.3	35.7	0.4[abc]
Work	14.9	33.1	0.1	22.8	32.2	0.3[abc]
Commute	1.2	2.7	0.0	2.5	3.5	0.1[abc]
Family care	37.9	27.4	46.3	39.8	35.0	51.4[ab]
Housework	23.6	17.1	28.9	18.6	16.1	24.6[abc]
Child care	8.6	6.0	10.7	12.6	10.6	17.2[abc]
Shopping	5.6	4.3	6.7	8.6	8.2	9.6[a]
Personal care	76.3	75.1	77.2	71.3	69.7	75.2[b]
Sleep	58.4	56.7	59.7	54.7	53.4	57.8[abc]
Meal	8.7	8.4	8.9	7.3	7.2	7.7[c]
Grooming	9.2	10.1	8.5	9.3	9.1	9.8
Total free time	37.7	29.6	44.3	31.6	27.7	41.0[abc]
Education	1.2	1.3	1.2	2.3	1.7	3.8[bc]
Religion	2.3	1.7	2.7	1.3	0.8	2.3[bc]
Organizations	1.9	1.4	2.3	0.6	0.5	1.0[bc]
Event	0.8	1.4	0.3	1.4	1.6	0.8[ab]
Visiting	6.8	5.3	8.0	6.1	5.8	6.8[a]
Fitness	0.8	0.9	0.8	1.4	1.4	1.5[c]
Hobby	2.9	2.1	3.6	1.6	1.4	2.2[c]
Television	14.1	10.3	17.1	11.5	9.6	16.2[abc]
Reading	2.6	2.4	2.8	1.4	1.5	1.1[c]
Stereo	0.4	0.2	0.5	0.2	0.1	0.4[b]
Communication	3.9	2.5	4.9	3.8	3.3	4.9[ab]
Total	168.0	168.0	168.0	168.0	168.0	168.0
Sample size (N)	(369)	(164)	(205)	(999)	(755)	(244)

Source: Authors' calculations from the 1975–76 Time Use in Economic and Social Accounts and the combined file of the 1998–99 Family Interaction, Social Capital and Trends in Time Use Study and the 2000 National Survey of Parents.
a. Employed and nonemployed in 1975 statistically significantly different, $p < 0.05$.
b. Employed and nonemployed in 2000 statistically significantly different, $p < 0.05$.
c. 1975 and 2000 estimates for all mothers statistically significantly different, $p < 0.05$.

**Table 6A.1   Comparison of 2000 Sloan Weekly Diary Study with 2000
March Current Population Survey**

	Percentage	
	Sloan Study	CPS
Families with		
One child	41.7	39.4
Two children	41.5	42.1
Three children	16.9	18.5
Father's education		
Less than B.A.	48.6	58.9
B.A.	28.0	26.7
More than a B.A.	23.4	14.4
Father's age		
Younger than thirty-five	19.4	21.9
Between thirty-five and forty-five	44.5	45.2
Older than forty-five	36.1	32.9

Source: Authors' calculations from the 2000 March Current Population Survey and the
2000 National Survey of Parents.

Table 8A.1 Activity Classification of 2002 PSID-CDS

Total paid work
Total paid work time, with commute. Includes:
Time spent on main or part-time jobs
Time spent on job search
Time spent on travel during work
Time spent on second job
Time spent on breaks at work

Total household work
Total time doing housework, child care, and shopping. Includes:
Time spent on food preparation
Time spent on food clean-up
Time spent on cleaning house
Time spent on outdoor cleaning
Time spent on clothes care
Time spent doing car maintenance (unless hobby)
Time spent on household paperwork
Time spent on plant care
Time spent on animal care

Time spent watching another person do household tasks
Time spent giving baby care to children age four and under
Time spent on care of children age five to seventeen
Time spent helping and teaching other children
Time spent reading to other children
Time spent playing with children as part of child care
Time spent on medical for other children
Time spent on unpaid babysitting for non-household children
Time spent on shopping for food
Time spent on shopping for clothes and household items
Time spent obtaining goods (for example, hanging out at the mall)

Time spent on personal care services
Time spent at medical appointment
Time spent on government and financial services
Time spent on car repair services
Time spent on other services
Time spent on errands
Time spent on travel related to obtaining goods and services

Total day care
Time spent in formal day care, nursery

Sleep
Time spent sleeping or napping
Meal
Time spent eating
Time spent on snacks (except at work)
Grooming
Time spent on showering and bathing
Time spent on medical care

Time spent on help and care to neighbors, friends

Time spent on personal hygiene and grooming

Time spent receiving child care related to personal care

Time spent on dressing

Time spent on other private activities

Time spent on travel related to personal care

Total personal care

Sum of Sleep, Meal, and Grooming

Total education

Total education time. Includes:

Time spent attending full-time school

Time spent on other classes

Time spent being tutored

Time spent on homework or studying

Time spent using library

Time spent using computer for homework

Time spent taking standardized tests or driver's ed

Time spent on education related travel

Home computer activities

Using computer for recreational purposes

Playing computer games

Using email

Shopping online

Religion

Time spent with religious groups

Time spent on religious practices (for example, weddings)

Organizations

Time spent at professional and union organizations

Time spent at special interest organizations

Time spent at political and civic organizations

Time spent at volunteer and helping organizations

Time spent at fraternal organizations

Time spent at child, youth or family organizations

Time spent at before or after school clubs (for example, drama, debate)

Time spent on travel related to organizations

Event

Time spent attending sporting events

Time spent on movies and videos

Time spent at theater

Time spent at museums, zoos, circuses, concerts

Visiting

Time spent on visiting and social activities

Time spent at parties and dances

Time spent at bars and lounges

Time spent on travel related to social activities

Sports

Time spent on active sports

Time spent on lessons in sports activities

Time spent on music or voice lessons

(Table continues on p. 222.)

Table 8A.1 Activity Classification of 2002 PSID-CDS (*continued*)

Time spent at organized meets, games, or practices	Time spent on music, drama or dance	Household conversations
Outdoors	Playing	Time spent complaining or in conversation with household members
Time spent on other out of doors.	Time spent on card, board, and social games	
Includes:	Time spent on unspecified indoor or outdoor play	Passive leisure
Time spent hunting, fishing, boating, camping, or walking	Time spent on travel to sports or active leisure	Time spent thinking and relaxing
Hobby		Time spent on travel related to passive leisure
Time spent on hobbies. Includes:	Television	Total free
Time spent on photography or scrapbooking	Time spent watching television	Sum of Home Computer Activities, Religion, Organizations, Events, Visiting, Sports, Outdoors, Hobby, Art Activities, Playing, Television, Reading, Household Conversations, Passive Leisure
Time spent working on cars	Reading	
Art activities	Time spent reading books, magazines, newspapers	
Time spent on domestic crafts	Time spent being read to, listening to a story	
Time spent in arts and literature		

Source: Authors' derivation from coding categories in the 2002 Panel Study of Income Dynamics Child Development Supplement (PSID-CDS) data codebook.

= Notes =

Chapter 2

1. Beginning in 2003, time diaries are being collected from much larger samples (12,000 to 20,000 per year) on an ongoing basis by the Bureau of Labor Statistics. This new collection, known as the American Time Use Survey (ATUS), uses the CPS as its sampling frame. These data first became available as we completed this project. The ATUS collection does not ascertain secondary activities but does provide a rich new source of information on time use in the United States, particularly time spent with children and in voluntary activities.

2. In the studies of Verbrugge and Gruber-Baldine (1993), average estimated weekly times totaled 187 hours, and their list of activities did not include time for churchgoing, shopping for durable goods or professional services, or adult education. In Hawes, Talarzyk, and Blackwell's (1975) national survey, estimated weekly activities averaged more than 230 hours. Because American culture judges people by what they do, portraying oneself as busy and industrious is often socially desirable. Hence people often construct answers that put them in a positive light. D. R. Chase and Geoffrey Godbey (1983), for instance, asked members of specific swimming and tennis clubs in State College, Pennsylvania, how many times they had used the club during the last twelve months and checked their responses against each club's sign-in system. In both cases, almost half of all respondents overestimated the actual number of times they participated by more than 100 percent.

3. Other methods include shadow studies, onsite observation, and "beeper" studies, as reviewed in appendix A.

4. A time-diary survey of almost 10,000 respondents from 1992 to 1994 was conducted for the Environmental Protection Agency (Robinson and Godbey 1999), but it is not included in our analyses because of its lack of sufficient family information.

5. We examined child care across all years, restricting 1985, 1995, and 2000 to respondents interviewed between October and December for comparability with the 1965 and 1975 samples. We found little variation in child care

223

between the fall and subsequent months for either mothers or fathers and hence use the full samples in later years in our analysis.

6. Our year 2000 time point in tables in subsequent chapters is based on the diaries collected in 1998 through 2001 in the two studies.

7. The sample was restricted to middle-class, dual-earner families because this was the target population of interest to the funder, the Alfred P. Sloan Foundation's Working Families Program headed by Kathleen Christensen.

Chapter 3

1. Gender specialization was probably at its peak after World War II during the U.S. Baby Boom. Unique economic circumstances bolstered sole wage earning on the part of the husbands, allowing men to earn a family wage (Levy 1998). Earlier in the twentieth century, husbands and wives were often both involved in the work of small family businesses or farms.

2. This point is significant because research suggests that stepparents may be less involved in child rearing than biological parents (Hofferth et al. 2002; Hofferth and Anderson 2004).

3. Some argue that the overburden cannot be measured in hours, as women continually do more family "mental managing" work. Others focus on the different qualities of women's and men's work, arguing that unpaid work has lower status and is more onerous. Still others point to deleterious consequences of women's economic dependency in the relatively common situation of divorce. Although these are important arguments, the ability to assess these is beyond the scope of our study.

Chapter 4

1. None of these measures double count child care time per se. However, if we were to add the second and third measures together with time spent in all the different primary activities over the course of the day, our second and third measures (ones that include secondary time in child care activities and all time with children) would result in totals greater than 24 hours.

2. See coding categories 22 to 25 in table 2.1.

3. This of course assumes that mothers' and fathers' time is additive and not redundant. To the extent that mother's and father's time overlaps, the differences between children in one-parent and two-parent homes may not be as great as these estimates suggest.

4. Although secondary activities were collected in 1965 and 1985, the data that were archived either do not include the secondary activity data (1985) or do not include sufficient detail about when the secondary activity took place (1965) to use comparably with the 1975 and 2000 data. Although we have summed measures of secondary child care on the 1965 data file, there is no

information on the simultaneous primary activities. We would be double counting some unknown proportion of child care time because we cannot subtract out the portion of secondary time that overlaps with primary child care time in 1965. In the 1995 study, secondary activities were not ascertained.

5. It is also possible that method affects the reporting of secondary activity because the 1975 data were collected in personal interviews whereas the 2000 data collections were done by telephone.

6. Television is included in free time but shown separately because it is such a large component of free time.

7. Only the difference for married fathers achieves statistical significance at the .05 level.

8. Tests of year-education interaction effects in multivariate models were not statistically significant. See Bianchi et al. (2004) for full regression results.

9. The differences between employed and nonemployed mothers sometimes appear larger in 2000 than in 1975, but in no case are the interactions between employment and year statistically different.

10. Data not shown.

Chapter 5

1. Counting total time in housework, married mothers do about 15 fewer hours per week than in the past. That is, when we add nonoverlapping secondary activity time in housework, women now do a bit more housework as a secondary activity than in the past.

2. Sample sizes were much smaller in 1995 than other years, perhaps making these estimates less reliable.

3. Theoretically, married mothers' and married fathers' reports should be equal. Our samples may be representative, but they do not include couples. It is also possible that men and women differ slightly in their reporting or perception of what time counts as being alone or with a spouse.

4. Although hours of sleep reported by mothers in 2000 are lower than in 1975, we do not make much of this change over time because using 1965 as our baseline would show no decrease. We have no explanation for why reported sleep hours should have risen between 1965 and 1975.

Chapter 6

1. Appendix table 6A.1 compares the Sloan Foundation weekly sample to comparable middle-A class, dual-earner families in the March 2000 CPS. Our weekly sample is strikingly similar to the CPS in terms of family size and father's age. The weekly sample is somewhat better educated than the more nationally representative CPS sample.

2. This could be a reporting artifact, because mothers may have filled out diaries for other members of the family. Certain activities may be more salient to them, thus creating the appearance of more similar primary activities than would otherwise be noted if reported by two individuals separately.

3. This is based on a Multiple Classification Analysis (MCA), adjusting for ages and numbers of children, and mothers' and fathers' paid work hours.

Chapter 7

1. Only currently employed parents were asked these questions. Thus, about 28 percent of our mothers (the majority of whom are homemakers), and about 5 percent of fathers (the temporarily unemployed, disabled, retired, or students) were excluded for this analysis.

2. These questions were also included in the 2000 General Social Survey to corroborate our findings in the 2000 NSP (see Milkie et al. 2004).

Chapter 8

1. There is some uncertainty about these estimates, however, as the question wording changed between surveys and the 1981 sample was extremely small (see Sandberg and Hofferth 2005).

Chapter 9

1. However, these single-site studies have been found to produce diary figures reflective of the nation as a whole (as noted in Szalai 1972 and Robinson and Godbey 1999).

2. For the with whom time in the United States (not shown in table 9.1) the parallel differences are 46 hours when children are in preschool and 29 hours when children are older, a highly significant difference, but less than a 2:1 ratio. In Canada, the difference is 52 versus 29 hours, which is closer to a 2:1 ratio.

Chapter 10

1. In 1985, respondents reported how much they liked activities on a scale of 1 (dislike) to 10 (like a lot). Paid work was rated a 7 compared with a rating of 6.6 for cooking and a much lower rating of 4.9 for cleaning (Robinson and Godbey 1999, table 25).

Appendix C

1. The first time-use studies conducted in the Netherlands date back to the 1930s, with time series data collections continuing into the 1950s and 1960s.

The present series began in 1975 and data were collected every five years, so that 2000 represented the sixth wave. The research combines two ways of gathering data. First is time-budget data collected by means of a weekly diary, in which respondents report their main activity for each quarter of an hour over the period of a full week in October, with the aid of a precoded list of activities. Second is ancillary activity-related information gathered before and after that week, by means of questionnaires.

Apart from several papers presented at the Annual Conferences of the International Association for Time Use Research, few Dutch studies on the time-use data have been published in English to date. To fill this void, a monograph on *Trends in Time* was published in spring 2004 (Van den Broek and Breedveld 2004). Full information in English about the Dutch Time Use Survey can be found at www.scp.nl.

2. In the Dutch data, every adult who indicated having a child under eighteen living at home was included in the analysis as a parent. Regrettably, the Dutch diary data do not contain time on child care as a secondary activity or the time spent with children.

References

Aldous, Joan, Gail M. Mulligan, and Thoroddur Bjarnason. 1998. "Fathering over Time: What Makes the Difference?" *Journal of Marriage and the Family* 60(4): 809–20.

Allen, Charles E. 1965. "Photographing the TV Audience." *Journal of Advertising Research* 5(1): 2–8.

Andrews, Frank M., James N. Morgan, John A. Sonquist, and Laura Klem. 1973. *Multiple Classification Analysis: A Report on a Computer Program for Multiple Regression Using Categorical Predictors.* Ann Arbor: Institute for Social Research, University of Michigan.

Babington, Charles. 1999. "Clinton Expands Family Leave Act for Federal Workers." *The Washington Post*, May 24, 1999, p. A02.

Bechtel, Robert, Clark Achepohl, and Roger Akers. 1972. "Correlates between Observed Behavior and Questionnaire Responses in Television Viewing." In *Television and Social Behavior, Reports and Papers*, vol. 4: *Television in Day-to-Day Life: Patterns and Use,* edited by Eli Abraham Rubenstein, George A. Comstock, and John Patrick Murray. Washington: U.S. Government Printing Office.

Becker, Gary S. 1991. *A Treatise on the Family,* rev. ed. Cambridge, Mass.: Harvard University Press.

Best, Joel. 1990. *Threatened Children: Rhetoric and Concern about Child-Victims.* Chicago: University of Chicago Press.

Bianchi, Suzanne M. 2000. "Maternal Employment and Time with Children: Dramatic Change or Surprising Continuity?" *Demography* 37 (November): 139–54.

Bianchi, Suzanne M., and John Robinson. 1997. "What Did You Do Today? Children's Use of Time, Family Composition, and the Acquisition of Social Capital." *Journal of Marriage and the Family* 59(May): 332–44.

———. 2005. National Survey of Parents (NSP). College Park: Survey Research Center, University of Maryland.

Bianchi, Suzanne M., and Daphne Spain. 1996. "Women, Work, and Family in America." *Population Bulletin* 51, No. 3 (December). Washington, D.C.: Population Reference Bureau.

Bianchi, Suzanne M., Sara B. Raley, and Melissa A. Milkie. 2006. " Taking on the Second Shift: Time Allocations and Time Pressures of U.S. Mothers and Fathers with Preschoolers." Unpublished manuscript. College Park: University of Maryland.

Bianchi, Suzanne M., John P. Robinson, and Stanley Presser. 2001. *Family Interaction, Social Capital, and Trends in Time Use Study (FISCT)*. College Park: Survey Research Center, University of Maryland.

Bianchi, Suzanne M., Vanessa Wight, and Sara B. Raley. 2005. "Maternal Employment and Activities with Children in the ATUS." Paper presented at the ATUS Early Results Conference, Bethesda, Md. (December 8, 2005).

Bianchi, Suzanne, Philip Cohen, Sara Raley, and Kei Nomaguchi. 2004. "Inequality in Parental Investment in Childrearing: Time, Expenditures, and Health." In *Dimensions of Social Inequality*, edited by Kathryn Neckerman. New York: Russell Sage Foundation.

Bianchi, Suzanne M., Melissa A. Milkie, Liana C. Sayer, and John P. Robinson. 2000. "Is Anyone Doing the Housework? Trends in the Gender Division of Household Labor." *Social Forces* 79(September): 191–228.

Bittman, Michael. 1995. "Recent Changes in Unpaid Work." Occasional Paper, Social Policy Research Centre. Sydney, Australia: The University of New South Wales.

———. 2000. "Now It's 2000: Trends in Doing and Being in the New Millennium." *Journal of Occupational Science* 7(3): 108–17.

Bittman, Michael, and Judith Wajcman. 2000. "The Rush Hour: The Character of Leisure Time and Gender." *Social Forces* 79(1): 165–89.

Blair-Loy, Mary. 2003. *Competing Devotions: Career and Family among Women Executives*. Cambridge, Mass.: Harvard University Press.

Blau, Francine. 1998. "The Well-being of American Women, 1970–1998." *Journal of Economic Literature* 36: 112–65.

Bond, James T., Ellen Galinsky, and Jennifer E. Swanberg. 1998. *The 1997 National Study of the Changing Workforce*. New York: Families and Work Institute.

Brown, Jane Delano, Kim Walsh Childers, Karl E. Bauman, and Gary G. Koch. 1990. "The Influence of New Media and Family Structure on Young Adolescents' Television and Radio Use." *Communication Research* 17(1): 65–82.

Bryant, W. Keith, and Cathleen D. Zick. 1996. "Are We Investing Less in the Next Generation? Historical Trends in Time Spent Caring for Children." *Journal of Family and Economic Issues* 17(3/4): 365–92.

Budig, Michelle J., and Paula England. 2001. "The Wage Penalty for Motherhood." *American Sociological Review* 66(2): 204–25.

Budig, Michelle J., and Nancy Folbre. 2004. "Child Care vs. Child-Minding: Measuring Activities, Responsibilities, and Time." In *Family Time: The Social Organization of Care*, edited by Nancy Folbre and Michael Bittman. New York: Routledge.

Burton, Linda M., ed. Forthcoming. *Adultified Children in Service Learning Programs: Considering the Needs of Youth Who Are "Growing Up a Little Faster."* Denver, Colo.: RMC Research Corporation.

Caplow, Theodore, Louis Hicks, and Ben J. Wattenberg. 2001. *The First Measured Century: An Illustrated Guide to Trends in America, 1900–2000*. Washington, D.C.: AEI Press.

Casper, Lynne M., and Suzanne M. Bianchi. 2002. *Continuity and Change in the American Family*. Thousand Oaks, Calif.: Sage Publications.

Chase, D. R., and Geoffrey C. Godbey. 1983. "Accuracy of Self-Reported Participation Rates: Research Notes." *Leisure Studies* 2(2): 231–35.

Christiansen, Shawn L., and Rob Palkovitz. 2001. "Why the 'Good Provider' Role Still Matters: Providing as a Form of Paternal Involvement." *Journal of Family Issues* 22(1): 84–106.

Cohen, Philip S., and Suzanne M. Bianchi. 1999. "Marriage, Children, and Women's Employment: What Do We Know?" *Monthly Labor Review* 122(12): 22–31.

Coleman, James. 1988. "Social Capital in the Creation of Human Capital." *American Journal of Sociology* 94(Supplement): 95–121.

Coleman, Mary T., and John Pencavel. 1993a. "Changes in Work Hours of Male Employees." *Industrial and Labor Relations Review* 46(2): 262–83.

———. 1993b. "Trends in Market Work Behavior of Women Since 1940." *Industrial and Labor Relations Review* 46(4): 653–76.

Coltrane, Scott. 1988. "Father-Child Relationships and the Status of Women: A Cross-Cultural Study." *The American Journal of Sociology* 93(5): 1060–95.

———. 1996. *Family Man: Fatherhood, Housework, and Gender Equity*. New York: Oxford University Press.

Converse, Philip E., and John P. Robinson. 1980. *Americans' Use of Time, 1965–1966*. First ICPSR Edition, ICPSR 7254 ed. Ann Arbor: Survey Research Center, Institute for Social Research, The University of Michigan.

Cooney, Teresa M., Frank A. Pedersen, Samuel Indelicato, and Rob Palkovitz. 1993. "Timing of Fatherhood: Is "On-Time" Optimal?" *Journal of Marriage and the Family*. 55(1): 205–15.

Coontz, Stephanie. 1992. *The Way We Never Were: American Families and the Nostalgia Trap*. New York: Basic Books.

Corsaro, William A. 2003. *We're Friends, Right? Inside Kids' Culture*. Washington, D.C.: Joseph Henry Press.

Council of Economic Advisers. 1999. "Families and the Labor Market, 1969–1999: Analyzing the 'Time Crunch.'" Washington: U.S. Government Printing Office.

Coverman, Shelley. 1985. "Explaining Husbands' Participation in Domestic Labor." *Sociological Quarterly* 26(1): 81–97.

Coverman, Shelley, and Joseph F. Sheley. 1986. "Change in Men's Housework and Child-Care Time, 1965–1975." *Journal of Marriage and the Family* 48(2): 413–22.

Crittenden, Ann. 2001. *The Price of Motherhood: Why the Most Important Job in the World is Still the Least Valued*. New York: Owl Books.

Crouter, Ann C., and Susan M. McHale. 2005. "Work, Family, and Children's Time: Implications for Youth." In *Work, Family, Health, and Well-Being*, edited by Suzanne M. Bianchi, Lynne M. Casper, and Rosalind Berkowitz King. Mahwah, N.J.: Lawrence Erlbaum.

Curtin, Richard, Stanley Presser, and Eleanor Singer. 2000. "Effects of Response Rate Changes on the Index of Consumer Sentiment." *Public Opinion Quarterly* 64(4): 413–28.

Csikszentmihalyi, Mihaly, and Reed Larson. 1984. *Being, Adolescent: Conflict and Growth in Teenage Years*. New York: Basic Books.

Daly, Kerry J. 1996. *Families & Time: Keeping Pace in a Hurried Culture*. Thousand Oaks, Calif.: Sage Publications.

———. 2001. *Minding the Time in Family Experience.* Amsterdam: Elsevier.

Davis, James Allan, and Tom W. Smith. 2000. *General Social Surveys, 1972–2000: Cumulative Codebook.* Storrs, Conn.: The Report Center for Public Opinion Research, University of Connecticut.

Deem, Rosemary. 1996. "No Time for a Rest? An Exploration of Women's Work, Engendered Leisure, and Holidays." *Time and Society* 5(1): 5–25.

Deutsch, Francine. 1999. *Halving it All: How Equally Shared Parenting Works.* Cambridge, Mass.: Harvard University Press.

DiLeonardo, Micaela. 1987. "The Female World of Cards and Holidays: Women, Families, and the Work of Kinship." *Signs: Journal of Women in Culture and Society* 12(3): 440–53

Drago, Robert, Robert Caplan, David Costanza, T. Brubaker, D. Cloud, S. Donohoe, N. C. Harris, and T. L. Riggs. 1998. "Time for Surveys: Do Busy People Complete Time Diaries?" *Society and Leisure* 21(2): 555–62.

Eccles, Jacquelynne, Bonnie Barber, Margaret Stone, and Janice Templeton. 2003. "Adolescence and Emerging Adulthood: The Critical Passage Ways to Adulthood." In *Well-Being: Positive Development across the Life Span,* edited by Marc H. Bornstein, Lucy Davidson, Corey L. M. Keyes, Kristin A. Moore, & The Center for Child Well-Being. Mahwah, N.J.: Lawrence Erlbaum.

Edin, Kathryn, and Maria Kefalas. 2005. *Promises I Can Keep: Why Poor Women Put Motherhood before Marriage.* Berkeley: University of California Press.

Ellwood, David, and Christopher Jencks. 2004. "The Spread of Single-Parent Families in the United States since 1960." In *The Future of the Family,* edited by Daniel P. Moynihan, Timothy M. Smeeding, and Lee Rainwater. New York: Russell Sage Foundation.

Ferree, Myra Marx. 1990. "Beyond Separate Spheres: Feminism and Family Research." *Journal of Marriage and the Family* 52(4): 866–84

Fields, Jason, Kristin Smith, Loretta E. Bass, and Terry Lugaila. 1994. *A Child's Day: Home, School, and Play (Selected Indicators of Child Well-Being).* Washington: U.S. Census Bureau.

Fisher, Kimberly, Andrew McCulloch, and Jonathan Gershuny. 1999. *British Fathers and Children: A Report for Channel 4 "Dispatches."* Channel 4 Dispatches. University of Essex: Institute of Social and Economic Research.

Frank, J. 1939. "Children and Their Leisure Time." *Childhood Education* 15(#): 389–92.

Furstenberg, Frank F., Jr. 1995. "Fathering in the Inner City: Paternal Participation and Public Policy." In *Fatherhood: Contemporary Theory, Research and Social Policy,* edited by William Marsiglio. Thousand Oaks, Calif.: Sage Publications.

Furstenberg, Frank F., Jr., Sheela Kennedy, Vonnie C. McLoyd, Rubén G. Rumbaut, Richard A. Settersten. 2004. "Growing Up is Harder to Do." *Contexts: Understanding People in their Social Worlds* 3(3): 33–41.

Gager, Constance T., and Laura Sanchez. 2003. "Two as One? Spouses' Personal Time Together, Marital Quality, and the Risk of Divorce." *Journal of Family Issues* 24(1): 21–50.

Galinsky, Ellen. 1981. *Between Generations: The Six Stages of Parenthood.* New York: Times Books.

———. 1999. *Ask the Children: What America's Children Really Think about Working Parents.* New York: Morrow.

Gareis, Karen, Rosalind Barnett, and Robert Brennan. 2003. "Individual and Crossover Effects of Work Schedule Fit: A Within-Couple Analysis." *Journal of Marriage and the Family* 65(2): 1041–54.

Gauthier, Anne H., Timothy M. Smeeding, and Frank F. Furstenberg, Jr. 2004. "Are Parents Investing Less Time in Children: Trends in Selected Industrialized Countries." *Population and Development Review* 30(4): 647–71.

Gershuny, Jonathan. 2000. *Changing Times: Work and Leisure in Postindustrial Society.* Oxford: Oxford University Press.

Gershuny, Jonathan, I. Miles, S. Jones, C. Mullings, G. Thomas, and S. Wyatt. 1986. "Time Budgets: Preliminary Analysis of a National Survey." *Quarterly Journal of Social Affairs* 2(1): 13–39.

Gershuny, Jonathan, and John P. Robinson. 1988. "Historical Changes in the Household Division of Labor." *Demography* 25(4): 537–52.

Gilbert, James 1986. *A Cycle of Outrage: America's Reaction to the Juvenile Delinquent in the 1950s.* New York: Oxford University Press.

Goldin, Claudia. 1990. *Understanding the Gender Gap: An Economic History of American Women.* New York: Oxford University Press.

———. 2004. "The Long Road to the Fast Track: Career and Family." *Annals of the American Academy of Political and Social Science* 596(1): 20–35.

Gornick, Janet C., and Marcia K. Meyers. 2003. *Families that Work: Policies for Reconciling Parenthood and Employment.* New York: Russell Sage Foundation.

Gupta, Sanjiv. 1999. "The Effects of Transitions in Marital Status on Men's Performance of Housework." *Journal of Marriage and the Family* 61(August): 700–11.

Hadaway, C. Kirk, Penny Long Marler, and Mark Chaves. 1993. "What the Polls Don't Show: A Closer Look at U.S. Church Attendance." *American Sociological Review* 58(6): 741–52.

Hamer, Jennifer. 2001. *What it Means to Be Daddy: Fatherhood for Black Men Living Away from Their Children.* New York: Columbia University Press.

Harvey, Andrew S., and David H. Elliot. 1983. *Time and Time Again.* Ottawa-Hull: Employment and Immigration Commission.

Hawes, Douglass K., W. Wayne Talarzyk, and Roger D. Blackwell. 1975. "Consumer Satisfactions from Leisure Time Pursuits." In *Advances in Consumer Research,* edited by Mary H. Schlinger. Chicago: Association for Consumer Research.

Hays, Sharon. 1996. *The Cultural Contradictions of Motherhood.* New Haven, Conn.: Yale University Press.

Hernandez, Donald J. 1993. *America's Children: Resources From Family, Government and the Economy.* New York: Russell Sage Foundation.

Hewlett, Sylvia Ann. 2002. *Creating a Life: Professional Women and the Quest for Children.* New York: Talk Miramax Books.

Hill, C. Russell, and Frank P. Stafford. 1974. "Allocation of Time to Pre-school Children and Educational Opportunity." *Journal of Human Resources* 9(3): 323–41.

———. 1980. "Parental Care of Children: Time Diary Estimates of Quantity, Predictability, and Variety." *Journal of Human Resources* 15(2): 219–39.

———. 1985. "Parental Care of Children: Time Diary Estimates of Quantity, Predictability, and Variety." In *Time, Goods, and Well-Being*, edited by F.T. Juster and Frank P. Stanfford. Ann Arbor: Survey Research Center, Institute for Social Research, University of Michigan.

Hochschild, Arlie. 1989. *The Second Shift: Working Parents and the Revolution at Home*. New York: Viking.

———. 1997. *The Time Bind: When Work Becomes Home and Home Becomes Work.* New York: Metropolitan Books.

Hofferth, Sandra L. 2003. "Race/Ethnic Differences in Father Involvement in Two-Parent Families: Culture, Context, or Economy." *Journal of Family Issues* 24(2): 185–216.

Hofferth, Sandra L., and Kermyt Anderson. 2004. "Are All Dads Equal? Biology versus Marriage as the Basis for Paternal Investment." *Journal of Marriage and Family* 65(1): 213–32.

Hofferth, Sandra, and John Sandberg. 2001a. "Changes in American Children's Use of Time, 1981–1997." In *Children at the Millennium: Where Have We Come from, Where Are We Going?* edited by T. Owens and S. Hofferth. Advances in Life Course Research Series. New York: Elsevier Science.

———. 2001b. "How American Children Spend Their Time." *Journal of Marriage and the Family* 63(2): 295–308.

Hofferth, Sandra, Joseph Pleck, Jeffrey Stueve, Suzanne M. Bianchi, and Liana C. Sayer. 2002. "The Demography of Fathers: What Fathers Do." In *Handbook of Father Involvement*, edited by Catherine Tamis-LeMonda and Natasha Cabrera. Mahwah, N.J.: Lawrence Erlbaum.

Huston, Aletha, John Wright, Janet Marquis, and Samuel Green. 1999. "How Young Children Spend Their Time: Television and Other Activities." *Developmental Psychology* 35(4): 912–25.

Jacobs, Jerry A. 1998. "Measuring Time at Work: An Assessment of the Accuracy of Self Reports." *Monthly Labor Review* 121(December): 42–53.

Jacobs, Jerry A., and Kathleen Gerson. 1998. "Who Are the Overworked Americans?" *Review of Social Economy* LVI(4): 442–59.

———. 2001. "Overworked Individuals or Overworked Families? Explaining Trends in Work, Leisure, and Family Time." *Work and Occupations* 28 (February): 40–63

———. 2004. *The Time Divide: Work, Family, and Gender Inequality.* Cambridge, Mass.: Harvard University Press.

Juster, F. Thomas. 1985. "The Validity and Quality of Time Use Estimates Obtained from Recall Diaries." In *Time, Goods, and Well-Being*, edited by F. Thomas Juster and Frank P. Stafford. Ann Arbor: Survey Research Center, Institute for Social Research, University of Michigan.

Juster, F. Thomas, and Frank P. Stafford. 1985. *Time, Goods, and Well-Being.* Ann Arbor: Survey Research Center, Institute for Social Research, University of Michigan.

Keeter, Scott, Carolyn Miller, Andrew Kohut, Robert Groves, and Stanley Presser. 2000. "Consequences of Reducing Nonresponse in a National Telephone Survey." *Public Opinion Quarterly* 64(2): 125–48.

Kiecolt, K. Jill. 2003. "Satisfaction with Work and Family Life: No Evidence of a Cultural Reversal." *Journal of Marriage and the Family* 65(1): 23–35.

Kinney, David A., Janet S. Dunn, and Sandra L. Hofferth. 2000. *Family Strategies for Managing the Time Crunch*. Paper presented at Conference on Work and Family: Expanding Horizons. San Francisco, Calif. (March 3–4, 2000).

Klerman, Jacob A., and Arleen Leibowitz. 1999. "Job Continuity among New Mothers." *Demography* 36(2): 145–55.

Kubey, Robert, and Mihaly Csikszentmihalyi. 1990. *Television and the Quality of Life: How Viewing Shapes Everyday Experience*. Hillsdale, N.J.: Lawrence Erlbaum.

Kurz, Demi. 2002. "Caring for Teenage Children." *Journal of Family Issues* 23(6): 748–67.

Lareau, Annette. 2000. "Social Class and the Daily Lives of Children: A Study from the United States." *Childhood* 7(2): 155–71.

———. 2002. "Invisible Inequality: Social Class and Childrearing in Black Families and White Families." *American Sociological Review* 67(October): 747–76.

———. 2003. *Unequal Childhoods: Class, Race, and Family Life*. Berkeley: University of California Press.

Lareau, Annette, Elliot B. Weininger, and Suzanne M. Bianchi. 2005. "Work-Family Conflicts, Gender and Children's Organized Leisure Activities." Unpublished manuscript. College Park: University of Maryland.

LaRossa, Ralph. 1988. "Fatherhood and Social Change." *Family Relations* 37(4): 451–57.

———. 1997. *The Modernization of Fatherhood: A Social and Political History*. Chicago: University of Chicago Press.

Larson, Reed W. 1998. "Implications for Policy and Practice: Getting Adolescents, Families, and Communities in Sync." In *Temporal Rhythms in Adolescence: Clocks, Calendars, and the Coordination of Daily Life*, edited by Ann Crouter and Reed W. Larson. San Francisco: Jossey-Bass.

———. 2001. "How U.S. Children and Adolescents Spend Time: What it Does (and Doesn't) Tell us about their Development." *Current Directions in Psychological Science* 10(5): 160–64.

Larson, Reed W., and Maryse Richards. 1991. "Daily Companionship in Late Childhood and Early Adolescence: Changing Developmental Contexts." *Child Development* 62(2): 284–300.

———. 1994. *Divergent Realities: The Emotional Lives of Mothers, Fathers, and Adolescents*. New York: Basic Books.

Larson, Reed W., and Suman Verma. 1999. "How Children and Adolescents Spend Time Across the World: Work, Play, and Developmental Opportunities." *Psychological Bulletin* 125(6): 701–36.

Larson, Reed W., Robert Kubey, and Joseph Colletti. 1989. "Changing Channels: Early Adolescent Media Choices and Shifting Investments in Family and Friends." *Journal of Youth and Adolescence* 18(6): 583–99.

Larson, Reed W., Maryse H. Richards, Giovanni Moneta, Grayson Holmbeck, and Elena Duckett. 1996. "Changes in Adolescents' Daily Interactions with Their Families from Ages 10 to 18: Disengagement and Transformation." *Developmental Psychology* 32(4): 744–54.

Leibowitz, Arleen. 1974. "Home Investments in Children." *Journal of Political Economy* 82(2): S111–S131.

———. 1977. "Parental Inputs and Children's Achievement." *Journal of Human Resources* 12(2): 242–51.

Levy, Frank. 1998. *The New Dollars and Dreams*. New York: Russell Sage Foundation.

Lundberg, Shelly, and Elaina Rose. 2000. "Parenthood and the Earnings of Married Men and Women." *Labour Economics* 7(6): 689–710.

———. 2002. "The Effects of Sons and Daughters on Men's Labor Supply and Wages." *Review of Economics and Statistics* 84(2): 251–68.

Marini, Margaret M., and Shelton, Beth A. 1993. "Measuring Household Work: Recent Experience in the United States." *Social Science Research* 22(4): 361–82.

Marsiglio, William. 1995. "Young Nonresident Biological Fathers." In *Single Parent Families: Diversity, Myths, and Realities*, edited by Shirley M. H. Hanson, Marsha L. Heims, Doris J. Julian, and Marvin B. Sussman. Binghamton, N.Y.: Haworth.

Martin, Steven P. 2000. "Diverging Fertility of U.S. Women Who Defer Childbearing Past Age 30." *Demography* 37(4): 523–33.

Maruani, Margaret. 2000. *Travail et Emploi des Femmes*. Paris: *La Découverte*.

Mattingly, Marybeth J., and Suzanne M. Bianchi. 2003. "Gender Differences in the Quantity and Quality of Free Time: The U.S. Experience." *Social Forces* 81(March): 999–1030.

Mattingly, Marybeth, and Liana C. Sayer. 2006. "Under Pressure: Trends and Gender Differences in the Relationship between Free Time and Feeling Rushed." *Journal of Marriage and Family* 68(February): 205–21.

Maume, David J., Jr., and Marcia L. Bellas. 2001. "The Overworked American or the Time Bind? Assessing Competing Explanations for Time Spent in Paid Labor." *American Behavioral Scientist* 44(March): 1137–56.

McLanahan, Sara S., and Gary Sandefur. 1994. *Growing Up with a Single Parent: What Hurts, What Helps*. Cambridge, Mass.: Harvard University Press.

Meeks, Carol, and Teresa Mauldin. 1990. "Children's Time in Structured and Unstructured Leisure Activities." *Lifestyles: Family and Economic Issues* 11(3): 257–81.

Michelson, William, ed. 1978. *Public Policy in Temporal Perspective*. The Hague: Mouton Press.

Milardo, Robert M., ed. 2001. *Understanding Families into the New Millennium: A Decade in Review*. Minneapolis, Minn.: National Council on Family Relations.

Milkie, Melissa A., and Pia Peltola. 1999. "Playing all the Roles: Gender and the Work-Family Balancing Act." *Journal of Marriage and the Family* 61(2): 476–90.

Milkie, Melissa A., Suzanne M. Bianchi, Marybeth J. Mattingly, and John P. Robinson. 2002. "Gendered Division of Childrearing: Ideals, Realities, and Relationship to Parental Well-Being." *Sex Roles* 47(1/2): 21–38.

Milkie, Melissa A., Marybeth J. Mattingly, Kei M. Nomaguchi, Suzanne M. Bianchi, and John P. Robinson. 2004. "The Time Squeeze: Parental Statuses and Feelings about Time with Their Children." *Journal of Marriage and the Family* 66(3): 739–61.

Miller, Daniel, and Guy Swanson. 1958. *The Changing American Parent: A Study in the Detroit Area*. New York: John Wiley & Sons.

Moen, Phyllis. 2003. *It's About Time: Couples and Careers*. Ithaca, N.Y.: ILR Press.

National Commission on Excellence in Education. 1983. *A Nation at Risk: The Imperative for Educational Reform.* Washington: U.S. Department of Education.

Neckerman, Kathryn M. 2004. *Dimensions of Social Inequality.* New York: Russell Sage Foundation.

Neimi, Iris. 1988. "Main Trends in Time Use From the 1920s to the 1980s." Unpublished manuscript. Statistics Finland.

Nock, Steven. 1998. *Marriage in Men's Lives.* New York: Oxford University Press.

———. 2001. "The Marriages of Equally Dependent Spouses." *Journal of Family Issues* 22(6): 755–75.

Nock, Steven L., and Paul William Kingston. 1988. "Time with Children: The Impact of Couples' Work-Time Commitments." *Social Forces* 67(1): 59–85.

Nomaguchi, Kei M., Melissa M. Milkie, and Suzanne M. Bianchi. 2005. "Time Strains and Psychological Well-Being: Do Dual-Earner Mothers and Fathers Differ?" *Journal of Family Issues* 26(6): 756–92.

Pacholok, Sally, and Anne H. Gauthier. 2004. "A Tale of Dual-Earner Families in Four Countries." In *Family Time: The Social Organization of Care,* edited by Nancy Folbre and Michael Bittman. London: Routledge.

Perry-Jenkins, Maureen. 2005. "Work in the Working Class: Challenges Facing Families." In *Work, Family, Health, and Well-Being,* edited by Suzanne M. Bianchi, Lynne M. Casper, and Rosalind Berkowitz King. Mahwah, N.J.: Lawrence Erlbaum.

Peterson, Richard R., and Kathleen Gerson. 1992. "Determinants of Responsibility for Child Care Arrangements among Dual-Earner Couples." *Journal of Marriage and Family* 54(3): 527–36.

Pleck, Joseph H. 1997. "Paternal Involvement: Levels, Sources, and Consequences." In *The Role of the Father in Child Development,* 3rd ed., edited by Michael E. Lamb. New York: John Wiley & Sons.

Presser, Stanley, and John Robinson. 2000. "Estimating Daily Activity Times: Comparing Three Approaches in Relation to Time Diaries." Paper presented at the annual meeting of the American Association for Public Opinion Research. Portland, Oregon (May 2000).

Presser, Stanley, and Linda Stinson. 1998. "Data Collection Mode and Social Desirability Bias in Self-Reported Religious Attendance." *American Sociological Review* 63(1): 137–45.

Pronovost, Gilles. 2002. "Les Temps Sociaux. Une Comparaison France-Canada-Québec," in HUET, Armel et SAEZ, Guy, dir. *Le règne des loisirs.* Paris. Éd. De l'Aube/DATAR.

Putnam, Robert. 2000. *Bowling Alone: The Collapse and Revival of American Community.* New York: Simon & Schuster.

Quinn, Robert P., and Graham L. Staines. 1979. *The 1997 Quality of Employment Survey: Descriptive Statistics with Comparison Data from the 1969–90 and the 1972–73 Surveys.* Ann Arbor: Survey Research Center, Institute for Social Research, University of Michigan.

Raley, Sara, Suzanne M. Bianchi, and Marybeth Mattingly. 2006. "How Dual are Dual-Income Couples? Documenting Change from 1970 to 2001." *Journal of Marriage and Family* 68(2): 11–28.

Reeves, Joy B., and Robert F. Szafran. 1996. "For What and For Whom Do You Need More Time?" *Time & Society* 5(2): 237–51.

Robinson, John P. 1976. *Changes in Americans' Use of Time, 1965–1975*. Cleveland, Ohio: Communication Research Center.

———. 1977. *How Americans Use Time: A Social-Psychological Analysis of Everyday Behavior*. Westport, Conn.: Praeger Publishers.

———. 1985. "The Validity and Reliability of Diaries versus Alternative Time Use Measures." In *Time, Goods, and Well-Being*, edited by F. Thomas Juster and Frank P. Stafford. Ann Arbor: Survey Research Center, Institute for Social Research, University of Michigan.

———. 1989. "Caring for Kids." *American Demographics* 11(7): 52–54.

———. 1993. "As We Like It." *American Demographics* 15(2): 26–28.

Robinson, John P., and Suzanne M. Bianchi. 1997. "The Children's Hours." *American Demographics* 19(12): 20–24.

Robinson, John P., and Ann Bostrom. 1994. "The Overestimated Workweek? What Time Diary Measures Suggest." *Monthly Labor Review* 117(8): 11–23.

Robinson, John P., and Jonathan I. Gershuny. 1994. "Measuring Hours of Paid Work: Time Diary vs. Estimate Questions." *Bulletin of Labour Statistics* xi–xvii. Geneva: International Labor Office.

Robinson, John P., and Geoffrey Godbey. 1999. *Time for Life: The Surprising Ways Americans Use Their Time*. 2nd ed. University Park: Pennsylvania State University Press.

Robinson, John P., and Melissa A. Milkie. 1998. "Back to Basics: Trends in and Role Determinants of Women's Attitudes toward Housework." *Journal of Marriage and the Family* 60(1): 205–18.

Robinson, Thomas N. 2001. "Television Viewing and Childhood Obesity." *Pediatric Clinics of North America* 48(4): 1017–25.

Rones, Philip L., Randy E. Ilg, and Jennifer M. Gardner. 1997. "Trends in Hours of Work Since the Mid-1970s." *Monthly Labor Review* (April): 3–14.

Salisbury, David, and Myron Lieberman. 2003. "Keeping the Nation at Risk." *The American Prowler*. (April 25, 2003).

Sanchez, Laura A., and Constance T. Gager. 2004. "Whose Time Is It? The Effect of Gender, Employment and Work/Family Stress on Housework." Paper presented at the Annual Meeting of the American Sociological Association. San Francisco, Calif. (August 13, 2004).

Sandberg, John F. and Sandra L. Hofferth. 2001. "Changes in Children's Time with Parents: United States, 1981–1997." *Demography* 38(3): 423–36.

———. 2005. "Changes in Children's Time with Parents: A Correction." *Demography* 42(2): 391–95.

Sayer, Liana. 2001. *Time Use, Gender and Inequality: Differences in Men's and Women's Market, Nonmarket, and Leisure Time*. Unpublished Ph.D. diss., College Park: University of Maryland, Department of Sociology.

Sayer, Liana, Anne H. Gauthier, and Frank F. Furstenberg. 2004. "Educational Differences in Parents' Time with Children: Cross-National Variations." *Journal of Marriage and Family* 66(5): 1152–69.

Sayer, Liana, Suzanne M. Bianchi, and John Robinson. 2004. "Are Parents Investing Less in Children? Trends in Mothers' and Fathers' Time with Children." *American Journal of Sociology* 110(1): 1–43.

Schor, Juliet B. 1991. *The Overworked American: The Unexpected Decline of Leisure.* New York: Basic Books.

Schuman, Howard, and Stanley Presser. 1981. *Questions and Answers in Attitude Surveys: Experiments on Question Form, Wording and Context.* Orlando, Fla.: Academic Press.

Shaw, Susan M. 1992. "Dereifying Family Leisure: An Examination of Women's and Men's Everyday Experiences and Perceptions of Family Time." *Leisure Sciences* 14(4): 271–286.

Skolnick, Arlene. 1991. *Embattled Paradise: The American Family in an Age of Uncertainty.* New York: Basic Books.

Smith, Kristin, Barbara Downs, and Martin O'Connell. 2001. "Maternity Leave and Employment Patterns: 1961–1995." *Current Population Reports,* Series P70, no. 79. Washington: U.S. Census Bureau.

Snyder, Thomas D., and Alexandra G. Tan. 2005. *Digest of Education Statistics, 2004.* Washington, D.C.: National Center of Education Statistics. Available only online: http://nces.ed.gov/programs/digest.

South, Scott J., and Glenna Spitze. 1994. "Housework in Marital and Nonmarital Households." *American Sociological Review* 59(3): 327–47.

Spain, Daphne, and Suzanne M. Bianchi. 1996. *Balancing Act: Motherhood, Marriage, and Employment among American Women.* New York: Russell Sage Foundation.

Statistics Canada. 1999. *Overview of the Uses of Time among Canadians in 1998.* Ottawa: Statistics Canada.

Stone, Philip J. 1972. "Child Care in Twelve Countries." In *The Use of Time: Daily Activities of Urban and Suburban Populations in Twelve Countries,* edited by Alexander Szalai. The Hague, Paris: Mouton.

Sutton-Smith, B. 1994. "Does Play Prepare the Future?" In *Toys, Play and Development,* edited by J. H. Goldstein. Cambridge: Cambridge University Press.

Szalai, Alexander, ed. 1972. *The Use of Time: Daily Activities of Urban and Suburban Populations in Twelve Countries.* The Hague, Paris: Mouton.

Thorne, Barrie. 1993. *Gender Play.* New Brunswick, N.J.: Rutgers University Press.

Thornton, Arland, and Linda Young-DeMarco. 2001. "Four Decades of Trends in Attitudes Toward Family Issues in the United States: The 1960s through the 1990s." *Journal of Marriage and the Family* 63(4): 1009–37.

Timmer, S., J. Eccles, and K. O'Brien. 1985. "How Children Use Time." In *Time, Goods and Well-Being,* edited by F. Thomas Juster and Frank P. Stafford. Ann Arbor: Survey Research Center, University of Michigan.

Townsend, Nicholas. 2002. *The Package Deal: Marriage, Work, and Fatherhood in Men's Lives.* Philadelphia: Temple University Press.

Van den Broek, Andries, and Koen Breedveld. 2004. *Trends in Time: The Use and Organization of Time in the Netherlands, 1975–2000.* The Hague, Netherlands: Social and Cultural Planning Office.

Verbrugge, Lois M., and D. Gruber-Baldine. 1993. *Baltimore Study of Activity Patterns.* Ann Arbor: Institute of Gerontology, University of Michigan.

Verrengia, Joseph B. 2005. "Families on a Treadmill: L.A. Parents, Kids going at Full Tilt to Get Everything Done." *Los Angeles Daily News,* March 19, 2005.

Vickery, Clair. 1977. "The Time-Poor: A New Look at Poverty." *Journal of Human Resources* 12(1): 27–48.

Waldfogel, Jane. 1997. "The Effect of Children on Women's Wages." *American Sociological Review* 62(2): 209–17.

Wang, Rong, Suzanne M. Bianchi, and Sara B. Raley. 2005. "Teenagers' Internet Use and Family Rules: A Research Note." *Journal of Marriage and Family* 67(5): 1249–58.

Warr, Mark, and Christopher B. Ellison. 2000. "Rethinking Social Reactions to Crime: Personal and Altruistic Fear in Family Households." *American Journal of Sociology* 106(3): 551–78.

Wartella, Ellen, and Sharon Mazzarella. 1990. "A Historical Comparison of Children's Use of Leisure Time." In *For Fun and Profit: The Transformation of Leisure into Consumption,* edited by R. Butsch. Philadelphia: Temple University Press.

Williams, Joan. 2000. *Unbending Gender: Why Family and Work Conflict and What To Do about It.* New York: Oxford University Press.

Wimbush, Erica, and Margaret Talbot, eds. 1988. *Relative Freedoms: Women and Leisure.* Milton Keynes/Philadelphia: Open University Press.

Zelizer, Viviana A. 1981. "The Price and Value of Children: The Case of Children's Insurance." *The American Journal of Sociology* 86(5): 1036–56.

———. 1994. *Pricing the Priceless Child: The Changing Social Value of Children,* 2nd ed. Princeton, N.J.: Princeton University Press.

Zick, Cathleen D., and Jane L. McCullough 1991. "Trends in Married Couples' Time Use: Evidence from 1977–78 and 1987–88." *Sex Roles* 24(7/8): 459–87.

Zick, Cathleen D., and W. Keith Bryant. 1996. "A New Look at Parents' Time Spent in Child Care: Primary and Secondary Time Use." *Social Science Research* 25(3): 260–80.

Zick, Cathleen D., W. Keith Bryant, and Eva Osterbacka. 2001. "Mothers' Employment, Parental Involvement, and the Implications for Children's Behavior." *Social Science Research* 30(1): 25–49.

═ Index ═

Boldface numbers refer to figures and tables.

adultification, 8
Alfred P. Sloan Foundation, 27, 224n7
American Time Use Survey, 174, 223n1
Australia. *See* multinational
  comparisons

Barnett, Rosalind, 39
Bellas, Marcia, 39
Bianchi, Suzanne, 15, 189, 196, 202
Bittman, Michael, 53, 100–101, 157, 174
Blackwell, Roger D., 223n2
Blair-Loy, Mary, 9–10, 12–14
Boy Scouts of America, 143
Brennan, Robert, 39
Bryant, W. Keith, 64–65, 78
Budig, Michelle, 11, 73
Burton, Linda, 8
busy families, adjustments made by,
  89, 111–12, 172; in Canada, 197–98;
  classification of activities, **214–15**;
  employed and nonemployed
  mothers, differences in activities of,
  108; employed and nonemployed
  mothers, differences in civic and
  family activities of, **110**; employed
  and nonemployed mothers, understanding changes made by, 107–10;
  family care and housework,
  changes in, 91–95, 165–67 (*see also*
  family care and housework); in
  France, 202; free time activities,
  changes in, 95–98, 164–67 (*see also*
  leisure); free time activities, quality

of, 100–103; multitasking, 68,
70–71, 98–100; in the Netherlands,
194–96; personal care and sleep,
changes in, 95–96, 165–66 (*see also*
personal care (including sleep));
primary activities, changes in,
89–98, 164–67; time with others,
changes in, 103–7; in the United
Kingdom, 191–92

Canada: parenting and child care,
  trends in, 196–200. *See also* multinational comparisons
Caplow, Theodore, 91
Casper, Lynne, 196
Chase, D. R., 223n2
Chenu, Alain, 174
childbearing, timing of, 4, 60, 87
child care. *See* parental time with
  children
childlessness, 4, 9–10, 60
children: anxiety of parents regarding
  activities of, 87; child-centeredness,
  ideal of, 126–27; childhood, changing ideas regarding, 7–9; diary
  activities of, 143–48; diary time,
  hours per week, **145**; differences in
  time use by family structure, hours
  per week, **151**; differences in time
  use by maternal employment
  hours per week, **150**; educated parents and, 5; educational activities
  of, 147–48; family, time spent with,

241